Lecture Notes in Computer S

Commenced Publication in 1973
Founding and Former Series Editors:
Gerhard Goos, Juris Hartmanis, and Jan van Le

T0259847

Paris Avgeriou (Ed.)

Software Engineering for Resilient Systems

4th International Workshop, SERENE 2012
Pisa, Italy, September 27-28, 2012
Proceedings

 Springer

Volume Editor

Paris Avgeriou
University of Groningen
Nijenborgh 9
9747 AG Groningen, The Netherlands
E-mail: paris@cs.rug.nl

ISSN 0302-9743   e-ISSN 1611-3349
ISBN 978-3-642-33175-6   e-ISBN 978-3-642-33176-3
DOI 10.1007/978-3-642-33176-3
Springer Heidelberg Dordrecht London New York

Library of Congress Control Number: 2012945542

CR Subject Classification (1998): D.4.5, D.2.1-2, D.2.4-5, D.2.11, C.2.4, H.4

LNCS Sublibrary: SL 2 – Programming and Software Engineering

Typesetting: Camera-ready by author, data conversion by Scientific Publishing Services, Chennai, India

Printed on acid-free paper

Springer is part of Springer Science+Business Media (www.springer.com)

Preface

The unprecedented level of complexity of modern software makes it difficult to ensure its resilience - the ability of the system to persistently deliver its services in a trustworthy way even when facing changes. Yet, we are observing the increasingly pervasive use of software in such critical infrastructures as transportation, health care, energy production etc. This trend urges the research community to develop powerful methods for assuring resilience of software-intensive systems. The SERENE workshop was established as a means of disseminating such research results and fostering discussion and cooperation between the growing resilience research community.

This volume contains the proceedings of the 4th International Workshop on Software Engineering for Resilient Systems (SERENE 2012). SERENE 2012 took place in Pisa, Italy, during September 27–28, 2012. The SERENE workshop is an annual event that brings together researchers and practitioners working on the various aspects of the software engineering life-cycle for resilient systems, especially design, verification, and assessment. In particular it covers such areas as:

- Modelling of resilience properties: formal and semi-formal techniques
- Requirements engineering and re-engineering for resilience
- Verification and validation of resilient systems
- Resilience prediction and experimental measurement
- Error, fault, and exception handling in the software life-cycle
- Empirical studies in the domain of resilient systems
- Relations between resilience and other system quality attributes
- Frameworks, patterns, and software architectures for resilience
- Resilience at run-time: metadata, mechanisms, reasoning, and adaptation
- Engineering of self-healing autonomic systems
- Quantitative approaches to ensuring resilience
- CASE tools for developing resilient systems

SERENE 2012 featured two invited speakers: Andrea Zisman and Nuno Ferreira Neves. Andrea Zisman is professor at the City University London (UK) and is considered a leading expert in service engineering in combination with resilience. She has worked, among others, in verification of service-based systems, consistency management and traceability of software artifacts, design and verification of secure software systems, and identification and composition of trusted services as well as development of trust framework for cloud infrastructures. Nuno Ferreira Neves is associate professor at the University of Lisbon (Portugal) and is a distinguished researcher in the area of fault and intrusion tolerance. He has worked on a range of topics, including security information and events management, critical infrastructure protection, dependable cloud computing, and intrusion-tolerant sensor networks.

The workshop was established by the members of the ERCIM working group SERENE. The group promotes the idea of resilient-centric development processes. It stresses the importance of extending the traditional software engineering practice with theories and tools supporting modelling and verification of various aspects of resilience. We would like to thank the SERENE working group for their hard work in publicizing the event and contributing to its technical program.

All submitted papers received at least three rigorous reviews. The accepted set, consisting of 12 high-quality submissions, allowed us to build a technically strong program that inspired lively discussion and future collaboration in the resilience community. We would like to express our gratitude to the Program Committee members and the additional reviewers who actively participated in reviewing and discussing the submissions. Of course, we would like to gratefully acknowledge and thank all the authors for their effort in submitting papers.

The organization of such a workshop is challenging. We would like to acknowledge the help of technical and administrative staff of CNR-ISTI, Newcastle University, and University of L'Aquila. SERENE 2012 was supported by ERCIM (European Research Consortium in Informatics and Mathematics), CNR-ISTI (Istituto di Scienza e Tecnologie dell'Informazione), and LASSY (Laboratory for Advanced Software Systems, University of Luxembourg).

July 2012   Paris Avgeriou
                                                            Program Chair

                                                    Felicita Di Giandomenico
                                                             General Chair

Organization

General Chair

Felicita Di Giandomenico   CNR-ISTI, Italy

Program Chair

Paris Avgeriou   University of Groningen, The Netherlands

Autumn School Director

Elena Troubitsyna   Åbo Akademi University, Finland

Steering Committee

Didier Buchs   University of Geneva, Switzerland
Henry Muccini   University of L'Aquila, Italy
Patrizio Pelliccione   University of L'Aquila, Italy
Alexander Romanovsky   Newcastle University, UK

Program Committee

Finn Arve Aagesen   NTNU, Norway
Mehmet Aksit   University of Twente, The Netherlands
Giovanna Di Marzo Serugendo   University of Geneva, Switzerland
Xavier Franch   Universitat Politècnica de Catalunya, Spain
Vincenzo Grassi   University of Rome Tor Vergata, Italy
Brahim Hamid   IRIT, France
Valerie Issarny   INRIA, France
Mohamed Kaaniche   LAAS-CNRS, France
Vyacheslav Kharchenko   National Aerospace University, Ukraine
Linas Laibinis   Åbo Akademi University, Finland
Tom Maibaum   McMaster University, Canada
Jose Carlos Maldonado   University of Sao Paulo, Brazil
Eda Marchetti   CNR, Italy
Raffaela Mirandola   Politecnico di Milano, Italy
Ivan Mistrik   Indep. Consultant, Germany
Henry Muccini   University of L'Aquila, Italy
Flavio Oquendo   European University of Brittany/IRISA-UBS, France

Andras Pataricza	BUTE, Hungary
Patrizio Pelliccione	University of L'Aquila, Italy
Anthony Savidis	FORTH, Greece
Peter Schneider-Kamp	University of Southern Denmark
Francis Tam	Nokia, Finland
Elena Troubitsyna	Åbo Akademi University, Finland
Apostolos Zarras	University of Ioannina, Greece

Subreviewers

Maurice H. Ter Beek
Silverio Martinez-Fernandez
Somayeh Malakuti
Nicolas Desnos
Pasqualina Potena

Table of Contents

Applying Formal Methods in Case Studies

Implementing Reusable Exception Handling Patterns with Compile-Time Metaprogramming

Yannis Lilis[1] and Anthony Savidis[1,2]

[1] Institute of Computer Science, FORTH
[2] Department of Computer Science, University of Crete
{lilis,as}@ics.forth.gr

Abstract. We investigate in depth the adoption of compile-time meta-programming to implement exception handling patterns. It is based on logic that is executed at compile-time and outputs source fragments which substitute the meta-code before compilation. Exception patterns are realized as metafunctions capable to transparently generate the invocation details and the appropriate exception handling layout. This way, programmers are relieved from underlying exception handling details, while the handling patterns can be standardized and directly reused. Pattern libraries of directly editable code are enabled, while the adoption of compile-time metaprogramming allows configuring the pattern deployment within the original client source based on application requirements. We examine key exception handling scenarios and we implement them as configurable and reusable pattern libraries in an existing meta-language.

Keywords: Exception handling patterns, design patterns, pattern implementation, compile-time metaprogramming.

1   Introduction

Exception handling [1] is a key mechanism supporting structured error recovery, being an essential ingredient for resilient software systems. It allows effectively decouple normal code from error handling code through distinctive try-catch control blocks. Once exceptions are raised with a throw statement the program control is transferred to the closest handler matching the raised exception. The same exception raised by different contexts may naturally be caught by different handlers, something dependent on the calling context which led to the statement raising the exception.

Ideally, exception handling in a language should facilitate the construction of handling code in a way that is modular and easy to reuse. But still the challenge of implementing modular, generic and directly reusable exception handler code remains an open issue for software developers. The main problem is that in real-life software systems the normal code and the handling code are frequently tightly coupled. An important factor in this context is that the exception handling logic is encompassed within syntactically distinct blocks, meaning the chances for applying language reuse approaches such as inheritance, abstraction, polymorphism and genericity, become de facto restricted. Finally, although there are well known good and bad practices

P. Avgeriou (Ed.): SERENE 2012, LNCS 7527, pp. 1–15, 2012.

regarding exception handling [2, 3], none of the established exceptions patterns can be directly reused in an implementation form across application contexts. In this context, we thought that once we manage to parameterize the syntactic structures, essentially treating syntax, and in effect source code, as a first-class value, we may succeed in realizing exception patterns in a directly implementable and deployable form. This line of thinking has driven us to consider compile-time metaprogramming, a powerful, promising and increasingly popularized programming approach which relies on a special set of features that must be offered by the language.

Compile-time metaprogramming is an advanced language feature enabling to mix programs with extra definitions that are executed at compile-time and transform the original source code of the program. Metaprograms are usually denoted with special language tags and operate on source code fragments in the form of abstract syntax trees (ASTs). Constructs are supported to directly create ASTs from source text (usually called *quasi-quotes*), to combine them with arbitrary ASTs produced by functions (usually called *escapes*), and to finally insert them as an integral part of the final source code that will be compiled (usually called *inlines*).

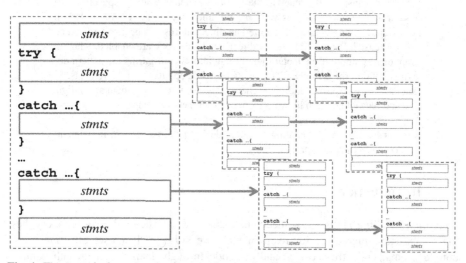

Fig. 1. The recursively-repeated structure of exception handling patterns generated via metaprogramming; *stmts* may contain exception handling code following the main pattern

Using metaprogramming, it is possible to express error handling patterns as parameterized source fragments in the form of *AST templates* with empty placeholders ready to host client-supplied code. Each pattern is implemented by a respective metafunction that can be invoked during compilation at the appropriate source context with the desirable parameters in order to generate a concrete instantiation of the exception handling pattern. Such patterns may in general encompass complex exception handling structures, combing arbitrary statements with nested and repeated try-catch blocks (Fig. 1). Nevertheless, the client code need only be aware of the pattern behavior, its corresponding metafunction and how to apply it. This way, not only programmers are relieved from underlying, sometimes transient, implementation details, but the exception handling patterns can be standardized and be directly reused. In this sense, it is possible to produce libraries of parameterized exception handling patterns, thus allowing configuring pattern deployment at generation-time based on the particular application requirements. This property is illustrated in Fig. 2. We support our claim by examining key exception handling scenarios and by providing all respective meta-implementations to eventually turn them into reusable pattern libraries.

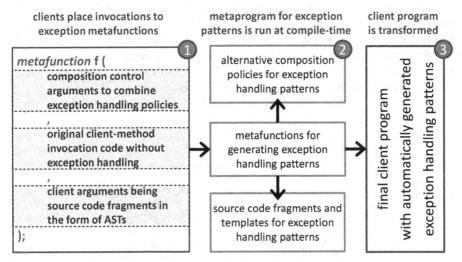

Fig. 2. Deploying library metaprograms to generate exception handling patterns

2 Exception Handling Patterns

Our work has been carried out in the context of the untyped object-based language *Delta* [4], thus, the implementations we present correspond to untyped exception handling. Since our approach has nothing to do with type checking and type systems, it can be well applied to any language, either typed or untyped, as long as they offer the required metaprogramming features. Some examples of languages that can directly use this approach include MetaML, Nemerle, MetaLua, Converge, Groovy, etc. Before discussing the exception handling patterns, we brief the metaprogramming elements offered by the *Delta* language, since they are adopted in all our patterns.

- *Quasi-quotes* (written <<...>>) may be inserted around most elements, such as expressions, statements, functions, etc., and convert them to the respective AST form. Quasi-quotes are the easiest way to create ASTs from source fragments.
- *Escape* (written ~(*expr*)) can be only used inside quasi-quotes to prevent converting *expr* to its AST form and evaluate it normally. Practically, escape is applied on expressions already carrying AST values that need to be incorporated within an AST being constructed via quasi-quotes. It can also be used on variables holding ground values to transform them into constant values in the generated AST.

- **Inline** (written *!(expr)*) will evaluate *expr* and then insert its value, which must be of AST type, into the source code point where the inlines resides.
- **Execute** (written *&stmt*) will evaluate *stmt* normally at compile-time. It allows including in a metaprogram any source code definition (e.g., variables, loops, functions, etc.), since in the Delta language a program is defined as a sequence of statements. Such definitions are not visible outside their enclosing metaprogram.

A simple example is provided in Fig. 3, where the RHS operand of the assignment is generated using metaprogramming. In particular, *foo* is a function available only at compile-time (prefixed with **&**) and its invocation combines the given argument with the AST declared within *foo's* body (*<<1+~x>>* part) to generate and return the AST of *1+2*. Then, the inline replaces the entire *!foo(<<2>>)* part with this AST value. Thus, finally the source code becomes *x=1+2*.

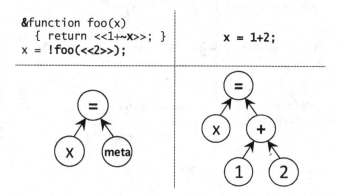

Fig. 3. Metaprograms as compile-time source-code transformations

2.1   Deploying Exception Handling

Design by Contract. Design by Contract (DbyC) [5] is a popular method towards self-checking code improving software reliability. It proposes contracts, constituting computable agreements between clients and suppliers. Clients have to respect method *preconditions* prior to invocation while suppliers guarantee that the associated *postconditions* will be satisfied once the invocation completes. Failure to satisfy the promised obligations, on either the client or the supplier side, constitutes a contract violation that will most likely result into an error, typically conveyed as an exception.

In this context, we will use metaprogramming to automatically generate contract verification code for the supplier class. More specifically, we will iterate the supplier class AST, seeking for precondition and postcondition tests. Once found, we use them to enrich the associated methods by inserting method entry code throwing an exception on contract violation. Additionally, we generate code for the class clients, automatically protecting method invocations that may actually raise contract exceptions with try-catch blocks. This way, we can either insert custom logic for specific contract violations, or allow uniform handling based on a predefined contract violation policy. The discussed functionality can be implemented with the following code.

```
&function DbyCSupplier (class) {   ← generator for the supplier class
   foreach (local m, class.getMethods()) {   ← iterate over class methods
      local pre_id = "pre_" + m.getName();   ← precondition method id
      if (class.hasMethod(pre_id))   ← does the precondition method exist ?
         m.body.push_front(   ← add source (AST) at the beginning of the method
         <<        ← source fragment as AST begins here
            if (not self[~pre_id]())   ← has precondition call failed?
               throw [                          ← then throw an exception
                  @class    : "ContractException",
                  @type     : "Precondition",
                  @classId   : ~(class.getName()),
                  @method   : ~(m.getName())
               ];
         >>        ← source fragment as AST ends here
         );
         …similar logic to add postcondition checking code at the method end here…
   }
}
```

A couple of compile-time generators for the DbyC clients are provided below:

```
&function DbyCClient (invocation_stmts, handler_stmts) {
   return <<   ← code template with parameters the invocation and the handler code
         try { ~invocation_stmts; }
         catch ContractException { ~handler_stmts; }
      >>;
}
&function DbyCClientLogging (invocation_stmts) {   ← a logger generator
   return   DbyCClient(                           ← uses basic client generator
         invocation_stmts,
         << log(ContractException) >>   ← handler only logs exception
      );
}
```

An example of using the DbyC generator for suppliers in a Stack class follows:

```
function Stack() {            function Stack() {
 return [                      return [
  method empty   {…},          method empty   {…},
  method pre_pop {…},          method pre_pop {…},
  method pop      {…},         method pop      {
                                  if (not self["pre_pop"]())
  !(DbyCSupplier(                   throw [
    context("class")      ⇨         @class    : "ContractException",
 ));                                @type     : "Precondition",
                                    @classId  : "Stack",
 ];                                 @method  : "pop"
}                                ];
context is a compile-time          … original body of pop method follows here…
operator providing the AST of    },
the current identified construct  ];
(here we request "class")      }
```

```
!(DbyCClient(                    try { st.pop(); }
  << st.pop() >>,          ⇨  catch ContractException
  << assert false; >>              { assert false; }
));
```

```
!(DbyCClientLogging(             try { st.pop(); }
  << st.pop() >>          ⇨  catch ContractException
));                                  { log(ContractException); }
```

Such an implementation can be modularly organized collecting all metafunctions that generate DbyC code in a library module, used during compilation by supplier and client classes. As shown in Fig. 4, apart from client-to-supplier normal dependencies, client and supplier modules have a meta-code dependency on the DbyC library. The same property applies to all exception pattern implementations we discuss later.

Fig. 4. Separation of software components involved in the DbyC exception pattern

Resource Failures. A typical error handling category relates to exceptions being raised due to resource failures. This includes scenarios where the system runs out of memory, a network connection fails, or a local database does not respond properly. Through metaprogramming we can reduce the boilerplate code required to test various resource failures, by automatic generation at the desirable client context. An implementation and its deployment are provided below.

```
&function Resources (alloc_stmts, handler_stms)
   { return <<try {~alloc_stmts;} catch e {~handler_stmts;}>>; }
&function InitialMemoryAllocation (alloc)
   { return Resources(alloc, <<print("No memory!"); exit();>>; }
&function NormalMemoryAllocation (alloc)
   { return Resources(alloc, <<Collector(); ~alloc;>>; }
```

```
!(InitialMemoryAllocation(<< x = malloc(10) >>));
!(NormalMemoryAllocation(<< y = malloc(20) >>));              ⇩
try { x = malloc(10); } catch e { print("No memory!"); exit(); }
try { y = malloc(20); } catch e { Collector(); y = malloc(20);}
```

High Level Architectural Exceptions. When implementing the interaction amongst high-level architectural components, the exceptions that can be raised are usually formalized and relate to predefined conditions that may fail during runtime. Along these lines, a component is aware of the exceptions that may be raised by a certain invocation and its reaction to them is typically predetermined: it either knows how to handle errors, in which case it deals with them directly, or it does not and just filters and propagates the exceptions to the calling component. These high-level exception interactions can be turned to metacode, inserted at the appropriate sites of component implementations. This allows standardizing exception interactions as component meta-data and can lead to cleaner code that is easier to understand and maintain. Such functionality can be achieved using the exception pattern implemented below.

```
&function ArchitecturalException (exception) {
   return [  ← returns a generator instance with meta methods for arch exceptions
      method Raise { return << throw ~exception; >>; },
      method Ensure(condition)  ← if the condition fails will raise an exception
         { return << if (not (~condition)) ~(self.Raise()); >>; },
      method Filter(invocation_stmts, filter_stmts) {
      return <<  ← upon an exception execute the filtering statements and rethrow
         try { ~invocation_stmts; }
         catch e { assert e==~exception; ~filter_stmts; throw e; }
         >>;
      },
      method Handle(invocation_stmts, handler_stmts) {
      return <<  ← handle an exception executing the given handler statements
         try { ~ invocation_stmts; }
         catch e { assert e == ~exception; ~handler_stmts; }
         >>;
      }
   ];
}
```

An example of invoking the *ArchitecturalException* metafunction at compile-time and the respective source code it introduces in its place is provided below:

```
&bank = ArchitecturalException("NegativeAmount");
!(bank.Ensure( << acc.amount >= 0 >>);
!(bank.Handle( << acc.Withdraw() >>, << acc.CancelTrans() >>);⇩
if (not (acc.amount >= 0)) throw "NegativeAmount";
try { acc.Withdraw(); }
catch e { assert e == "NegativeAmount"; acc.CancelTrans(); }
```

Multiple Repeating Catch Blocks. A common scenario encountered in exception handling relates to small source fragments, even single statements, which may raise multiple distinct exceptions. Such code fragments may be found in various independent locations of the program but the error handling strategy is usually similar. A typical example of this scenario is the use of sockets, where various things may go wrong (e.g. *IOException, ConnectException, TimeoutException, SecurityException,* etc.), but each of them is usually handled in a custom manner. For instance, upon a *TimeoutException* the program will typically wait and retry the operation after some time, upon an *IOException* it will try to reestablish the IO stream, upon a *SecurityException* it may try to elevate security privileges or notify the user about insufficient permissions, and so on. Such cases require introducing comprehensive cascading catch blocks that cannot be abstracted via polymorphism or genericity in any manner. But it is possible to introduce metafunctions capturing the cascaded exception handling logic and insert it at the appropriate client sites thus accomplishing the desirable exception handling behavior. This is demonstrated by the following code:

```
&function Cascading (invocation_stmts, alt_handlers) {
   ast = nil;          ← will hold the AST enumerating all handler entries
   foreach (type^of exception : handler^for exception, alt_handlers)
     ast = <<          ←make AST associating exceptions type with handler code
              ~ast, { ~type : function{ ~handler; } }
           >>;
   return <<
     try { ~invocation_stmts; }
     catch e {
        D = [~ast];                  ← inserts previously made AST of handlers
        f = D[e.type];               ← get handlers dispatcher for this exception
        if (f) f(); else throw e;    ← if the handler exists call it else throw
     }
   >>;
}

&FILE_IO_Handlers = [   ← hash table as <exception type>: <handler code>
   {"EOFException"                  : << reader.close(); >>   },
   {"FileNotFoundException"         : << print("no file")>>   },
   {"UnknownEncodingException"      : << load_encodings()>>   }
];
!(Cascading(              ← generator produces the cascaded handling logic
   << reader = FileReader("foo.abc"); reader.read(); >>,
   FILE_IO_Handlers
));
try { reader = FileReader("foo.abc"); reader.read(); }
catch e {
   D = [
     {"EOFException"               : function {reader.close();  }},
     {"FileNotFoundException"      : function {print("no file");}},
     {"UnknownEncodingException"   : function {load_encodings();}}
   ];
   f = D[e.type]; if (f) f(); else throw e;
}
```

Our examples are untyped so the cascading catch blocks are modeled through a single catch block, using a dispatcher to choose a handler via the runtime exception type tag. In a typed language, the generated code would consist of successive catch blocks for typed exceptions, each with the respective handler invocation.

2.2   Exception Policies

Exception handling is known to be a global design issue [6] that affects multiple system modules, mostly in an application-specific way. In this sense, it should be possible to select a specific exception handling policy for the entire system or apply different policies for different components of the system. Using typical object-oriented techniques, the only solution would be to abstract the desired exception handling policy within a function (or object method) and place a corresponding invocation to every applicable catch block. However, it does not avoid the boilerplate code required for declaring the handler and performing the function call, nor does it support arbitrary exception handling structures or context-dependent information. As before, each policy will be implemented through a respective metafunction and it will be used in multiple different contexts and call sites. Additionally, it is possible to parameterize the actual policy being applied, thus allowing the interchangeable use of different policies based simply on configuration parameters and without requiring even a single change at the actual call sites inside client code. We have implemented a set of exception handling policies incorporating some of the strategies discussed in [7]. Specifically we support the following use cases implemented in the code below:

- *None* – Do not handle exceptions
- *Inaction* – Ignore any raised exceptions
- *Logging* – Log any raised exceptions
- *Retry* – Repeatedly attempt an operation that raised an exception
- *Cleanup Rethrow* – Perform any cleanup actions and propagate the exception
- *Higher Level Exception* – Raise a higher level exception
- *Guarded Suspension* – Suspend execution until a condition is met and then retry

```
&function None (stmts) { return stmts; }← no handling, just return stmts
&function Inaction (stmts)
      { return << try { ~stmts; } catch e {} >>; }
&function Logging (stmts)
      { return << try { ~stmts; } catch e { log(e); } >>; }
&function ConstructRetry (data) { ← constructor for a custom retry policy
   return function (stmts) { ←return a function implementing the code pattern
      return <<                  ←the returned function returns an AST
         for (local i = 0; i < ~(data.attempts); ++i)
            try { ~stmts; break; } ← try & break loop when successful
            catch e { Sleep(~(data.delay)); } ←catch & wait before retrying
         if (i == ~(data.attempts))         ←maximum attempts were tried?
            { ~(data.failure_stmts); } ←then give-up & invoke failure code
      >>;
   };
}
&function ConstructCleanupRethrow (cleanup_smts) {
   return function (smts) {
   return <<
      try { ~stmts; }   ←try the code and on error cleanup and rethrow
      catch e { ~cleanup_stmts; throw e; }
   >>;
   };
}
&function ConstructHigherLevelException (exception) {
   return function (stmts) {
   return <<
      try { ~stmts; }  ←try the code and on error throw a higher-level exception
      catch e { throw [ ~exception, @source : e ]; }
   >>;
   };
}
```

```
&function ConstructGuardedSuspension(condition) {
  return function (stmts) { return <<
    while (true)
      try { ~stmts; break; }        ←try the given code and break on success
      catch e { while (not ~condition); }  ←else wait condition to hold
    >>;
  };
}
```

An example of using metaprogramming to create exception handling policies and the respective source code generated by their deployment is provided below:

```
&Policies.Install("LOG", Logging);
&Policies.Install("RETRY", ConstructRetry([
  @attempts : 5, @delay : 1000, @fail : <<post("FAIL")>>
]));
```

```
                                     for (i = 0; i < 5; ++i)
&p = Policies.Get("RETRY");  ⇨     try     { f(); break; }
!p(<<f()>>);                        catch e { Sleep(1000); }
                                     if (i == 5) { post("FAIL"); }

&p = Policies.Get("LOG");    ⇨ try { g(); }
!p(<<g()>>);                   catch e { log(e); }
```

The policy implementations are straightforward, placing the given invocation code in a *try* block and the handler logic in a *catch* block. Notably, the pattern for expressing the handler policy is specified once and reused across all generated *catch* blocks. This way, programmers need not be aware of the pattern details or be forced to implement it multiple times; policies are standardized within a library and can be reused based on the application requirements.

Some of the policies discussed require no additional information to be expressed (e.g. *Inaction*, or *Logging*), while others receive such information as construction parameters. For example, the *Retry* policy requires the number of attempts for retrying the operation, the delay to wait between them in case an exception occurs and code to be executed if all attempts fail. *It is important to note that any parameters are required only once upon construction and are not repeated per policy application.* This relieves programmers from repeatedly supplying the required parameters, but more importantly, it allows the invocation style of policy metaprograms to be uniform, allowing them to be used interchangeably without changes in their call sites.

An approach for parameterized exception handling policies is presented in [8] through a library filtering already caught exceptions. This means boilerplate code is repeated per handler, but more importantly it cannot support scenarios with more elaborate exception handling logic (for example *Retry, Guarded Suspension*, etc.).

2.3   Process Modeling Patterns

Exception handling is not limited to the scope of specific functions or software modules, but also applies in the more general context of a process model. In both cases it is important to specify the normal execution path as well as the possible exceptional behaviors along with the tasks required to handle them properly. In this sense, exception handling patterns observed in the one world can also be beneficial to the other. To this end, we adopt the *trying other alternatives* and *inserting behavior* process modeling patterns described in [9] and provide for them meta-implementations.

Trying other Alternatives. It is possible for a single task to be accomplished in multiple ways, possibly involving different components and relying on different conditions. Instead of explicitly using such information in the code structure, it is preferable to abstract the functionality in distinct operations, where all of them achieve the same task, and if one fails another alternative may be tried in its place. Below we provide an exception handling pattern implementation for this scenario. The *alternatives* argument contains a list with the alternative code fragments for the given task, while the *ex* argument is the exception that signals failure of a task so as to try an alternative.

```
&function TryAlternatives (alternatives, ex) {
    ast = << local success = false; >>;   ← guard for successful alternative
    foreach (local alt, alternatives)
        ast = << ~ast;                     ← merge with previously produced AST
            if (not success)               ← skip rest of alternatives if task has succeeded
                try { ~alt; success = true; } ← if no exception we succeeded
                catch e { if (e != ~ex) throw e; } ← throw all other exceptions
        >>;
    return << ~ast; if (not success) throw ~ex; >>;  ← throw if all fail
}
```

An example of invoking the *TryAlternatives* metafunction at compile-time and the respective source code it introduces in its place is provided below:

```
&alternatives = list_new(<<hotel1.Book()>>, <<hotel2.Book()>>);
&Order(alternatives);      ← optionally apply client-specific ordering
!(TryAlternatives(alternatives, "FullyBookedException"));   ⇩
local success = false;
if (not success)
    try { hotel1.Book(); success = true; }
    catch e { if (e != "FullyBookedException") throw e; }
if (not success)
    try { hotel2.Book(); success = true; }
    catch e { if (e != "FullyBookedException") throw e; }
if (not success) throw "FullyBookedException";
```

Inserting Behavior. When errors occur during the execution of a series of tasks, they may not be fatal, but may instead require specific actions to be performed to fix the problems that caused them. This inserted behavior may have to be executed directly after the occurrence of an error before any later tasks are executed, (*immediate fixing*), or it may be possible to just note the error and handle it accordingly after all tasks are completed (*deferred fixing*). Below we provide a pattern implementation supporting both scenarios. The *tasks* argument contains all relevant information (normal code, exceptions that they may raise and handler code) about the tasks to be executed, while the *immediate* argument specifies when to apply the error handling code.

```
&function InsertBehavior (tasks, immediate) {
  ast = nil, err = nil, i = 0;
  foreach (local task, tasks) {
    ast = << ~ast;                    ←merge with previously produced AST if any
      try { ~(task.stmts); }     ←insert the task-related stmts

    catch e {
        if (e != ~(task.except)) throw e;    ←throw all other exceptions
        ~(immediate ? task.handler : << errors[~i] = true >>);
      } ←if immediate-fixing insert directly the task handler else record the error
    >>;
    if (not immediate)  ←if deferred fixing insert code to handle recorded errors
      err = << ~err; if(errors[~i]) { ~(task.handler); } >>;
    ++i;
  }
  return immediate ? ast : << local errors=[]; ~ast; ~err >>;
}
```

```
!(InsertBehavior(list_new(          try { LoadConfig(); }
[ @stmts: << LoadConfig()>>,        catch e {
  @except: "NotFound",                if(e!="NotFound") throw e;
  @handler : <<LoadDefault()>> ],     LoadDefault();
 [@stmts: <<SendData()>>,           }
  @except: "ConnError",             try { SendData(); }
  @handler :<<RepairConn()>> ]      catch e {
), true));                            if(e!="ConnError") throw e;
                                      RepairConn();
                                    }
```

2.4   Pattern Combinations

The previously discussed patterns target different implementation layers ranging from low level operations on sockets to high level component interactions towards a common task. All these patterns are orthogonal and can be combined with each other to form more elaborate and custom exception handling styles (Fig. 5). It is important to note that using this approach the pattern combination maintains a linear code complexity level. Even though the generated code may contain multiple levels of nested and/or cascading catch blocks, the original code involves mainly independent pattern implementations, typically provided as a library, and the pattern combination that essentially behaves as a code decoration process. For example, consider the task of

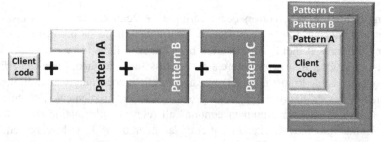

Fig. 5. Modular composition of exception-handling patterns as decorator stacks

booking a hotel. Various alternative hotel objects may be available for booking, each object involving DbyC contractual tests, while the system may adapt a retry policy to handle any raised exceptions. Clearly, addressing all these requirements by manually inserting exception handling code would result into error-prone code that will be hard to read, understand and maintain. However, using metaprogramming we can combine applications of the *Retry Policy*, *Try Alternatives* and *Design by Contract* patterns.

```
!(Policies.Get("RETRY")(    ←apply the Retry pattern
  TryAlternatives(          ←apply the Try Alternatives pattern
    list_new(
      DbyCClientLogging(<<hotel1.Book()>>),  ←apply DbyC pattern
      DbyCClientLogging(<<hotel2.Book()>>),  ←apply DbyC pattern
    ), "FullBookedException"
  )
));
```

⇩

```
for (local i = 0; i < 5; ++i)
  try {                          ← try-catch generated by Retry
    local success = false;
    if (not success)
      try {                      ← try-catch generated by TryAlternatives
        try { hotel1.Book(); }   ← try-catch generated by DbyC
        catch ContractException { log(ContractException); }
        success = true;
      } catch e { if (e != "FullyBookedException") throw e; }
      ...if statement with similar code structure for alternative hotel2.Book();
      if (not success) throw "FullyBookedException";
      break;
  } catch e { Sleep(1000); }
if (i == 5) { post("FAIL"); }
```

3   Related Work

Our work targets the delivery of modular and reusable error handling code. As such, it is closely related to aspect-oriented programming (AOP) [10], an approach for improving the separation of crosscutting concerns in software design and implementation. In this context, there is a lot of work in the direction of separating exception handling code from application code and modularizing it into aspects.

Introductory texts [10, 11] describe exception handling as a potential target for applying AOP and there are refactoring catalogues [12, 13] that include procedures for moving exception-handling code to aspects; however they do not assess the suitability or effectiveness of the approach. An initial study on this subject [14] showed that aspects can decrease the number of LOC, but a later more in-depth study [15] showed that there are cases where aspects may bring more harm than good. In general, current AOP languages have some limitations when used for exception handling. Firstly, they cannot express certain exception handlers without leading to program anomalies [16]. Secondly, they do not help much in making the interface between normal and error handling code explicit [15]. Additionally, aspectizing context dependent handlers requires introducing artificial changes, thus causing software maintenance issues [17]. Finally, mixing exception handling with AO programs can hinder program reliability as the exception flow is complicated, leading to several possible bugs [18].

Using metaprogramming to generate exception handling code structures can help overcoming limitations found in AO solutions. Firstly, the exception handling code is generated *in-place* meaning that any required context is directly available to it, avoiding the need for explicitly providing it as additional aspect parameters. Secondly, code generation allows creating any code structure including nested and cascading exception handlers without having to specify multiple advices. Additionally, combining multiple exception handling patterns is explicit and straightforward; there can be no conflicts from independently deployed aspects where no ordering is specified. Finally, metaprogramming allows parameterizing code structures and thus combining similar functionality, something not always possible through typical AO advice. Table 1 highlights the pros and cons of each approach with respect to exception handling.

Table 1. Comparison of AOP and metaprogramming in the context of exception handling

	Aspects	Metaprograms
Automation	☑ Pointcuts match multiple sites	☒ Pattern is repeated per site
Combination	☒ May impose explicit ordering	☑ Free user-defined ordering
Context	☒ Handlers depending on local context break encapsulation	☑ Handlers are generated in-place and always access local context
Reuse	☒ Similar code fragments must be repeated every time ☑ Reuse via aspect inheritance	☑ Similar code fragments can be composed and reused as ASTs ☑ Reuse via metafunctions
Expressiveness	☒ Bound by pattern matching	☑ Allows any handler scenario

4   Conclusion

We have presented a methodology for implementing exception handling patterns as reusable and composable libraries. Our approach is based on compile-time metaprogramming and relies on two axes: (i) encapsulating and abstracting the pattern logic as a metacode library manipulating source fragments as ASTs; and (ii) applying the metacode during compilation to generate the pattern implementation details based on the exception handling parameters of the application. As AST fragments can express any source code structure, this approach can support any exception handling pattern as well as any of their possible combinations, regardless of the complexity.

Essentially, metaprogramming relieves programmers from maintaining error-prone implementation details and allows them to easily use and combine exception handling pattern libraries. We examined various exception handling scenarios, from typical cases involving DbyC and resource failures, to generic policies and process modeling patterns. For each of them we applied our methodology and expressed the handling patterns with metafunctions. As part of the evaluation process, we also applied it on various projects. Results showed that the effort required in producing, understanding and maintaining exception handling code is reduced, while developers noted that patterns allowed them to better separate normal code from error handling code.

Overall, we consider this work to be a step forward in enabling directly programmable standardized exception handling patterns. The adoption of compile-time metaprogramming allows reuse and modularity beyond what is possible with current object-oriented and aspect-orientated practices.

References

1. Goodenough, J.B.: Exception handling: Issues and a proposed notation. Communications of the ACM 18(12), 683–696 (1975)
2. Doshi, G.: Best practices for exception handling (2003),
   http://www.onjava.com/pub/a/onjava/2003/11/19/
   exceptions.html (accessed May 11, 2012)
3. McCune T.: Exception-handling antipatterns (2006),
   http://today.java.net/pub/a/today/2006/04/06/
   exceptionhandling-antipatterns.html (accessed May 11, 2012)
4. Savidis, A.: Delta Language (2010),
   http://www.ics.forth.gr/hci/files/plang/Delta/Delta.html
   (accessed May 11, 2012)
5. Bertrand, M.: Design by Contract. In: Mandrioli, D., Meyer, B. (eds.) Advances in Object-Oriented Software Engineering, pp. 1–50. Prentice Hall (1991)
6. Garcia, A., Rubira, C., Romanovsky, A., Xu, J.: A comparative study of exception handling mechanisms for building dependable object oriented software. Journal of Systems and Software 59(2), 197–222 (2001)
7. Wirfs-Brock, R.: What it Really Takes to Handle Exceptions in Use Cases. In: Use 2002 Conference Proceedings, pp. 341–370 (2002)
8. Newton, K.: The Exception Handling Application Block. From. The Definitive Guide to the Microsoft Enterprise Library, pp. 221–257. Apress (2007)
9. Lerner, B.S., Christov, S., Osterweil, L.J., Bendraou, R., Kannengiesser, U., Wise, A.: Exception handling patterns for process modelling. IEEE Transactions on Software Engineering 36(2), 162–183 (2010)
10. Kiczales, G., Lamping, J., Mendhekar, A., Maeda, C., Lopes, C., Loingtier, J., Irwin, J.: Aspect-Oriented Programming. In: Aksit, M., Auletta, V. (eds.) ECOOP 1997. LNCS, vol. 1241, pp. 220–242. Springer, Heidelberg (1997)
11. Laddad, R.: AspectJ in Action. Manning 512 (2003)
12. Cole, L., Borba, P.: Deriving refactorings for Aspectj. In: Proc. of the 4th ACM Conference on Aspect-Oriented Software Development, Chicago, USA, pp. 123–134 (March 2005)
13. Laddad R. Aspect-Oriented refactoring, parts 1 and 2. The Server Side (2003),
   http://www.theserverside.com (accessed May 11, 2012)
14. Lippert, M., Lopes, C.V.: A study on exception detection and handling using aspect-oriented programming. In: Proc. of the 22nd ICSE, Limerick, Ireland, pp. 418–427 (June 2000)
15. Castor, F., Cacho, N., Figueiredo, E., Maranhao, R., Garcia, A., Rubira, C.: Exceptions and aspects: The devil is in the details. In: Proceedings of the 14th SIGSOFT FSE, Portland, U.S.A., pp. 152–162 (November 2006)
16. Castor, F., Garcia, A., Rubira, C.: Extracting Error Handling to Aspects: A Cookbook. In: Proceedings of the 23rd ICSM, Paris, France (2007)
17. Greenwood, P., Bartolomei, T., Figueiredo, E., Dosea, M., Garcia, A., Cacho, N., Sant'Anna, C., Soares, S., Borba, P., Kulesza, U., Rashid, A.: On the Impact of Aspectual Decompositions on Design Stability: An Empirical Study. In: Bateni, M. (ed.) ECOOP 2007. LNCS, vol. 4609, pp. 176–200. Springer, Heidelberg (2007)
18. Coelho, R., Rashid, A., von Staa, A., Noble, J., Kulesza, U., Lucena, C.: A catalogue of bug patterns for exception handling in aspect-oriented programs. In: Proc. of the 15th Conference on Pattern Languages of Programs, New York, NY, USA, pp. 1–13 (2008)

A Case Study in Formal Development of a Fault Tolerant Multi-robotic System

Inna Pereverzeva[1,2], Elena Troubitsyna[2], and Linas Laibinis[2]

[1] Turku Centre for Computer Science
[2] Åbo Akademi University
Joukahaisenkatu 3-5, 20520 Turku, Finland
{inna.pereverzeva,elena.troubitsyna,linas.laibinis}@abo.fi

Abstract. Multi-robotic systems are typical examples of complex multi-agent systems. The robots – autonomic agents – cooperate with each other in order to achieve the system goals. While designing multi-robotic systems, we should ensure that these goals remain achievable despite robot failures, i.e., guarantee system fault tolerance. However, designing the fault tolerance mechanisms for multi-agent systems is a notoriously difficult task. In this paper we describe a case study in formal development of a complex fault tolerant multi-robotic system. The system design relies on cooperative error recovery and dynamic reconfiguration. We demonstrate how to specify and verify essential properties of a fault tolerant multi-robotic system in Event-B and derive a detailed formal system specification by refinement. The main objective of the presented case study is to investigate suitability of a refinement approach for specifying a complex multi-agent system with co-operative error recovery.

Keywords: Event-B, formal modelling, refinement, fault tolerance, multi-robotic system.

1 Introduction

Over the last decade, the field of autonomous multi-robotic systems has grown dramatically. There are several research directions that are continuously receiving significant attention: autonomous navigation and control, self-organising behaviour, architectures for multi-robot co-operation, to name a few. The robot co-operation is studied from a variety of perspectives: delegation of authority and control, heterogeneous versus homogeneous architectures, communication structure etc. In this paper we focus on studying the fault tolerance aspects of multi-robotic co-operation. Namely, we show by example how to formally derive a specification of a multi-robotic system that relies on dynamic reconfiguration and co-operative error recovery to achieve fault tolerance.

Our paper presents a case study in formal development of a cleaning multi-robotic system. That kind of systems are typically employed in hazardous areas. The system has a heterogenous architecture consisting of several stationary devices, base stations, that coordinate the work of respective groups of robots.

P. Avgeriou (Ed.): SERENE 2012, LNCS 7527, pp. 16–31, 2012.

A base station assigns a robot to clean a certain segment. Since both base stations and robots can fail, the main objective of our formal development is to formally specify co-operative error recovery and verify that the proposed design ensures goal reachability, i.e., guarantees that the whole territory will be eventually cleaned. The proposed development approach ensures goal reachability "by construction". It is based on refinement in Event-B [2] – a formal top-down approach to correct-by-construction system development. The main development technique – refinement – allows us to ensure that a resulting specification preserves the globally observable behaviour and properties of the specifications it refines. The Rodin platform [8] automates modelling and verification in Event-B.

In this paper we demonstrate how to formally define a system goal and, in a stepwise manner, *derive* a detailed specification of the system architecture. While refining the system specification, we gradually introduce a representation of the main elements of the architecture – base stations and robots – as well as failures and the fault tolerance mechanisms. Moreover, we identify the main properties of a fault tolerant multi-robotic system and demonstrate how to formally specify and verify them as a part of the refinement process. In particular, we show how to derive a mechanism for cooperative error recovery in a systematic way.

Traditionally, the behaviour of multi-robotic systems is verified by simulation and model checking. These approaches allow the designers to investigate only a limited number of scenarios and require a significant reduction of the state space. In our paper, we discuss advantages and limitations of a refinement approach to achieve full-scale verification of a multi-robotic system.

The paper is structured as follows. In Section 2 we briefly overview the Event-B formalism. Section 3 describes the requirements for our case study – a multi-robotic cleaning system – and outlines the development strategy. Section 4 presents a formal development of the cleaning system and demonstrates how to express and verify its properties in the refinement process. Finally, in Section 5 we conclude by assessing our contributions and reviewing the related work.

2 Modelling and Refinement in Event-B

The Event-B formalism – a variation of the B Method [1] – is a state-based formal approach that promotes the correct-by-construction development paradigm and formal verification by theorem proving. In Event-B, a system model is specified using the notion of an *abstract state machine* [2]. An abstract state machine encapsulates the model state represented as a collection of variables and defines operations on the state, i.e., it describes the *behaviour* of the modelled system. Usually, a machine has an accompanying component, called *context*, which may include user-defined carrier sets, constants and their properties given as a list of model axioms. In Event-B, the model variables are strongly typed by the constraining predicates. These predicates and the other important properties that must be preserved by the model constitute model *invariants*.

The dynamic behaviour of the system is defined by a set of atomic *events*. Generally, an event has the following form:

$$e \mathrel{\widehat{=}} \textbf{any } a \textbf{ where } G_e \textbf{ then } R_e \textbf{ end},$$

where e is the event's name, a is the list of local variables, the *guard* G_e is a predicate over the local variables of the event and the state variables of the system. The body of the event is defined by the next-state relation R_e. In Event-B, R_e is defined by a *multiple* (possibly nondeterministic) assignment over the system variables. The guard defines the conditions under which the assignment can be performed, i.e., when the event is *enabled*. If several events are enabled at the same time, any of them can be chosen for execution non-deterministically. If an event does not have local variables, it can be described simply as:

$$e \mathrel{\widehat{=}} \textbf{when } G_e \textbf{ then } R_e \textbf{ end}.$$

Event-B employs a top-down refinement-based approach to system development. A development starts from an abstract system specification that non-deterministically models the most essential functional requirements. In a sequence of refinement steps, we gradually reduce non-determinism and introduce detailed design decisions. In particular, we can add new events, split events as well as replace abstract variables by their concrete counterparts, i.e., perform *data refinement*. When data refinement is performed, we should define so called *gluing invariant* as a part of the invariant of the refined machine. The gluing invariant defines the relationship between the abstract and concrete variables.

Often a refinement step introduces new events and variables into the abstract specification. The new events correspond to the stuttering steps that are not visible at the abstract level, i.e., they refine implicit *skip*. To guarantee that the refined specification preserves the global behaviour of the abstract machine, we should demonstrate that the newly introduced events *converge*. To prove it, we need to define a *variant* – an expression over a finite subset of natural numbers – and show that the execution of new events decreases it. Sometimes, convergence of an event cannot be proved due to a high level of abstraction. Then the event obtains the status *anticipated*. This obliges the designer to prove, at some later refinement step, that the event indeed converges.

The consistency of Event-B models, i.e., verification of well-formedness and invariant preservation as well as correctness of refinement steps, is formally demonstrated by discharging the relevant proof obligations generated by the Rodin platform [8]. Rodin also provides an automated tool support for proving.

3   Multi-robotic Systems

Our paper focuses on formal modelling and development of multi-robotic systems that should function autonomously , i.e., without human intervention. Such kind of systems are often deployed in hazardous areas, e.g., nuclear power plants, disaster areas, minefields, etc.

Typically, the main task or *goal* that a multi-robotic system should accomplish is split between the deployed robots. The robot activities are coordinated by a number of stationary units – base stations. Since both robots and base stations may fail, to ensure success of the overall goal we should incorporate the fault tolerance mechanisms into the system design. These mechanisms rely on co-operative error recovery that allows the system dynamically reallocate functions from the failed agents to the healthy ones.

Designing co-operative error recovery for multi-agent systems is a notoriously complex task. The complexity is caused by several factors: asynchronous communication, a highly decentralised system architecture and the lack of the "universally known" global system state. Yet, the designers should guarantee that the system goals are achievable despite failures. A variety of failure modes and scenarios makes verification of goal reachability of the co-operative error recovery difficult and time-consuming. Therefore, there is a clear need for rigorous approaches that support scalable design and verification in a systematic manner.

Next we present the requirements of our case study – a multi-robotic system for cleaning a territory. Then we will demonstrate how we can formally develop the system in Event-B and prove its essential properties.

3.1   A Case Study: Cleaning a Territory

The goal of the system is to get a certain territory cleaned by robots. The whole territory is divided into several *zones*, which in turn are further divided into a number of *sectors*. Each zone has a *base station* that coordinates the cleaning activities within the zone. In general, one base station might coordinate several zones. In its turn, each base station supervises a number of robots attached to it by assigning cleaning tasks to them.

A robot is an autonomous electro-mechanical device that can move and clean. A base station may assign a robot a specific sector to clean. Upon receiving the assignment, the robot autonomously moves to this sector and performs cleaning. After successfully completing its mission, the robot returns back to the base station to receive a new assignment. The base station keeps track of the cleaned and non-cleaned sectors. Moreover, the base stations periodically exchange the information about their cleaned sectors.

While performing the given task, a robot might fail which subsequently leads to a failure to clean the assigned sector. We assume that a base station is able to detect all the failed robots attached to it. In case of a robot failure, the base station may assign another active robot to perform the failed task.

A base station might fail as well. We assume that a failure of a base station can be detected by the others base stations. In that case, the healthy base stations redistribute control over the robots coordinated by the failed base station.

Let us now to formulate the main requirements and properties associated with the multi-robotic system informally described above.

(PR1) *The main system goal: the whole territory has to be cleaned.*

(PR2) *To clean the territory, every its zone has to be cleaned.*

(PR3) *To clean a zone, every its sector has to be cleaned.*

(PR4) *Every cleaned sector or zone remains cleaned during functioning of the system.*

(PR5) *No two robots should clean the same sector.* In other words, a robot gets only non-assigned and non-cleaned sectors to clean.

(PR6) *The information about the cleaned sectors stored in any base station has to be consistent with the current state of the territory.* More specifically, if a base station sees a particular sector in some zone as cleaned, then this sector is marked as cleaned in the memory of the base station responsible for it. Also, if a sector is marked as non-cleaned in the memory of the base station responsible for it, then any base station sees it as non-cleaned.

(PR7) *Base station cooperation: if a base station has been detected as failed then some base station will take the responsibility for all the zones and robots of the failed base station.*

(PR8) *Base station cooperation: if a base station has no more active robots, a group of robot is sent to this base station from another base station.*

(PR9) *Base station cooperation: if a base station has cleaned all its zones, its active robots may be reallocated under control of another base station.*

The last three requirements essentially describe the co-operative recovery mechanisms that we assume to be present in the described multi-robot system.

3.2 Formal Development Strategy

In the next section we will present a formal Event-B development of the described multi-system robotic system. We demonstrate how to specify and verify the given properties (PR1)–(PR9). Let us now give a short overview of this development and highlight formal techniques used to ensure the proposed properties.

We start with a very abstract model, essentially representing the system behaviour as a process iteratively trying to achieve the main goal (PR1). The next couple of data refinement steps decompose the main goal into a set of subgoals, i.e., reformulate it in the terms of zones and sectors. We will define and prove the relevant gluing invariants establishing a formal relationship between goals and the corresponding subgoals.

While the specification remains highly abstract, we postulate goal reachability property by defining *anticipate* status for the involved events. Once, as a result of the refinement process, the model becomes sufficiently detailed, we change the event status into *convergent* and prove their termination by supplying the appropriate variant expression.

Next we introduce different types of agents (i.e., base stations and robots). The base stations coordinate execution of the tasks required to achieve the corresponding subgoal, while the robots execute the tasks allocated on them. We formally define the relationships between different types of agents, as well as agents and respective subgoals. These relationships are specified and proved as invariant properties of the model.

The consequent refinement steps explicitly introduce agent failures, the information exchange as well as co-operation activities between the agents. The integrity between the local and the global information stored within base stations is again formulated and proved as model invariant properties.

We assume that communication between the base stations as well as the robots and the base stations is reliable. In other words, messages are always transmitted correctly without any loss or errors. The main focus of our development is on specifying and verifying the co-operative recovery mechanisms.

4   Development of a Multi-robotic System in Event-B

4.1   Abstract Model

We start our development by abstractly modelling the described multi-robotic system. We aim to ensure the property (PR1). The main system goal is to clean the whole territory. The process of achieving this goal is modelled by the simple event Body presented below. A variable $goal \in STATE$ models the current state of the system goal. It obtains values from the enumerated set $STATE = \{incompl, compl\}$, where the value $compl$ corresponds to the situation when the goal is achieved, otherwise it is equal to $incompl$. The system continues its execution until the whole territory is not cleaned, i.e., while $goal$ stays $incompl$.

```
Body ≙
status anticipated
  when
      goal ≠ compl
  then
      goal :∈ STATE
  end
```

The event Body has the status $anticipated$. This means that goal reachability is postulated rather than proved. However, at some refinement step it also obliges us to prove that the event or its refinements converge, i.e., to prove that the process of achieving goal eventually terminates.

4.2   First Refinement: Zone Cleaning

Our initial model represents the system behaviour at a high level of abstraction. The objective of our first refinement step is to elaborate on the process of cleaning the territory. Specifically, we assume that the whole territory is divided into n zones, where $n \in \mathbb{N}$ and $n \geq 1$, and aim at ensuring the property (PR2).

We augment our model with a representation of subgoals. We also associate the notion of a *subgoal* with the process of *cleaning a particular zone*. A subgoal is achieved only when the corresponding zone is cleaned. A new variable *zones* represents the current subgoal status for every zone:

$$zones \in 1..n \to STATE.$$

In this refinement step we perform a data refinement: we replace the abstract variable *goal* with a new variable *zones*. To establish the relationship between those variables, we formulate the following gluing invariant:

$$goal = compl \Leftrightarrow zones[1..n] = \{compl\}.$$

The invariant can be understood as follows: the territory is considered to be cleaned if and only if its every zone is cleaned. Hence, hereby we have formalised the property (PR2). The refined event Body is presented below:

```
Body ≙ refines Body
status anticipated
  any z, res
  when
      z ∈ 1..n ∧ zones(z) ≠ compl ∧ res ∈ STATE
  then
      zones(z) := res
  end
```

Moreover, while a certain subgoal is reached, it stays such, i.e., the system always progresses towards achieving its goals. Thereby we ensure the property (PR4).

4.3   Second Refinement: Sector Cleaning

In the next refinement step we further decompose system subgoals into a set of subsubgoals. Specifically, we assume that each zone in our system is divided into k sectors, where $k \in \mathbb{N}$ and $k \geq 1$, and aim at formalising the property (PR3). We establish the relationship between the notion of a subsubgoal (or simply *a task*) and the process of *cleaning a particular sector*. A task is completed when the corresponding sector is cleaned. A new variable *territory* represents the current status of each sector:

$$territory \in 1 \ldots n \to (1 \ldots k \to STATE).$$

The refinement step is again an example of a data refinement. Indeed, we replace the abstract variable *zones* with a new variable *territory*. The following gluing invariant expresses the relationship between subgoals and subsubgoals (tasks) and correspondingly ensures the property (PR3):

$$\forall j \cdot j \in 1 \ldots n \Rightarrow (zones(j) = compl \Leftrightarrow territory(j)[1 \ldots k] = \{compl\}).$$

The invariant postulates that a zone is cleaned if and only if each of its sectors is cleaned.

The abstract event Body is further refined. It is now models cleaning of a previously non-cleaned sector s in a zone z. The task is achieved when this sector is eventually cleaned, i.e., *result* becomes *compl*.

```
Body  ≘ refines Body
status anticipated
  any z, s, result
  when
      zone ∈ 1..n  ∧ s ∈ 1 .. k  ∧ territory(z)(s) ≠ compl  ∧ result ∈ STATE
  then
      territory(z) := territory(z) ⊴ {s ↦ result}
  end
```

Let us observe that the event Body also preserve the property (PR4).

At this refinement step we have achieved a sufficient level of detail to introduce an explicit representation of the agents – base stations and robots. This constitutes the main objective of our next refinement step.

4.4   Third Refinement: Introducing Agents

We start by defining, in the model context, the abstract finite set $AGENTS$ and its disjointed non-empty subsets RB and BS that represent the robots and the base stations respectively. To define a relationship between a zone and its supervising base station, we introduce the variable *responsible*, which is defined as the following total function:

$$responsible \in 1 \ldots n \to BS.$$

Each robot is supervised by a certain base station. During system execution robots might become inactive (failed). We model the relationship between robots and their supervised station by a variable *attached*, defined as partial function:

$$attached \in RB \nrightarrow BS.$$

The new function variables $asgn\_z$ and $asgn\_s$ model respectively the zone and the sector assigned to a robot to clean. When a robot is idle, i.e., it does not have a task assigned to it, the corresponding function value is 0:

$$asgn\_z \in RB \nrightarrow 0 \ldots n, \; asgn\_s \in RB \nrightarrow 0 \ldots k.$$

We require that only the robots that have a supervisory base station might receive a cleaning task:

$$dom(attached) = dom(asgn\_z), \; dom(asgn\_z) = dom(asgn\_s).$$

Now we can formulate the property (**PR5**) – *no two robots can clean the certain sector at the same time* – as a model invariant:

$$\forall rb1, rb2 \cdot rb1 \in dom(attached) \wedge rb2 \in dom(attached) \wedge asgn\_z(rb1) = asgn\_z(rb2) \wedge$$
$$asgn\_s(rb1) \neq 0 \wedge asgn\_s(rb2) \neq 0 \wedge asgn\_s(rb1) = asgn\_s(rb2) \Rightarrow rb1 = rb2.$$

To coordinate the cleaning process, a base station stores the information about its own cleaned sectors and periodically updates information about the status of the other cleaned sectors. Therefore, we assume that each base station has a "map" – a knowledge about all sectors of the whole territory. To model this, we introduce a new variable, $local\_map$:

$$local\_map \in BS \rightarrow (1 \ldots n \nrightarrow (1 \ldots k \rightarrow STATE)).$$

The "maps" are defined only for the base stations that have any zone cleaning to coordinate, i.e., $bs \in ran(responsible)$:

$$\forall bs \cdot bs \in ran(responsible) \Rightarrow local\_map(bs) \in 1 \ldots n \rightarrow (1 \ldots k \rightarrow STATE),$$
$$\forall bs \cdot bs \in BS \wedge bs \notin ran(responsible) \Rightarrow local\_map(bs) = \varnothing.$$

The abstract variable $territory$ represents the global knowledge on the whole territory. For any sector and zone, this global knowledge has to be consistent with the information stored by the base stations. Namely, if in the local knowledge of any base station bs a sector s is marked as cleaned, i.e., $local\_map(bs)(z)(s) = compl$, then it should be cleaned according to the global knowledge as well, i.e., $territory(z)(s) = compl$; and vice versa: if a sector s is marked as non-cleaned in the global knowledge, i.e., $territory(z)(s) = incompl$, then it remains non-cleaned according the local knowledge of any base station bs, i.e., $local\_map(bs)(z)(s) = incompl$. To establish those relationships, we formulate and prove the following invariants:

$$\forall bs, z, s \cdot bs \in ran(responsible) \wedge z \in 1 \ldots n \wedge s \in 1 \ldots k \Rightarrow$$
$$(local\_map(bs)(z)(s) = compl \Rightarrow territory(z)(s) = compl),$$

$$\forall bs, z, s \cdot bs \in ran(responsible) \wedge z \in 1 \ldots n \wedge s \in 1 \ldots k \Rightarrow$$
$$(territory(z)(s) = incompl \Rightarrow local\_map(bs)(z)(s) = incompl).$$

For each base station, the local information about its zones and sectors always coincides with the global knowledge about these zones and sectors:

$$\forall bs, z, s \cdot bs \in ran(responsible) \wedge z \in 1 \ldots n \wedge responsible(z) = bs \wedge s \in 1 \ldots k \Rightarrow$$
$$(territory(z)(s) = incompl \Leftrightarrow local\_map(bs)(z)(s) = incompl).$$

All together, these three invariants formalise the property (PR6).

A base station assigns a cleaning task to its attached robots. This behaviour is modelled by a new event NewTask. In the event guard, we check that the assigned sector s is not cleaned yet, i.e., $local\_map(bs)(z)(s) = incompl$, and no other robot is currently cleaning it. The last condition can be formally expressed as $s \notin ran((dom(asgn\_z \rhd \{z\})) \lhd asgn\_s)$, i.e., the sector s is not assigned to any robot that performs cleaning in the zone z:

```
NewTask ≙
  any bs, rb, z, s
  when
    bs ∈ BS ∧ rb ∈ dom(attached) ∧ attached(rb) = bs ∧ z ∈ 1 .. n ∧
    responsible(z) = bs ∧ asgn_z(rb) = 0 ∧ s ∈ 1 .. k ∧ asgn_s(rb) = 0 ∧
    local_map(bs)(z)(s) = incompl ∧ s ∉ ran((dom(asgn_z ▷ {z})) ◁ asgn_s)
  then
    asgn_s(rb) := s
    asgn_z(rb) := z
  end
```

The robot failures have impact on execution of the cleaning process. The cleaning task cannot be performed if a robot assigned for this task has failed. To reflect this behaviour in our model, we refine the abstract event Body by two events TaskSuccess and TaskFailure, which respectively model successful and unsuccessful execution of the task. If the task has been successfully performed by the assigned robot rb, its supervising base station bs changes the status of the sector s to cleaned, i.e., we override the previous value of $local\_map(bs)(z)(s)$ by the value $compl$.

```
TaskSuccess ≙ refines Body
  status convergent
  any bs, rb, z, s
  when
    bs ∈ BS ∧ rb ∈ dom(attached) ∧ attached(rb) = bs ∧
    z ∈ 1 .. n ∧ responsible(z) = bs ∧ asgn_z(rb) = z ∧
    s ∈ 1 .. k ∧ asgn_s(rb) = s ∧ local_map(bs)(z)(s) = incompl
  then
    territory(z) := territory(z) ⊲ {s ↦ compl}
    local_map(bs) := local_map(bs) ⊲ {z ↦ local_map(bs)(z) ⊲ {s ↦ compl}}
    asgn_s(rb) := 0
    asgn_z(rb) := 0
    counter := counter − 1
  end
```

The dual event TaskFailure abstractly models the opposite situation caused by a robot failure. As a result, all the relationships concerning the failed robot rb are removed:

```
TaskFailure ≙ refines Body
  status convergent
  any bs, rb, z, s
  when
    bs ∈ BS ∧ rb ∈ dom(attached) ∧ attached(rb) = bs ∧
    z ∈ 1 .. n ∧ responsible(z) = bs ∧ asgn_z(rb) = z ∧
    s ∈ 1 .. k ∧ asgn_s(rb) = s ∧ local_map(bs)(z)(s) = incompl
  then
    territory(z) := territory(z) ⊲ {s ↦ incompl}
    asgn_s := {rb} ⩤ asgn_s
    asgn_z := {rb} ⩤ asgn_z
    attached := {rb} ⩤ attached
  end
```

At this refinement step, we are ready to demonstrate that the events TaskSuccess and TaskFailure converge. To prove it, we define the following variant expression over system variables:

$$counter + card(dom(attached)),$$

where $counter$ is an auxiliary variable that stores the number of all non-cleaned sectors of the whole territory. The initial value of $counter$ is equal to $n * k$. When a robot fails to perform a task, it is removed from the corresponding set of the attached robots $dom(attached)$. This in turn decreases the value of $card(dom(attached))$ and consequently the whole variant expression. On the other hand, when a robot succeeds in cleaning a sector, the variable $counter$ decreases and consequently the whole variant expression decreases as well. If there are no sectors to clean, the events become disabled and the system terminates.

A base station keeps track of the cleaned and non-cleaned sectors and repeatedly receives the information from the other base stations about their cleaned sectors. This knowledge is inaccurate for the period when the information is sent but not yet received. In this refinement step we abstractly model receiving the information by a base station. In the next refinement step, we are going to define this process of information broadcasting more precisely.

The new event UpdateMap models updating the local map of a base station bs. Here we have to ensure that the obtained information is always consistent with the global one. Specifically, the base station updates a sector s as cleaned only if it has this status according to the global knowledge, i.e., $territory(z)(s) = compl$.

```
UpdateMap ≙
  any bs, z, s
  when
      bs ∈ BS ∧ z ∈ 1 .. n ∧ s ∈ 1 .. k ∧
      responsible(z) ≠ bs ∧ bs ∈ ran(responsible)∧
      territory(z)(s) = compl
  then
      local_map(bs) := local_map(bs) ⊲ {z ↦ local_map(bs)(z) ⊲ {s ↦ compl}}
  end
```

In this refinement step we also introduce an abstract representation of the base station co-operation defined by the property (PR7). Namely, we allow to reassign a group of robots from one base station to another. This behaviour is defined by the event ReassignRB. In the next refinement steps we will elaborate on this event and define the conditions under which this behaviour takes place.

Additionally, we model a possible redistribution between the base stations their pre-assigned responsibility for zones and robots. This behaviour is defined in the new event GetAdditionalResponsibility presented below. The event guard defines the conditions when such a change is allowed. A base station bs_j can take the responsibility for a set of new zones zss if it has the accurate knowledge about these zones, i.e., the information about their cleaned and non-cleaned sectors. Specifically, in the guard we check that the global status of each sector s from the zone z, i.e., $territory(z)(s)$, coincides with the local information that the base station bs_j has about this sector. In that case, we reassign responsibility for the zone(s) zss and the robots rbs to the base station bs_j:

```
GetAdditionalResponsibility ≘
  any bs_i, bs_j, rbs, zs
  when
    bs_i ∈ BS ∧ bs_j ∈ BS ∧ zs ⊂ 1 .. n ∧
    zs = dom(responsible ▷ {bs_i}) ∧ rbs ⊂ dom(attached) ∧
    rbs = dom(attached ▷ {bs_i}) ∧ bs_i ≠ bs_j ∧ bs_j ∈ ran(responsible) ∧
    (∀z, s·z ∈ zs ∧ s ∈ 1 .. k ⇒ territory(z)(s) = local_map(bs_j)(z)(s))
  then
    responsible := responsible ⩤ (zs × {bs_j})
    attached := attached ⩤ (rbs × {bs_j})
    asgn_s := asgn_s ⩤ (rbs × {0})
    asgn_z := asgn_z ⩤ (rbs × {0})
    local_map(bs_i) := ∅
  end
```

Modelling this behaviour allows us to formalise the property (PR9). Our next refinement step will elaborate on our chosen communication model that is needed to achieve such co-operative recovery.

4.5   Fourth Refinement: A Model of Broadcasting

In the fourth refinement step we aim at defining an abstract model of broadcasting. After receiving a notification from a robot about successful cleaning the assigned sector, a base station updates its local map and broadcasts the message about the cleaned sector to the other base stations. In its turn, upon receiving the message, each base station correspondingly updates its own local map. We assume that the communication between base stations is reliable: no message is lost and eventually every base station receives it. In further refinement steps, this model of the broadcasting can be further refined by a more concrete mechanism.

To model the described behaviour, we introduce a new relational variable, msg, that models the message broadcasting buffer:

$$msg \in BS \leftrightarrow (1 .. n \times 1 .. k).$$

If a message $(bs \mapsto (z \mapsto s))$ belongs to this buffer, this means that the sector s from the zone z has been cleaned, i.e., $territory(z)(s) = compl$. The first element of the message, bs, determines the base station the message is sent to. We formulate this property by the following system invariant:

$$\forall z, s·z \in 1 .. n \land s \in 1 .. k \land (z \mapsto s) \in ran(msg) \Rightarrow territory(z)(s) = compl.$$

If there are no messages in the msg buffer for any particular base station then the local map of this base station is accurate, i.e., it coincides with the global knowledge about the teritory:

$$\forall bs, z, s·z \in 1 .. n \land s \in 1 .. k \land bs \in ran(responsible) \land (bs \mapsto (z \mapsto s)) \notin msg \Rightarrow$$
$$territory(z)(s) = local\_map(bs)(z)(s),$$

$$\forall bs·bs \in ran(responsible) \land bs \notin dom(msg) \Rightarrow$$
$$(\forall z, s·z \in 1 .. n \land s \in 1 .. k \Rightarrow territory(z)(s) = local\_map(bs)(z)(s)).$$

After receiving a notification about successful cleaning of a sector, a base station marks this sector as cleaned in its local map and then broadcasts the message about it to other base stations. To model this, we refine the abstract event TaskSuccess. Specifically, in the event body we add a new assignment $msg := msg \cup (bss \times \{z \mapsto s\})$ to add a new message to the broadcasting buffer.

We also refine the abstract event UpdateMap. In particular, we replace the guard $territory(z)(s) = compl$ by the guard $(bs \mapsto (z \mapsto s)) \in msg$. This guard checks that there is a message for the base station bs about the cleaned sector s from the zone z. As a result of the event, the base station bs reads the message and marks the sector s in the zone z as cleaned in its local map.

```
UpdateMap ≙ refines UpdateMap
  any bs, z, s
  when
      bs ∈ BS ∧ z ∈ 1 .. n ∧ s ∈ 1 .. k  ∧ responsible(z) ≠ bs ∧
      bs ∈ ran(responsible)  ∧ (bs ↦ (z ↦ s)) ∈ msg
  then
      local_map(bs) := local_map(bs) ⊕ {z ↦ local_map(bs)(z) ⊕ {s ↦ compl}}
      msg := msg \ {bs ↦ (z ↦ s)}
```

4.6   Fifth Refinement: Introducing Robot Failures

Now we aim at modelling possible robot failures and elaborate on the abstract events concerning robot and zone reassigning. We start by partitioning the robots into active and failed ones. The current set of all active robots is defined by a new variable $active$ with the following invariant properties:

$$active \subseteq dom(attached), \ active \subseteq dom(asgn\_s), \ active \subseteq dom(asgn\_z).$$

Initially all robots are active, i.e., $active = RB$. A new event RobotFailure models possible robot failures that can happen at any time during system execution:

```
RobotFailure ≙
  any rb
  when
      rb ∈ active ∧ card(active) > 1
  then
      active := active \ {rb}
  end
```

We make an assumption that the last active robot can not fail and add the corresponding guard $card(active) > 1$ to the event RobotFailure to restrict possible robot failures. Let us note that for multi-robotic systems with many homogeneous robots this constraint is not unreasonable.

A base station monitors all its robots and detects the failed ones. The abstract event TaskFailure abstractly models such robot detection.

To formalise the property (PR8), we should model a situation when some base station bs_j does not have active robots anymore, i.e., $dom(attached \rhd \{bs\_j\}) \nsubseteq active$. In that case, some group of active robots rbs has to be sent to this base station bs_j from another base station bs_i. This behaviour is modelled by the event ReassignNewBStoRBs that refines the abstract event ReassignRB. As a result, all the robots from rbs become attached to the base station bs_j:

```
ReassignNewBStoRBs ≙ refines ReassignRB
  any bs_i, bs_j, rbs
  when
      bs_i ∈ BS ∧ bs_j ∈ BS ∧ rbs ⊂ active ∧
      ran(rbs ◁ attached) = {bs}  ∧ bs_i ∈ ran(responsible) ∧
      ran(rbs ◁ asgn_s) = {0}  ∧ rbs ≠ ∅ ∧ bs_j ∈ ran(responsible) ∧
      bs_i ≠ bs_j  ∧ bs_i ∈ ran(rbs ◁ attached) ∧ dom(attached ▷ {bs_j}) ⊄ active
  then
      attached := attached ⊕ (rbs × {bs_j})
  end
```

This event can be further refined by a concrete procedure to choose a particular base station that will share its robots (e.g., based on load balancing).

Finally, to ensure the property (PR9) , let us consider the situation when all the sectors for which a base station is responsible are cleaned. In that case, all the active robots of the base station may be sent to some other base station that still has some unfinished cleaning to co-ordinate. This functionality is specified by the event SendRobotsToBS (a refinement of the event ReassignRB):

$$
\begin{array}{l}
\text{SendRobotsToBS} \ \widehat{=}\ \text{refines ReassignRB} \\
\quad \textbf{any } bs\_i, bs\_j, rbs \\
\quad \textbf{when} \\
\qquad bs\_i \in operating \wedge bs\_j \in operating \wedge rbs \subset active \wedge \\
\qquad ran(rbs \lhd attached) = \{bs\_i\} \ \wedge bs\_i \in ran(responsible) \wedge \\
\qquad ran(rbs \lhd asgn\_s) = \{0\} \ \wedge rbs \neq \varnothing \ \wedge bs\_j \in ran(responsible) \wedge \\
\qquad bs\_i \neq bs\_j \ \wedge bs\_i \in ran(rbs \lhd attached) \ \wedge rbs = dom(attached \rhd \{bs\_i\}) \wedge \\
\qquad (\forall z \cdot z \in 1 \ .. \ n \wedge responsible(z) = bs\_i \Rightarrow local\_map(bs\_i)(z)[1 \ .. \ k] = \{compl\}) \\
\quad \textbf{then} \\
\qquad attached := attached \lhd\!\!\!- (rbs \times \{bs\_j\}) \\
\quad \textbf{end}
\end{array}
$$

4.7   Sixth Refinement: Introducing Base Station Failures

In the final refinement step presented in the paper, we aim at specifying the base station failures. Each base station might be either operating or failed. We introduce a new variable $operating$ to define the set of all operating base stations. The corresponding invariant properties are as follows.

$$operating \subseteq BS,$$

$$\forall bs \cdot bs \in BS \wedge local\_map(bs) = \varnothing \ \Rightarrow \ bs \notin operating.$$

Also, similarly to the event RobotFailure, we introduce a new event BaseStationFailure to model a possible base station failure.

In the fourth refinement step we assumed that a base station can take over the responsibility for the robots and zones of another base station. This behaviour was modelled by the event GetAdditionalResponsibility. Now we can refine this event by introducing an additional condition – only if a base station is detected as failed, another base station can take over its responsibility for the respective zones and robots:

$$
\begin{array}{l}
\text{GetAdditionalResponsibility} \ \widehat{=}\ \text{refines GetAdditionalResponsibility} \\
\quad \textbf{any } bs\_i, bs\_j, za, rbs \\
\quad \textbf{when} \\
\qquad bs\_i \in BS \wedge bs\_j \in operating \wedge zs \subset 1 \ .. \ n \wedge \\
\qquad zs = dom(responsible \rhd \{bs\_i\}) \ \wedge rbs \subset active \ \wedge rbs = dom(attached \rhd \{bs\_i\}) \wedge \\
\qquad bs\_i \neq bs\_j \ \wedge bs\_j \notin dom(msg) \ \wedge bs\_i \notin operating \\
\quad \textbf{then} \\
\qquad responsible := responsible \lhd\!\!\!- (zs \times \{bs\_j\}) \\
\qquad attached := attached \lhd\!\!\!- (rbs \times \{bs\_j\}) \\
\qquad asgn\_s := asgn\_s \lhd\!\!\!- (rbs \times \{0\}) \\
\qquad asgn\_z := asgn\_z \lhd\!\!\!- (rbs \times \{0\}) \\
\qquad local\_map(bs\_i) := \varnothing \\
\quad \textbf{end}
\end{array}
$$

As a result of the presented refinement chain, we arrived at a centralised model of the multi-robotic system. We can further refine the system to derive its distributed implementation, relying on the modularisation extension of Event-B to achieve this.

5   Discussion

Assessment of the Development. The development of the presented multi-robotic system has been carried out with the support of the Rodin platform [8]. We have derived a complex system specification in six refinement steps. In general, the refinement approach has demonstrated a good scalability and allowed us to model intricate dependencies between the system components. We have been able to express and verify all the desired properties defined for our system. Therefore, we can make a general conclusion about suitability of the refinement technique for formal development and verification of the multi-robotic systems.

However, we have also identified a number of problems. Firstly, in spite of seeming simplicity, the relationships between the base stations, zones and sectors have been modelled using quite complex nested data structures (functions). The Rodin platform could not comfortably handle the proofs involving manipulations with the nested functions and required rather time-consuming interactive proving efforts. Secondly, the Rodin platform does not support the direct assignment to a function with nested arguments. For instance, instead of simply specifying $local\_map(bs)(z)(s) := compl$, we have to express it as the following intricate statement $local\_map(bs) \vartriangleleft \{z \mapsto local\_map(bs)(z) \vartriangleleft \{s \mapsto compl\}\}$, i.e., use the overriding relation twice. These two problems can be alleviated with a mathematical extension of the Rodin platform that is currently under development.

Despite certain technical difficulties, we have found the refinement approach as such to be beneficial for deriving precise requirements and the corresponding model of a multi-robotic system. In the refinement process, we have discovered a number of subtleties in the system requirements. The proving effort has helped us to localise the present problems and ambiguities and find the appropriate solutions. For instance, we had to impose extra restrictions on the situations when a base station takes a new responsibility for other zones and robots. Moreover, we had to make our assumptions about robot failures more precise.

Related Work. Formal modelling of multi-agent systems has been undertaken in [10,9,11]. The authors have proposed an extension of the Unity framework to explicitly define such concepts as mobility and context-awareness. Our modelling have pursued a different goal – we have aimed at formally guaranteeing that the specified agent behaviour achieves the pre-defined goals. Formal modelling of fault tolerant MAS in Event-B has been undertaken by Ball and Butler [3]. They have proposed a number of informally described patterns that allow the designers to incorporate well-known (static) fault tolerance mechanisms into formal models. In our approach, we have implemented a more advanced fault tolerance scheme that relies on goal reallocation and dynamic reconfiguration to guarantee goal reachability.

The foundational work on goal-oriented development has been done by van Lamsweerde [4]. The original motivation behind the goal-oriented development was to structure the requirements and derive properties in the form of temporal logic formulas that the system design should satisfy. Over the last decade, the goal-oriented approach has received several extensions that allow the designers to link it with formal modelling [5,6,7]. These works aimed at expressing temporal logic properties in Event-B. In our work, we have relied on goals to facilitate structuring of the system behaviour and derived a detailed system model that satisfies the desired properties by refinement.

Conclusions. In this paper we have presented a formal development of a fault tolerant multi-robotic system. The development has been carried out by refinement in Event-B. As a result of the formal development process, we have achieved the desired goal – formally specified the complex system behaviour and proved the desired properties. The formal development has allowed us to uncover missing requirements and rigorously define the relationships between agents. The refinement approach has also allowed us to derive a complex mechanism for cooperative error recovery in a systematic manner.

Our approach has demonstrated a number of advantages comparing to various process-algebraic approaches used for modelling multi-agent systems. The reliance on a proof-based verification has allowed us to derive a quite complex model of the behaviour of a multi-agent robotic system. We have not needed to avoid complex data types and could comfortably express intricate relationships between the system goals and the employed agents. As a result, our approach scales well with respect to the number of system states, agents, and their complex interactions. We believe that, once the mentioned technical difficulties of handling complex nested functions are resolved in the Rodin platform, Event-B and the associated tool set will provide a suitable framework for formal modelling of complex multi-robotic systems.

References

1. Abrial, J.-R.: The B-Book: Assigning Programs to Meanings. Cambridge University Press (2005)
2. Abrial, J.-R.: Modeling in Event-B. Cambridge University Press (2010)
3. Ball, E., Butler, M.: Event-B Patterns for Specifying Fault-Tolerance in Multi-agent Interaction. In: Butler, M., Jones, C., Romanovsky, A., Troubitsyna, E. (eds.) Methods, Models and Tools for Fault Tolerance. LNCS, vol. 5454, pp. 104–129. Springer, Heidelberg (2009)
4. van Lamsweerde, A.: Goal-Oriented Requirements Engineering: A Guided Tour. In: RE, pp. 249–263 (2001)
5. Landtsheer, R.D., Letier, E., van Lamsweerde, A.: Deriving tabular event-based specifications from goal-oriented requirements models. Requirements Engineering 9(2), 104–120 (2004)
6. Matoussi, A., Gervais, F., Laleau, R.: A Goal-Based Approach to Guide the Design of an Abstract Event-B Specification. In: 16th International Conference on Engineering of Complex Computer Systems. IEEE (2011)
7. Ponsard, C., Dallons, G., Philippe, M.: From Rigorous Requirements Engineering to Formal System Design of Safety-Critical Systems. ERCIM News (75), 22–23 (2008)

8. Rodin: Event-B Platform, `http://www.event-b.org/`
9. Roman, G.-C., Julien, C., Payton, J.: A Formal Treatment of Context-Awareness. In: Wermelinger, M., Margaria-Steffen, T. (eds.) FASE 2004. LNCS, vol. 2984, pp. 12–36. Springer, Heidelberg (2004)
10. Roman, G.-C., Julien, C., Payton, J.: Modeling adaptive behaviors in Context UNITY. Theoretical Computure Science, 376, 185–204 (2007)
11. Roman, G.-C., McCann, P., Plun, J.: Mobile UNITY: Reasoning and Specification in Mobile Computing. ACM Transactions of Software Engineering and Methodology (1997)

Fault-Tolerant Interactive Cockpits
for Critical Applications: Overall Approach

Camille Fayollas[1,2,3], Jean-Charles Fabre[3], David Navarre[2],
Philippe Palanque[2], and Yannick Deleris[1]

[1] AIRBUS Operations, 316 Route de Bayonne, 31060, Toulouse, France
Yannick.Deleris@airbus.com
[2] ICS-IRIT, University of Toulouse, 118 Route de Narbonne, F-31062, Toulouse, France
{fayollas,navarre,palanque}@ irit.fr
[3] LAAS-CNRS, 7 avenue du colonel Roche, F-31077 Toulouse, France
Jean-Charles.Fabre@laas.fr

Abstract. The deployment of interactive facilities in avionic digital cockpits for critical applications is a challenge today. The dependability of the user interface and its related supporting software must be consistent with the criticality of the functions to be controlled. The approach proposed in this paper aims at describing how fault prevention and fault tolerance techniques can be combined to address this challenge. Following the ARINC 661 standard, a model-based development of interactive objects (namely widgets and layers) aims at providing zero-default software. Regarding remaining software faults in the underlying runtime support and also physical faults, the approach is based on fault tolerance design patterns, like self-checking components and replication techniques. The proposed solution relies on the space and time partitioning provided by the executive support following the ARINC 653 standard. Defining and designing resilient interactive cockpits is a necessity in the near future as these command and control systems provide a great opportunity to improve maintenance and evolutivity of avionic systems.

Keywords: Interactive Systems, Self Checking Components, Widgets, Dependability, Fault Tolerance, Resilient Computing.

1 Introduction

In the late 70's the aviation industry developed a new kind of display system integrating multiple displays and known as "glass cockpit". Using integrated displays it was possible to gather under a single screen a lot of information usually statically attached to multiple independent traditional mechanical gauges. This generation of glass cockpits uses several displays with electronic technology. It receives information from aircraft system applications of embedded equipment, then processes and displays this information to crew members. In order to send controls to the aircraft systems, the crew members have to use physical buttons usually made available next to the displays. Control and display are processed independently (different hardware and

P. Avgeriou (Ed.): SERENE 2012, LNCS 7527, pp. 32–46, 2012.

software) and without integration. This is something that is about to change radically with interactive cockpit applications which have started to replace (e.g. with Airbus A380) the glass cockpit. The main reason is that it makes possible to integrate information from several aircraft systems in a single user interface in the cockpit. This integration is nowadays required in order to allow flight crew to handle the always increasing number of instruments which manage more and more complex information. Such integration takes place through interactive applications featuring graphical input and output devices and interaction techniques as in any other interactive contexts (web applications, games, home entertainment, mobile devices …). The interactive system in the cockpit is called Control and Display System (CDS). It performs various operational services of major importance for flight crew and allows the display of aircraft parameters using LCD screens (as in the glass cockpit), but it also allows the pilots to graphically interact with these parameters using a keyboard and a mouse to control aircraft systems.

If the information displayed on (or controlled by) the CDS is critical, its general architecture must be fault-tolerant. Similarly, on the user side, the information flow between the pilot and the CDS has to ensure safe flight operations, avoiding the entering of wrong or incomplete data and displaying only correct information (with respect to the inner state of the aircraft). Ensuring such dependability of information is not an easy task due to the high number of hardware and software components involved.

In this paper, we propose an approach for assessing dependability of interactive cockpits. The approach is based on conventional fault tolerance techniques applied to interactive objects, at various abstraction levels. The approach also relies on the error confinement facilities provided by the runtime support, namely an ARINC 653 operating system kernel [2]. Such runtime platform provides both space and time partitioning. Today the interaction is devoted to non-critical avionic functions and the management of the interaction is located into one partition for the whole interactive system. The basic idea is to design fault tolerant interactive entities using multiple partitions providing error confinement on redundant Display Units.

The paper is organized as follows. In section 2 we describe the problem statement in more details before illustrating the architecture of interactive cockpits using the A380 example in section 3. We put focus in this section to the organization of a digital interactive system following the ARINC 661 standard [1]. In section 4, we describe our approach to improve the dependability of interactive systems for avionic critical applications. The architecture of our fault tolerant solution is described in section 5 and is based on a conventional approach for fault tolerant computing in avionics, the COM-MON approach [15]. Section 6 concludes this paper.

2   Problem Statement

It is worth noting that, currently, the interactive approach is only used in avionics for non-safety critical functions. The challenge is now to use this interactive approach for critical functions.

The interactive system can be viewed at various levels of abstraction, from individual widgets at the bottom level up to more complex interactive entities associated to so-called user applications, namely the interactive counterpart of avionic functions. The specifications of interactive objects (widgets and layers) are defined in the ARINC 661 standard. Such complex system is subject to faults that can impair the correct rendering of information and the delivery of input information to avionic functions. In this work, we focus on dependability issues of the CDS, as a computer-based system so the type of faults considered ranges from software to hardware faults and we do not consider human errors. We understand that such errors are definitely of interest as far as man-machine interface and interactive systems are considered. However the evolution of conventional cockpits to total digital cockpits is a revolution and raises the challenge of its dependability with respect to conventional software and hardware faults. The dependability of such complex computer-based systems should be as high as possible depending on the associated failure cases considered: as far as critical functions are concerned, the system must be developed in compliance with the highest assurance level, so-called DAL A (Design Assurance Level A) according to the D0178B development process standard [15].

The approach proposed in this work is two-fold and relies both on fault prevention and fault tolerance approaches. To deal with software faults, we advocate the use of a model-based approach of interactive applications, limiting as far as possible software faults in the resulting interactive entities. A formalism based on Petri Nets is used to formalize the specifications of interactive objects (widgets and layers). This formal representation of the interactive objects is interpreted at runtime by a virtual machine. Regarding physical faults, we advocated a fault tolerance approach relying on the *N-Self Checking Programming* paradigm [3] and taking advantage of the ARINC 653 features and redundant hardware.

The long-term interest of such digital cockpit is its flexibility. The lifetime of a civil aircraft is about 40 years and is subject to many evolutions and updates. This digital cockpit approach vs. the physical approach offers a clear benefit in this respect, provided the dependability of the interactive system is guaranteed when changes occur. This calls thus for resilient computing [15] solutions by definition, which is the long-term aim of this work.

3   Interactive Cockpit Architecture

3.1   Cockpit Architecture Overview: An Example

In this paper, we will take the example of the Airbus A380 cockpit (see **Fig. 1**). The interactive control and display system (CDS) of the Airbus A380 is composed of 2 input devices called KCCUs (Keyboard and Cursor Control Unit) and 8 output devices called DUs (Display Unit). Only some of the 8 DUs allow the crew to use the interactivity, the other ones are only used for displaying information.

A DU device is composed of a LCD screen, a graphic processing unit and a central processing unit running an ARINC 653 [2] operating system kernel. The software responsible for the interactivity is processed in the DU within one partition.

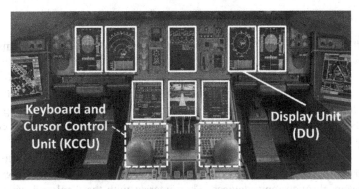

Fig. 1. Airbus A380 interactive cockpit

The type of user interfaces that can be proposed on these DUs is based on ARINC 661 specification [1]. Beyond that user interface aspect, ARINC 661 specification also defines the communication protocol (see **Fig. 2**(c)) between the various architectural components of an interactive cockpit (see **Fig. 2**). The ARINC 661 is based on client-server architecture.

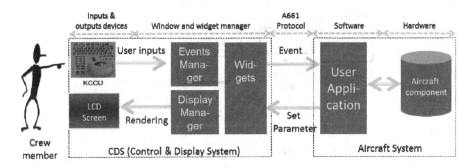

Fig. 2. Simplified Architecture compliant with ARINC 661 specification standard : (a) Crew; (b) CDS, (c) ARINC 661 Protocol; (d)Aircraft System

The server is part of the CDS (Control & Display System) in **Fig. 2** (b) and it is composed of the following elements:

- *Input and output devices*: KCCUs (Keyboard and Cursor Control Unit) and LCD screens. They allow crew members to interact with the application.
- *Window and widget managers*: composed of an event manager, a display manager and a set of graphical elements (called widgets) distributed in a set of windows rendered on the LCD screens. For instance, the CDS is responsible for handling the creation of widgets, managing KCCU graphical cursors, dispatching the events to the corresponding widgets and the rendering of graphical information on the LCD screens.

The CDS manages information for two types of clients:

- *Aircraft Systems* (**Fig. 2**(d)): information to and from aircraft systems flows through dedicated so-called User Applications (UAs) which are applications featuring a graphical user interface for a given avionic function. They process the event notifications sent by the widgets (and might trigger commands on the physical aircraft components).They can also update the widgets (by calling update methods called SetParameters) in order to provide feedback to the flight crew according to state changes which occurred in the aircraft systems.
- *Crew members* (**Fig. 2** (a)): they have the responsibility of flying the aircraft by monitoring the aircraft systems through the LCD screens and controlling the aircraft system through input devices. They interact with the displayed widgets. For instance, they can click on a button in order to trigger a command, enter a numeric value in an EditBoxNumeric to send a value to an avionic function.

3.2   Interactive Software Organisation

The cockpit interactive user interfaces use a windowing concept (see **Fig. 3**) that can be compared to a desktop computer system windowing.

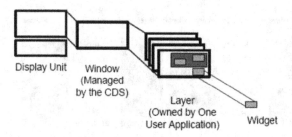

Fig. 3. ARINC 661 windowing concept

Each DU display surface is divided into windows. Each window can be subdivided in one or more layers. A layer is associated to one UA and represents the display and the interactive facilities required by an avionic function. The UA and the CDS share data within this layer and its hierarchical structure. The layer hierarchical structure can be seen as a widget tree. The layer is the highest level of this tree. The widgets are the basic interactive components such as:

- Pushbutton: dedicated to commands triggering.
- Radio buttons: selection of one option amongst a set of available ones.
- EditBoxNumeric: for entering numeric values.

The construction of the structural widget tree is made possible by specials widgets called ***containers*** that can contain other widgets. We called the containers *parents* and the widgets they contain *children*.

4   Overall Approach

In this section, we first present the main assumptions we make, the functional failures we want to prevent and the fault model we consider to select the appropriate fault tolerance strategies. Then we propose our approach for embedding dependability mechanisms within an interactive cockpit. Our approach is two-fold, we first use a model-based approach to develop our software and deal with software faults, then we introduce well-known dependability mechanisms to deal with physical faults.

4.1   Main Hypotheses and Functional Failures to Cover

The focus of this paper is on the interactive system dependability, more precisely, the CDS dependability. Human-errors are out of the scope of our study, the target being here the dependability of CDS as a computer-based system. As the CDS is a really large and complex entity, we decided to focus first on the server reliability. To concentrate on this problem, we assume the following:

- The communication between the CDS and aircraft system is reliable. The data transfer is without corruption and this can easily be achieved using conventional reliable protocols on a FIFO communication channel.
- The reliability of user applications (UA), the display related part of an avionic function, is out of the scope of this work, we consider that all information received by the CDS from aircraft systems is correct.
- The displays of the CDS are reliable, graphical commands sent to the LCD screen are always correctly displayed.
- The KCCU is sending reliable data to the server.

Our main interest is to ensure that the server processes correctly input events from crew members, and send graphical commands to the LCD screen according to the data received from user applications. Three possible failures must be avoided:

- **Erroneous Display:** Transmission of an erroneous value to the display according to the data received from aircraft systems (e.g. a widget receives the value x to render and transmits to the display another value);
- **Erroneous Control:** Transmission of a different action from the one done by crew members (e.g. a crew member clicks on Button1 but the event Click-Button2 is sent to the application);
- **Inadvertent Control:** Transmission of an action without any crew members' action (e.g. an event click is sent to the application without crew action on input devices).

The fault model considered in our study encompasses physical faults ranging from crash faults, due to a power supply failure of an electronic board for instance, to more subtle faults like Single Event Effects [15]. Regarding software faults, the model-based design approach proposed in the next section aims at limiting very much the introduction of design faults in the development process. Furthermore, to consider transient software faults the interactive software and the base executive software, namely the ARINC 653 kernel will be developed at the highest assurance level (DAL A) and thus considered as a zero-default piece of software.

4.2   Using ICO Formal Modeling to Design Interactive Cockpits

In the domain of the design of safety-critical interactive systems, the use of a formal specification technique is extremely valuable because it provides non-ambiguous, complete and concise models. The advantages of using such formalisms are widened if they are provided with formal analysis techniques that allow proving properties about the design [3], thus giving an early verification to the designer before the application is actually implemented [5].

The Interactive Cooperative Objects (ICO) is a formal description technique dedicated to the specification and verification of interactive systems [11]. It uses concepts borrowed from the object-oriented approach (dynamic instantiation, classification, encapsulation, inheritance, client/server relationship) to describe the structural or static aspects of interactive systems, and uses high-level Petri nets [7] to describe their dynamic or behavioural aspects. As an extension of the Cooperative Objects formalisms it has been designed to describe behavioural aspects of objects-based distributed systems [4]. The formalism is able to handle the specific aspects of interactive systems. In a nutshell, the ICO formalism can be described as follows:

- ICO is Petri net based, suitable to specify the behaviour of event driven-interactive systems and concurrent human-computer interactions, but also able to describe the inner states of the Interactive Application.
- The formalism enables the handling of more complex data structure (typed places and tokens, transitions with actions and preconditions, variable names on arcs).
- ICO objects react to external events according to their internal state and they can produce events.
- An object is defined as the set of four elements: an extended Petri Net describing the behaviour of the interactive object, a presentation part, and two functions (the activation function and the rendering function) that make the link between the co-operative objet and the presentation part (events from input devices and output on the LCD screens).

In previous work [3], we have proposed the use of ICO formal modeling for describing in a complete and unambiguous way both standard widgets and interactive applications following ARINC 661 specifications.

Any widget corresponds to a collection of interconnected Petri Nets. For instance, the ICO model of the PicturePushButton (PPB) may be divided in 7 sub-parts (one handling mouse click events and the other 6 for managing one parameter each: *Visible, Enable, PictureReference, LabelString, StyleSet, Highlighted*).

To illustrate the model, we show in **Fig. 4** the handling of mouse click events. The PicturePushButton has two internal states: it can be (i) pressed or (ii) released. State changes are due to user actions (mouse down events, mouse click events). The mouse click events are relayed to the widget via the processMouseClicked method. They are handled only if the widget is enable and visible. In this case, the event A661_EvtSelection is triggered; otherwise, the mouse click events are discarded. **Fig. 4** is only a small part of the entire PicturePushButton ICO model, which is composed of 37 places and 24 transitions. It is modeled as (i) the various states it can be in (e.g. visible, enable, pressed), (ii) the set of method calls he can process (e.g. processMouseClick, setLabelString), (iii) the set of events it can trigger (e.g. A661_EvtSelection) and (iv) when such events are triggered (see **Fig. 4**). The entire behavioral description of the PPB can be found in [14].

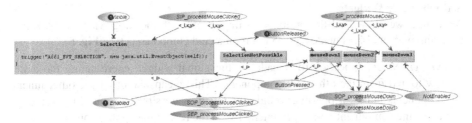

Fig. 4. ICO model of the management of mouse click events for the PicturePushButton

4.3   Introducing Dependability Mechanisms into Interactive Cockpits

Many dependability strategies rely on the notion of self-checking component as introduced in [3] and [15], ideally grouping a function and its corresponding controller. A self-checking component provides error-confinement and can be thus considered as a fail-stop component. The error detection coverage of a self-checking component is expected to be very high, making thus replication strategies possible to provide service continuity. This concept has been used for many safety-critical functions in avionic systems: the COM/MON approach [15] is the basis for various N-Self-Checking Programming (NSCP)-based architectures [3]. We decided to apply the self-checking approach to two abstraction levels of our interactive system, the first one being the widgets, the second one being the layers.

According to [3], "*a self-checking software component consists of either a variant and an acceptance test or two variants and a comparison algorithm*". In accordance with this definition, we can generalize a self-checking component to a *functional component* associated with a *controller* or *checker*. Then, several options can be considered for the implementation of a self-checking interactive object:

- **Option 1:** A copy of the functional component (called *controller* or *checker*) and a voting mechanism (called *comparator*).
- **Option 2:** A diversified variant of the functional component (as a *controller*) and a voting mechanism (the *comparator*)
- **Option 3:** A safety properties checker, the controller being responsible in this case for the verification of a number of safety properties associated to the interactive object semantics in its operational context.

In the two first self-checking options, the functional and the controller components are processing inputs at the same time, the comparator then compares both outputs and sends an error if the functional outputs and the controller ones are different. Both options tolerate transient software faults, the second aiming at tolerating design faults.

In the last self-checking options, the safety properties checker checks some properties defined as safety ones. We check if the outputs are consistent with the inputs. This last option tolerates transient faults or remaining design faults that impair the safety properties.

Self-Checking Widgets

As a start, we have used the option 1 to implement self-checking widgets. A self-checking widget [14] is made up of 5 interconnected components (see **Fig. 5**):

- *The self-checking widget* (or façade) is the global widget, coordinating the data flow to and from the other sub-components. This encapsulation of the other inner components makes it possible to hide (as much as possible) the self-checking nature of the component which can interact with the rest of the application.
- *The dispatcher*: events received by the self-checking widget are received by the dispatcher. The dispatcher duplicates this event and sends it both to the functional and controller using a simple atomic broadcast protocol (all or nothing semantics).
- *The functional* component is the behavioral model of the non-fault-tolerant widget. The outputs are sent both to the self-checking widget and the comparator.
- *The controller* is a second version of the widget. It only implements the functionalities that have to be supervised by the controller. The controller sends its output to the comparator.
- *The comparator* is in charge of comparing the functional and controller outputs.

The dispatcher and the comparator have obviously important roles and should be zero-default. They are quite simple and are subject to intensive testing.

The comparator raises errors that may invalidate outputs as shown in **Fig. 5**. Two kinds of comparison that can be performed: one related to parameters modification and the other related to event notification. When the comparator receives an output from the functional component (resp. the controller) it waits for the corresponding output from the controller (resp. the functional component). Following the reception of these two outputs, 3 types of errors can occur: (i) one of the outputs is not received, (ii) one of the outputs is received too late with respect to the defined temporal window, (iii) the outputs don't carry the same value. In case of error, the comparator raises an error event.

One of the key aspects of the proposed architecture is that it allows the segregation of the five sub-components (e.g. each sub-component may be executed on different processors with different resources). Indeed, a self-checking mechanism is not enough to ensure fault-tolerance if a fault occurring on one component might interfere with the behavior of another component. This would be the case if all the components of the architecture were executed in the same partition. ARINC 653 [2] defines such partitioning in avionic systems and our contribution relies on this notion (section 5).

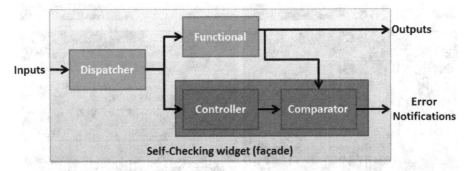

Fig. 5. Self-checking widget functional architecture

As presented in **Fig. 5**, adding fault-tolerance mechanism to the PicturePushButton is the result of the merge of the five subparts of the self-checking component architecture (the self-checking-component façade, the dispatcher, the functional, i.e. the classic non-self-checking widget as presented in section 4.3, the controller and the comparator). Each component is modeled in a different Petri Net model. For lack of space, we will not present these components here.

Self-Checking Layers

The approach presented above is very generic as it can be applied to each widget, without any knowledge of the application: as explained in section 3, the widget is the basic interactive component. Therefore, this approach can be resource consuming. Indeed, to cover both transient and permanent hardware faults, we need to isolate the functional component and its controller in different partitions (see section 5). In addition, self-checking interactive objects must be replicated on different display units, following the principle of N-Self Checking Programming. Four partitions on 2 DUs for every widget does not seem acceptable due to resource overheads. It is worth noting that an interactive application can contain a lot of widgets, the partition number will then be really very high (a standard user application requires about several hundreds of widgets) even if not every widgets will be considered as critical and then will need to be fault-tolerant.

To solve this issue, we propose to apply the self-checking mechanism to an upper level: the layer. The layer is a logical unit merging all the widgets for one application, for one UA. In this case, the objective is not to validate every output at the widget level, but safety properties related to a sequence of interactions between the layer and its attached UA. The granularity of the verification is done in this case at a more abstract and semantic level.

To illustrate more concretely a layer, we give an example in **Fig. 6** containing one layer grouping 138 widgets: it is an interactive cockpit application called Flight Control Unit (FCU) Backup. The FCU is a hardware panel (i.e. several electronic devices such as buttons, knobs, displays ...) providing two types of services: Electronic Flight Information System (EFIS) and Auto Flight System (AFS).

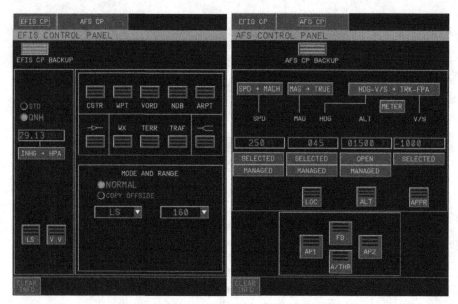

Fig. 6. Snapshot of the FCU Backup application in Airbus A380 (left EFIS, right AFS)

The FCU Backup application (see **Fig. 6**) is designed as an ARINC 661 layer to re-cover all FCU functions in case of failure of the physical FCU. It is composed of two interactive pages: EFIS Control Panel (CP) and AFS CP and is displayed on two of the eight LCD screens (for the A380) in the cockpit, one for the Captain and the other for the First Officer. Both crew members can interact with the application via the KCCUs which gathers in the same hardware component a keyboard and a trackball.

As the layer is directly connected to an application, it is easy to define safety assertions associated with the application semantics. Beyond self-checking widgets and generic se-quences of widget actions, we have to consider safety properties that can be checked.

A simple example can be found on the FCU-Backup application (see **Fig. 6**). The EditBoxNumeric on the left of EFIS CP displays the atmospheric pressure. It can be displayed in two different units (inHg or hPa). The atmospheric pressure unit is cho-sen using the PicturePushButton just behind the EditBoxNumeric. A safety property correspond to the verification that the unit and value are modified in a right way upon a click on the PicturePushButton.

A self-checking layer implementation relies in part on a controller as a *safety properties checker* (option 3 defined in section 4.3). Furthermore, as explained pre-viously, the layer is a very big and complex entity and thus very complicated to mod-el. The application of the self-checking pattern to a layer is of interest when safety properties have to be checked, because of their semantic nature.

5   Fault-Tolerant Architecture

The self-checking interactive objects (widgets and layers) aim at improving the error detection coverage regarding the fault model described previously. The execution of an interactive object developed using ICO relies on several software layers: a Petri Net simulator (e.g. PetShop [11] in our case) or code generated from the model, a virtual machine (a JVM in our case), display and event managers belonging to the CDS and at last the ARINC 653 operating system kernel.

To cover both transient faults and permanent hardware faults, it is mandatory to take into account error confinement areas to isolate the functional part and the controller part of the self-checking objet, whatever it is a widget or a layer.

5.1   Architectural Issues

Ideally the functional part should be located in one partition, the controller in a second partition and the dispatcher and the comparator in a third partition. A simplification can be to locate the controller, the dispatcher and the comparator in a single partition, the three components being considered as a verification logic. A partition providing space and time segregation prevent faults having an impact on both the function and its controller counterpart.

To tolerate crash faults, two copies of the self-checking widget should be located on two different DUs, as a physical unit. Only one is considered active at a given point in time. This approach follows the *N-Self-Checking Components* principle early mentioned in this paper. Because interactive objects hold a persistent state, a *master-slave* replication strategy is mandatory. Two design patterns of duplex protocols can be envisaged: a checkpointing-based strategy (primary-backup replication protocol) or an active replication strategy (e.g. a leader-follower replication protocol). In short the architecture can be sketched as follows:

a)   the functional part F1 of the interactive object is located in P1 on DU1
b)   the controller part C1 of the interactive object is located in P1 on DU2
c)   a replica of the functional part F2 is located on P2 on the DU2
d)   the controller part C2 of the functional part replica is located in P2 on DU1

Fig. 7 illustrates these implementation choices: F1/C1 is the master and F2/C2 is the slave. The slave does not interact with the crew, only the master does. This means that inputs from the crew on the master ICO object are forwarded to the slave object. Events produced by the slave, if it is an active copy, are not forwarded to the UA, only events from the master are delivered to the UA. More details on design patterns for resilient computing can be found in [8].

Each partition contains an ARINC 661 server, implemented as an ICO model allowing the communication between the ICO interactive object (layer or widget) and the UA or the input and output devices. In order to execute ICO models all partitions include a JVM on top of which our Petshop tool is running. This is the option we consider now in our experiments, which is conformant to the fault assumptions early described. This option does not consider remaining development faults within the Petshop tool or the JVM, i.e. common mode faults in the executive software. We come back to this point in the next section.

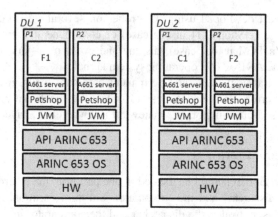

Fig. 7. Fault tolerant architecture

It is worth noting that the proposed fault tolerant architecture implementation is using 2 DUs. Yet, depending on the requirements, other implementations with 3 or more DUs can also be studied based on this principle.

5.2   Performance Issues: Discussion

The performance of the architectural solution proposed in the previous section can be analyzed through different angles: dependability and resource overheads.

From a dependability viewpoint, the proposed solution relies first on the use of a model-based development that minimizes the introduction of design faults. The ARINC 661 standard defines the behavior of the widgets and a non-ambiguous description is obtained using the ICO formalism. The model is interpreted at runtime and implements the expected interactive objects for a given avionic function through a so-called user application (UA). The communication between the interactive object and the UA or the input and output devices is insured by an ARINC 661 server modeled in ICO. The execution relies on a specific Petri Net interpreter running on top of a JVM. The remaining design faults in the executive support (Petshop, the JVM, or even the server) can be a problem for critical applications. To address this issue, a first solution can be to use the Petri Net interpreter in one partition for the functional part (F1/P1/DU1 in **Fig. 7**) and generate code for the controller (C1/P1/DU2). The controller is a copy of the functional part, but in this case the runtime image is different. One can also consider using several implementations of the JVM (diversification) in different partitions. A similar approach based on different ADA runtime supports has been used in the B777 architecture [17].

Whatever the option is, the space and time partitioning provided by the ARINC 653 kernel clearly isolates the functional part of a self-checking interactive object from other ICO objects running in different partitions. Errors due to memory faults and infinite loops have no side effects on ICO objects running in companion partitions on the same DU. In options 2 and 3 proposed in Section 4.3, the controller differs from the functional interactive objects. A reduced version of the functional interactive object specification can be implemented as a controller if some aspects of the ICO object have no impact on dependability and can be ignored. Moving forward with this approach leads in fact to the third option, where the controller only checks safety properties, i.e. executes user-defined executable assertions. A white box approach enables assertions to benefit from deeper observability of the ICO object behavior.

Whatever the implementation option is (widget or layer), the resource overhead (timing, communication, etc.) has to be considered. We plan to provide measures related to (i) the complexity of the model (number of states and transitions) but also (ii) to communication overheads (number and size of messages) between functional and controller partitions.

6   Conclusion and Perspectives

In this paper, we have shown that safety critical applications (such as interactive cockpits applications) raise specific concerns with regard to fault-tolerance and resilience. We have presented an approach to increase safety critical interactive system resilience by enriching them with fault-tolerance mechanisms. We proposed to introduce a self-checking mechanism at two abstraction levels of the interactive system: the widget and the layer.

These two approaches can be used separately or jointly. The design choice (self-checking widget or self-checking layer) is left open to the UA designer according to the criticality of the avionic function considered in general, but also with respect to the criticality of the parameter (or event) to be obtained or the parameter to be displayed. For instance, the UA designer can choose to use the layer approach yet, he can use jointly the widget approach for really critical information. We also presented an architecture compliant with our approach. To go further, we are currently applying our approach to the FCU Backup application mentioned in the paper.

The approach presented in this paper has been implemented in Java as a first proof of concepts, but the final implementation might be different. We are currently investigating in more details the notion of self-checking layer and plan to implement the FCU Backup case study on a realistic platform.

Acknowledgment. This work is partly funded by Airbus under the contract R&T Display System X31WD1107313.

References

1. ARINC 661 Cockpit Display System Interfaces to User Systems. ARINC Specification 661. Airlines Electronic Engineering Committee (2002)
2. ARINC 653 Avionics Application Software Standard Interface. ARINC Specification 653. Airlines Electronic Engineering Committee, July 15 (2003)
3. Barboni, E., Conversy, S., Navarre, D., Palanque, P.: Model-Based Engineering of Widgets, User Applications and Servers Compliant with ARINC 661 Specification. In: Doherty, G., Blandford, A. (eds.) DSVIS 2006. LNCS, vol. 4323, pp. 25–38. Springer, Heidelberg (2007)

4. Bastide, R., Sy, O., Palanque, P.: A formal notation and tool for the engineering of CORBA systems. Concurrency: Practice and Experience (Wiley) 12, 1379–1403 (2000)
5. Degani, A., Heymann, M.: Analysis and Verification of Human-Automation Interfaces. Human Centered Computing: Cognitive, Social and Ergonomic Aspects. In: Proceedings of the 10th Int. Conf. on HCI, vol. 3, pp. 185–189. Erlbaum, Mahwah (2003)
6. DO-178B: Software Considerations in Airbone Systems and Equipment Certification. RTCA Inc., EUROCAE (December 1992)
7. Genrich, H.J.: Predicate/Transitions Nets. In: Jensen, K., Rozenberg, G. (eds.) High-Levels Petri Nets: Theory and Application, pp. 3–43. Springer, Heidelberg (1991)
8. Gibert, V., Machin, M., Fabre, J.-C., Stoicescu, M.: Design for Adaptation of Fault Tolerance Strategies. Rapport LAAS no 12198, 35 p (April 2012)
9. Laprie, J.-C.: From Dependability to Resilience. In: IEEE/IFIP International Conference on Dependable Systems and Networks, Anchorage, Alaska, USA (June 2008)
10. Laprie, J.-C., Arlat, J., Béounes, C., Kanoun, K.: Definition and Analysis of hardware and software Fault-Tolerant Architectures. IEEE Computer 23(7), 39–51 (1990)
11. Navarre, D., Palanque, P., Bastide, R.: A Tool-Supported Design Framework for Safety Critical Interactive Systems in Interacting with computers, vol. 15/3, pp. 309–328. Elsevier, Amsterdam (2003)
12. Navarre, D., Palanque, P., Ladry, J.-F., Barboni, E.: ICOs: a Model-Based User Interface Description Technique dedicated to Interactive Systems Addressing Usability, Reliability and Scalability. ACM Trans. on Computer-Human Interaction 16(4), 1–56 (2009)
13. Normand, E.: Single-event effects in avionics. IEEE Transactions on Nuclear Science 43(2), 461–474 (1996)
14. Tankeu-Choitat, A., Navarre, D., Palanque, P., Deleris, Y., Fabre, J.-C., Fayollas, C.: Self-checking components for dependable interactive cockpits using formal description techniques. In: Proc. of 17th IEEE Pacific Rim Int. Symp. on Dependable Computing (PRDC 2011), Pasadena, California, USA (2011)
15. Traverse, P., Lacaze, I., Souyris, J.: Airbus Fly-by-Wire: A Total Approach to Dependability. In: Proceedings 18th IFIP World Computer Congress, Building the Information Society, Toulouse, France, August 22-27, pp. 191–212 (2004)
16. Yau, S.S., Cheung, R.C.: Design of self-Checking Software. In: Proc. Int. Conf. on Reliable Software, pp. 450–457. IEEE Computer Society Press, Los Angeles (1975)
17. Yeh, Y.C. (Bob): Design Considerations in Boeing 777 Fly-By-Wire Computers. In: Third IEEE International High-Assurance Systems Engineering Symposium, p. 64 (1998)

Linking Modelling in Event-B with Safety Cases

Yuliya Prokhorova[1,2] and Elena Troubitsyna[2]

[1] TUCS – Turku Centre for Computer Science
[2] Department of Information Technologies, Åbo Akademi University
Joukahaisenkatu 3-5 A, 20520 Turku, Finland
{Yuliya.Prokhorova,Elena.Troubitsyna}@abo.fi

Abstract. Safety cases are adopted in the certification process of many safety-critical systems. They justify why a system is safe and whether the design adequately incorporates safety requirements defined in a system requirement specification. The use of formal methods facilitates modelling and verification of safety-critical systems. In our work, we aim at establishing a link between formal modelling in Event-B and constructing a safety case. We propose an approach to incorporating safety requirements in a formal specification in such a way that it allows the developers to derive a safety case sufficient to demonstrate safety. We present a small case study illustrating the proposed approach.

Keywords: Event-B, formal specification, safety case, safety requirements, safety-critical systems.

1 Introduction

The use of formal methods in specification and verification of safety-critical systems has increased during the last decade. However, Habli and Kelly [1] point out that the use of an evidence generated from formal analysis is still an open issue in the system certification process. Basir et al. in [2] also state that formal methods, specifically formal proofs, provide justification for the validity of claims and widely deployed in software development. Nevertheless, the formal proofs are often too complex which causes uncertainties about trustworthiness of using formal proofs as the evidence in safety cases of safety-critical systems.

Another open issue related to the formal modelling process is whether the obtained formal model adequately represents safety requirements described in a system requirement specification. Several works address the question of requirements elicitation and traceability into a formal model [3,4,5]. Formal proofs as the evidence are only reasonable if those proofs are demonstrated to support incorporated safety requirements.

In this paper, we propose an approach to linking formal modelling in Event-B [6,7] with safety cases. We give the classification of safety requirements and define how each class can be represented in a formal specification. Additionally, we propose to split up a safety case into two main branches: argumentation over safety requirements and argumentation over the whole design. We define a number of invariants and theorems to support the argumentation. We use the

P. Avgeriou (Ed.): SERENE 2012, LNCS 7527, pp. 47–62, 2012.

Event-B framework to automatically generate the respective proof obligations which can be used in the safety case as the evidence that requirements have been met. The approach permits the developers to obtain a consistent system specification that allows for deriving a "sufficient" safety case. The problem what amount or what types of evidence to consider as "sufficient" is addressed in [8]. The authors determine the sufficiency of the evidence as *"its capability to address specific explicit safety assurance claims in a safety argument"*.

The paper is structured as follows. The safety case concept and modelling in Event-B principles are described in Section 2. In Section 3 we present our approach. In particular, in Subsection 3.1 we classify safety requirements and show the corresponding elements of an Event-B model. The link between Event-B and the main parts of a system safety case (represented using GSN) is given in Subsection 3.2. The verification support provided by the Event-B formalism for safety case arguments is discussed in Subsection 3.3. We illustrate our approach by an example – the sluice gate control system in Section 4. Finally, in Section 5 we give concluding remarks as well as discuss future and related work.

2   Background

2.1   Safety Cases

A safety case is *"a structured argument, supported by a body of evidence that provides a compelling, comprehensible and valid case that a system is safe for a given application in a given operating environment"* [9,10].

A claim or a requirement, a safety argument and an evidence are the main elements of a safety case. Bishop and Bloomfield [10] define a *claim* to be the property of the system or some subsystem, while Kelly [11] defines a *requirement* as the safety objectives that must be addressed to assure safety. An *evidence* is the information extracted from analysis, testing or simulation of the system. The evidence makes the basis of the safety argument. An *argument* is a link between the evidence and the claim or requirements.

To represent the elements of a safety case and the relationships that exist between these elements, a graphical argumentation notation called *Goal Structuring Notation (GSN)* has been proposed by Kelly [11]. The principal elements of the notation are shown in Fig. 1.

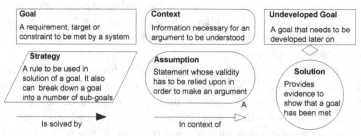

Fig. 1. Principal elements of GSN (detailed description is given in [11,12])

The safety case constructed in terms of GSN shows how goals (claims) are decomposed into sub-goals until the claim can be supported by the direct evidence (solution). It also defines the argument strategies and the context in which goals are declared. GSN has been adopted by a wide range of European companies from different domains: avionics, submarines, railways, etc. [1].

2.2   Modelling in Event-B

Event-B [6,7] is a state-based formal method for system level modelling and analysis. It is an extension of the B Method [13] that aims at facilitating modelling of parallel, distributed and reactive systems. Automated support for modelling and verification in Event-B is provided by the Rodin Platform [6].

In Event-B system models are defined using the notion of an *abstract state machine*. An abstract machine encapsulates the state (the variables) of a model and defines operations (events) on its state. The machine is uniquely identified by its name *MachineName*. The state variables of the machine are declared in the **VARIABLES** clause and initialised in the *INITIALISATION* event. The variables are strongly typed by the constraining predicates in terms of invariants given in the **INVARIANTS** clause. The data types and constants of the model are stated in a separate component called **CONTEXT**, where their properties are postulated as axioms. The behaviour of the system is determined by a number of atomic **EVENTS**. An event can be defined as follows:

$$e \mathrel{\hat{=}} \textbf{ANY } lv \textbf{ WHERE } g \textbf{ THEN } R \textbf{ END}$$

where lv is a list of local variables, the guard g is the conjunction of predicates defined over model variables, and the action R is a composition of assignments on the variables executed simultaneously.

The guard denotes when an event is enabled. If several events are enabled simultaneously then any of them can be chosen for execution non-deterministically. If none of the events is enabled then the system deadlocks. An assignment to a variable can be either deterministic or non-deterministic.

The semantics of Event-B events is defined using before-after predicates [14]. A before-after predicate (BA) describes a relationship between the system states before and after execution of an event. To verify correctness of a specification, one needs to prove that the model preserves its invariants, i.e., each event e_i of the model preserves the given invariant:

$$A(d,c), \; I(d,c,v), \; g_i(d,c,v), \; BA_i(d,c,v,v') \; \vdash \; I(d,c,v') \qquad \text{(INV)}$$

where A stands for the conjunction of the axioms, I is the conjunction of the invariants, g_i is the guard of the event e_i, BA_i is the before-after predicate of this event, d stands for the sets, c are the constants, and v, v' are the variable values before and after event execution.

2.3   Refinement and Verification in Event-B

Event-B employs a top-down refinement-based approach to formal development of a system. The development starts from an abstract specification of the system and continues with stepwise unfolding of system properties by introducing new variables and events into the model. We call such kind of a refinement a *superposition refinement*. Moreover, Event-B formal development supports data refinement, allowing us to replace some abstract variables with their concrete counterparts. In this case, the invariant of a refined model formally defines the relationship between the abstract and concrete variables; this type of invariants is called a *gluing invariant*.

To verify correctness of a refinement step, one needs to discard a number of *proof obligations (PO)* for a refined model. For brevity, here we show only a few essential ones. The full list of proof obligations can be found in [7].

Let us introduce a shorthand $H(d, c, v, w)$ which stands for the hypotheses while $I(d, c, v)$ and $I'(d, c, v, w)$ are respectively the abstract and refined invariants and v, w are respectively the abstract and concrete variables.

The event guards in a refined model can only be strengthened in refinement:

$$H(d, c, v, w),\ g'_i(d, c, w) \vdash g_i(d, c, v) \tag{GRD}$$

where g_i, g'_i are respectively the abstract and concrete guards of the event e_i.

The *simulation* proof obligation (SIM) requires to show that the action (i.e., assignment on the state variables) of a refined event is not contradictory to its abstract version:

$$H(d, c, v, w),\ g'_i(d, c, w),\ BA'_i(d, c, w, w') \vdash \exists v'.BA_i(d, c, v, v') \wedge I'(d, c, v', w') \tag{SIM}$$

where BA_i, BA'_i are respectively the abstract and concrete before-after predicates of the same event e_i.

Finally, the Event-B formalism allows us to define theorems either in the context $T(d, c)$ or in the machine $T(d, c, v)$. The *theorem* proof obligation (THM) ensures that a proposed theorem is indeed provable. The first variant is defined for a theorem in a context:

$$A(d, c) \vdash T(d, c) \tag{THM}$$

The second variant is defined for a theorem in a machine:

$$A(d, c), I(d, c, v) \vdash T(d, c, v) \tag{THM}$$

The described proof obligations are automatically generated by the Rodin Platform [6] that supports Event-B. Additionally, the tool attempts to automatically prove them. Sometimes it requires user assistance by invoking its interactive prover. However, in general the tool achieves high level of automation (usually over 80%) in proving.

3   An Approach to Linking Modelling in Event-B with Safety Cases

In this section, we present an approach that establishes a link between formal modelling of a system in Event-B and deriving a safety case for this system. We aim at obtaining the safety case where the argumentation is based on formal reasoning and supported by discharging proof obligations. To achieve this goal, we firstly give the classification of the safety requirements and show how each class is treated within the Event-B framework. Secondly, we show how the safety requirements, invariants and theorems as well as proofs for them correspond to the elements of the safety case. Finally, we provide verification support for safety case arguments by defining safety invariants and theorems formally.

3.1 Requirements Classification

Let us now give a classification of safety requirements. To provide the reader with the classification of safety requirements, we adopt and modify the taxonomy proposed by Bitsch [15]. Following his approach, we divide safety requirements into two groups: *Static Safety Requirements* and *Dynamic Safety Requirements*. The former are those properties that must hold for the whole formal model. The latter are those properties that must be true only in certain model states.

The *Dynamic Safety Requirements (DSRs)* cover a large group of safety requirements. To simplify the task of mapping them on the Event-B framework, we decompose the *Dynamic Safety Requirements* class into two sub-classes: *DSRs about General Access Guarantee* and *DSRs about Chronological Succession.*

To ensure safety of a certain class of control systems, we should prove that these systems are deadlock free. Therefore, DSRs about General Access Guarantee are defined as requirements which describe the necessity to provide an access to some property or to reach some state. While developing a formal model of a safety-critical control system, we also might deal with requirements that are dependent on the chronological occurrences of some properties, e.g., requirements that define fault tolerance procedures. Since fault detection, isolation and recovery actions are strictly ordered, we also need to preserve their sequence in a formal model of a system. The DSRs about Chronological Succession reflect such requirements. Hence, these sub-classes of DSRs are addressed differently in a formal model. Furthermore, the proposed classification can be extended with respect to, for example, timing properties. However, we leave such sub-classes out of the scope of this paper.

To define how each class of safety requirements can be treated in Event-B, we have analysed several works that aim at tracing requirements in a formal specification in Event-B [3,4,5]. For instance, Méry and Singh [3] propose to represent safety requirements as invariants or theorems, while Jastram et al. [4] incorporate them as invariants and before-after predicates of events. Additionally, in [5] Yeganefard and Butler state that requirements can be modelled in Event-B as guards or actions of events. All these works show the mapping between particular requirements and the Event-B structure. However, they do not consider the classification of the safety requirements. In contrast, we create the link between the requirements classification and their representation in Event-B as shown in Table 1. We propose to model *Static Safety Requirements* in the Event-B framework as invariants or incorporate them in the process of guards strengthening in refinement while *Dynamic Safety Requirements*, in general, can be related to after predicates or actions simulation in refinement. *DSRs about General access*

Table 1. Mapping of the safety requirements classification on the Event-B framework

Safety requirements class	Event-B framework
Static Safety Requirements	Invariants; Guards strengthening in refinement
Dynamic Safety Requirements	After predicates; Actions simulation in refinement
Dynamic Safety Requirements about General access guarantee	Deadlock freedom
Dynamic Safety Requirements about Chronological succession	Events order

guarantee are represented as the deadlock freedom condition, while *DSRs about Chronological succession* are defined as events order in Event-B.

As soon as all safety requirements are assigned to respective classes and the mapping on Event-B is done, we can argue that the system is safe.

3.2   Linking Safety Cases with the Event-B Framework

To provide an argument that the system is safe, we build a system safety case using GSN (Fig. 2). We introduce the main **Goal** *"(G1): System is safe"* that is considered in the **Context** of formal modelling in Event-B *(C1)*. Additionally, we propose to split up the overall process of the safety case derivation into two main parts: argumentation over each safety requirement and argumentation that the design is satisfactory. To represent this in terms of GSN, we introduce two respective **Strategies**: *"(S1): Argument over each safety requirement"* and *"(S2): Argument that design is satisfactory"*.

The complete safety case with respect to the system safety requirements is obtained by providing an evidence that the safety requirements listed in the Requirements Document (RD) are derived and adequately formalised. For this purpose, we introduce an **Assumption** *"(A1): All safety requirements are derived from RD"*. We support this assumption by performing hazard analysis. In this case, our goal is to obtain the safety requirements list *(G2)*. The **Solution** (or the evidence) is to conduct one or a combination of well-known hazard analysis techniques such as Failure Modes and Effects Analysis (FMEA), HAZard and OPerability analysis (HAZOP), Preliminary Hazard Analysis (PHA), etc.

We arrange the derived safety requirements according to the classification proposed in Section 3.1. Therefore, we introduce several **Sub-goals** (or goals) that correspond to the given safety requirements classes and their mapping on Event-B (proposed in Table 1):

(G3): Static Safety Requirements (invariants)
(G4): Static Safety Requirements (guards strengthening in refinement)
(G5): Dynamic Safety Requirements (after predicates)
(G6): Dynamic Safety Requirements (actions simulation in refinement)
(G7): Dynamic Safety Requirements. General access guarantee
        (deadlock freedom)
(G8): Dynamic Safety Requirements. Chronological succession (events order)

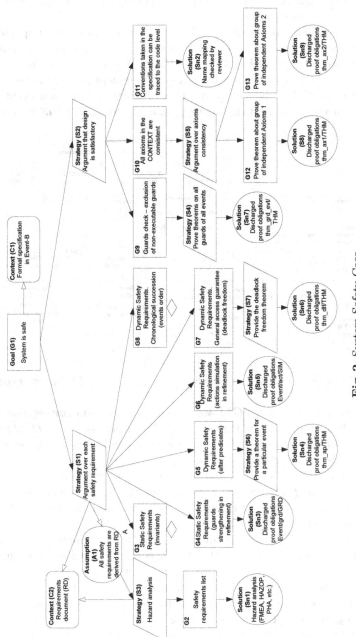

Fig. 2. System Safety Case

The goals *(G4)* and *(G6)* simply require a solution that can be provided in terms of Event-B by discharged proof obligations *(Sn3)* and *(Sn5)*, respectively. However, the goals *(G3)*, *(G5)*, *(G7)* and *(G8)* need to be decomposed before deriving the evidence for them.

The safety requirements given as invariants *(G3)* must be supported by an argumentation concerning their proper formalisation: assumption *(A3.1)* and respective strategy *(S3.3)* as shown in Fig. 3. We also need to prove that the invariant holds for all events by providing an argument over each event independently, e.g., *(G3.1)*. The discharged proof obligations for each event serve as solutions for this branch of the safety case, e.g., *(Sn3.1)*, *(Sn3.2)*, etc.

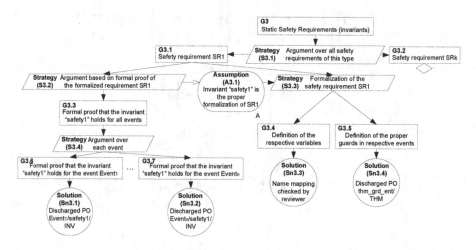

Fig. 3. Safety Case for Static Safety Requirements of Invariant Type

To decompose the goal *(G5)*, we introduce a theorem stating that an after predicate holds for a particular event *(S6)*. The proof obligation *(Sn4)* supports this claim. Respectively, for *(G7)* we provide a deadlock freedom theorem *(S7)* and the evidence *(Sn6)* as shown in Fig. 2.

To produce the evidence for the dynamic safety requirements about chronological succession *(G8)*, we propose to adopt the flow approach introduced by Iliasov [16]. However, due to the lack of space, we omit the detailed description of the respective safety case.

Despite the fact that safety requirements might be adequately represented in a formal specification, the goal "*(G1): System is safe*" can still be unreachable. The design (the formal specification) can contain inconsistency and improper representation of physical components in terms of variables, constants and sets. Therefore, we need to show that our design is consistent and adequate as well. We consider such **Sub-goals** as "*(G9): Guards check – exclusion of non-executable guards*", "*(G10): All axioms in the CONTEXT are consistent*" and "*(G11): Conventions taken in the specification can be traced to the code level*". To support the first subgoal, theorems on all guards of all events have to be introduced in the specification *(S4)* and the derived proof obligations can serve as solutions *(Sn7)*. The second sub-goal requires argumentation over axioms consistency which leads to the decomposition of this goal into sub-goals *(G12)*, *(G13)*. This level sub-goals represent different groups of independent axioms. To provide the evidence, we propose to introduce and prove theorems for consistency of each group of axioms, e.g., *(Sn8)* and *(Sn9)*. The solution to the third sub-goal is the name mapping checked by a reviewer *(Sn2)*. The reader can consult Fig. 2 for recalling the precise meaning of abbreviations.

3.3   Verification Support for Safety Case Arguments

In the previous subsection, we created the link between safety cases and the Event-B framework. Now, we show the formalisation of this link, i.e., how the proposed invariants and theorems can be postulated in Event-B and which proof obligations support them.

First, let us consider the classes of safety requirements that simply require an evidence and can be implemented in a refinement step, i.e., "*(G4)*: *Static Safety Requirements (guards strengthening in refinement)*" and "*(G6)*: *Dynamic Safety Requirements (actions simulation in refinement)*".

In a refinement step an abstract variable, e.g., abs_var_k, can be replaced by some new concrete variables $conc\_var$. For instance, the variable that represents a failure of a system might be replaced by variables representing failures of concrete system units (sensors, actuators, etc.). For such a data refinement, we introduce a gluing invariant of the form: $abs\_var_k = VALUE \Leftrightarrow P(conc\_var)$, where P is a predicate on new concrete variables.

To illustrate the considered classes of requirements, we introduce the abstract event *Event_Name* that contains one local variable and its refinement *New_Evt_Name* as shown in Fig. 4. The label $@grd_i$ stands for the *i-th* guard of an event whilst $@act_j$ represents the *j-th* action of an event. Since we replace the abstract local variable n by a concrete value TRUE in the refinement, we

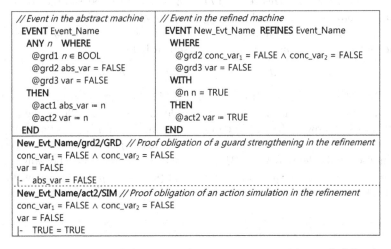

Fig. 4. The example of abstract and concrete events with proof obligations

need to provide a *witness* for it (the **WITH** clause). The witness substitutes the disappearing local variable with a new variable or a concrete value.

To support these safety requirements in the safety case, we provide the proofs that are instances of (GRD) and (SIM), respectively for *(Sn3)* and *(Sn5)*.

Next, we state the Static Safety Requirements *(G3)* as safety invariants of the model, i.e., $I(d, c, v)$. The respective proof obligations (INV) serve as the evidence for the safety case and are automatically generated for all model events.

Now, we formalise the Dynamic Safety Requirements implemented as after predicates "*(G5): Dynamic Safety Requirements (after predicates)*". The simplification of the event definition by omitting local variables does not affect the generality of the proposed approach since any event containing local variables can always be rewritten in a simpler form. Hence, the definition of an event presented in Section 2.2 can be given as the relation: $e(v, v') = g_e(v) \land BA_e(v, v')$. Then, *before(e)* represents a set of all possible pre-states defined by the guard of an event e while *after(e)* is a set of all possible post-states of the event e [16]:

$$before(e) = \{v \in \Sigma \mid I(v) \land g_e(v)\}$$
$$after(e) = \{v' \in \Sigma \mid I(v') \land (\exists v \in \Sigma \cdot I(v) \land g_e(v) \land BA_e(v, v'))\}$$

where Σ corresponds to a model state space defined by all possible values of the vector v (i.e., a set of system variables).

Thereafter, we assume that $q(v')$ is a certain desired post-state. We can verify that this post-state is always established by proving the following theorem:

$$\forall v' \cdot v' \in after(e) \Rightarrow q(v')$$

This theorem serves as the strategy *(S6)* in the respective branch of the safety case while the discharged proof obligation of the type (THM) defined for a machine provides the solution *(Sn4)*.

Another class of the Dynamic Safety Requirements is the requirements about general access guarantee *(G7)*. We represent this class within an Event-B model as the deadlock freedom theorem *(S7)*. This theorem is postulated as the disjunction of guards of all model events $g_1(d, c, v) \lor ... \lor g_m(d, c, v)$. The instance of the (THM) proof obligation for a machine given in Section 2.3 provides the evidence for the safety case *(Sn6)* and is shown below:

$$A(d, c), \ I(d, c, v) \ \vdash \ g_1(d, c, v) \lor ... \lor g_m(d, c, v)$$

Please note that the application of this rule is not compulsory, since not all systems need to be deadlock free. For example, if the system allows the manual operation or shutdown when failure occurs, the model can be deadlocked.

To verify that our formal specification (the design) is satisfactory and there are no non-executable guards *(G9)*, we introduce theorems for checking guards *(S4)*. We base our reasoning on the notion of post- and pre-states as well. The following theorem guarantees that there are no non-executable guards in the model:

$$\forall i \, \exists j \cdot i \neq j \land after(e_j) \Rightarrow before(e_i)$$

This theorem states that for each event e_i there exists an event e_j that enables it (i.e., e_j enables e_i). The exceptions are the initialisation event, which is always enabled at the beginning of the simulation independently of other events, and events without guards, i.e., their guards are always true. The provided theorem and the respective proof obligation ensure that each event of the model is enabled at least once, i.e., the model does not include events with non-executable guards.

The inconsistency in the model axioms has an impact on the whole model *(G10)*. If axioms contradict to each other, the model is falsifiable, i.e., we cannot guarantee its correctness any more. To avoid this, we define theorems for all groups of independent axioms in the model CONTEXT *(S5)*:

$$\exists\, d, c \cdot A_1(d, c) \wedge \ldots \wedge A_n(d, c)$$

The generated proof obligation, e.g., *(Sn8)*, is an instantiation of the (THM) proof obligation for a context given in Section 2.3.

At this point, we have classified safety requirements and have shown how each class can be treated in the formal specification. Additionally, we have defined the link between the Event-B framework and safety cases. In the next section we illustrate our approach by a realistic system – the sluice gate control system.

4   Case Study – Sluice Gate Control System

The sluice gate control system shown in Fig. 5 is a typical representative of a safety-critical control system. This system controls a sluice that connects areas with dramatically different pressures [17]. The purpose of the system is to adjust the pressure in the sluice area. The system consists of two doors – *door1* and *door2* that can be operated independently of each other and a pressure chamber pump that changes the pressure in the sluice area (i.e., the room). To guarantee safety, a door can be opened only if the pressure in the locations it connects is equalized. Moreover, at most one door can be opened at any moment and the pressure chamber pump can only be switched on when both doors are closed. The sluice gate control system is equipped with the sensors and actuators (motors) as shown in Fig. 5.

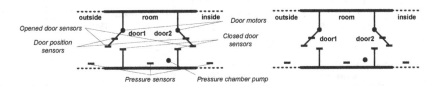

Fig. 5. Sluice Gate System

For the sake of brevity, here we show only those parts of the specification that are relevant to the approach we present. More details on the specification can be found in [17].

Fig. 6 gives an example of a static safety requirement formalisation that represents guards strengthening in the refinement for "*SR1: The system failure occurs*

// Event in the abstract machine	// Event in the refined machine

EVENT Prediction
  WHERE
    @grd1 flag = PRED
    @grd2 Failure = FALSE
    @grd3 Stop = FALSE
  THEN
    @act1 flag ≔ ENV
END
	EVENT Prediction **REFINES** Prediction
	  WHERE
	    @grd1 flag = PRED
	    @grd2 door1_fail = FALSE ∧ door2_fail = FALSE ∧ pressure_fail = FALSE
	    @grd3 Stop = FALSE
	  THEN
	    @act2 d1_exp_min ≔ min_door(door1_position↦door1_motor)
	    ...
	END

Prediction/grd2/GRD // Proof obligation of a guard strengthening in the refinement
flag = PRED
door1_fail = FALSE ∧ door2_fail = FALSE ∧ pressure_fail = FALSE
Stop = FALSE
⊢ Failure = FALSE	

Fig. 6. The event *Prediction* and the respective proof obligation

if and only if either the door1 component fails, or the door2 component fails, or the pressure pump fails".

The event *Prediction* taken as an example models the prediction of the expected values of sensors based on the current state of the system and physical laws of components operation. Later, the obtained information permits the system to detect faults of components by the comparison between expected values and the received ones.

The dynamic safety requirement *"SR2: To handle a system failure, the systems should stop its operation"* is formalised as an action simulation in the refinement step. The event *SafeStop* depicted in Fig. 7 represents the refinement of the abstract event *ErrorHandling*. The deterministic assignment to the variable *Stop* substitutes the non-deterministic assignment to this variable with value TRUE. Additionally, the refined event is supported with the respective witness (@res res = TRUE). The generated proof obligation of the type (SIM)

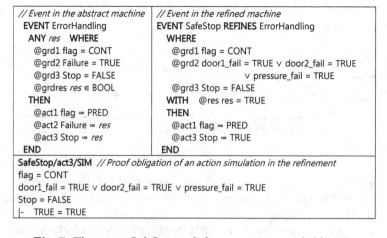

Fig. 7. The event *SafeStop* and the respective proof obligation

shows that the assignment to the state variable *Stop* of the refined event is not contradictory to its abstract version.

Such safety requirements as: *"SR3: Both doors cannot be opened simultaneously"*, *"SR4: If the pressure inside the room is not equal neither to the pressure of the outside area nor to the pressure of the inside area, the doors must remain closed"*, *"SR5: The pressure pump can be switched on only if both doors are closed"*, etc. can be formalised as invariants. Therefore, let us show only the safety case for SR5 (Fig. 8). We introduce the invariant *"safety5"* as a formalisation of SR5: $failure = FALSE \land pump \neq PUMP\_OFF \Rightarrow (door1\_position = 0 \land door2\_position = 0)$.

Fig. 8. Safety Case for the Safety Requirement SR5

To support the claim that *"safety5"* holds for all events of the model, we state an argument over each event and discard the proof obligations of the type (INV). For brevity, here we show only the event *Pressure_High* that models the increase of the pressure inside the room and display the proof obligation ensuring that *"safety5"* holds for this event (Fig. 9).

EVENT Pressure_High **REFINES** NormalSkip	Pressure_High/safety5/INV
WHERE	failure = FALSE ∧ pump ≠ PUMP_OFF ⇒
@grd1 door1_position = 0	door1_position = 0 ∧ door2_position = 0
@grd2 door2_position = 0	door1_position = 0
@grd3 pressure_value = PRESSURE_OUTSIDE	door2_position = 0
@grd0_1 flag = CONT	pressure_value = PRESSURE_OUTSIDE
@grd0_2 failure = FALSE	flag = CONT
@grd0_3 Stop = FALSE	failure = FALSE
THEN	Stop = FALSE
@act1 flag ≔ PRED	⊢ failure = FALSE ∧ PUMP_INC≠PUMP_OFF ⇒
@act2 pump ≔ PUMP_INC **END**	door1_position = 0 ∧ door2_position = 0

Fig. 9. The event *Pressure_High* and the respective proof obligation

Let us consider the dynamic safety requirement formalised as an after predicate: *"SR6: If the pressure value in the room is equalised to the pressure value of the inside area, the pump should be switched off"*. The desired post-state q for this safety requirement is $pump = PUMP\_OFF$. The event *Pressure_Highed* models this case and has the set of all possible post-states $after(Pressure\_Highed)$ as shown in Fig. 10. Here we omit showing other model variables since the event *Pressure_Highed* does not modify them, i.e., they remain the same. The given

EVENT Pressure_Highed **REFINES** NormalSkip	*after(Pressure_Highed)* =
WHERE	
@grd2 pump = PUMP_INC	{ (pump, flag, pressure_value, failure, Stop, ...) |
@grd3 pressure_value = PRESSURE_INSIDE	pump = PUMP_OFF $\land$
@grd0_1 flag = CONT	flag = PRED $\land$
@grd0_2 failure = FALSE	pressure_value = PRESSURE_INSIDE $\land$
@grd0_3 Stop = FALSE	failure = FALSE $\land$
THEN	Stop = FALSE }
@act1 flag ≔ PRED	
@act2 pump ≔ PUMP_OFF **END**	$q \triangleq$ pump = PUMP_OFF

Fig. 10. The event *Pressure_Highed*

$after(Pressure\_Highed)$ implies that q is true. The proof obligation of the type (THM) provides the evidence for the respective branch of the safety case.

Due to manual handling of a system failure, the sluice gate control system has a deadlock. There is an event that sets the variable *Stop* to TRUE (the event *SafeStop* in Fig. 7), while none of the events assigns FALSE to it. To reset the variable *Stop*, the system should be restarted. Therefore, we do not include the deadlock freedom branch in the system safety case.

Finally, we support our modelling of the sluice gate control system with argumentation over the whole design. To exclude non-executable guards, all events are supported by the respective theorems. The generated proof obligations of the type (THM) serve as the evidence. The consistency of axioms is also checked and proved for the sluice gate system through discarding the corresponding theorems in the model *CONTEXT*.

Since we have defined one-to-one mapping between a safety case and a formal model, we can use this mapping to generate the safety case from the model.

5   Related Work and Conclusions

5.1   Related Work

The work presented by Basir et al. [2,12] is dedicated to formal program verification using a safety case construction. It establishes a link between automatically generated program code and a formal analysis, based on automated theorem proving. The authors focus on natural deduction (ND) style proofs and explain how to construct the safety cases by converting the ND proof tree into corresponding safety case elements. Unlike [2,12], in our work we do not go so deeply in the proof obligations semantics provided by Event-B and do not introduce inference rules [7] as elements of the safety case. We rather guide the modelling of safety-critical systems in Event-B and use the proofs as an evidence for a safety case.

Habli and Kelly [1] consider two standards, DO-178B and the UK Defence Standard 00-56, to analyse how formal analysis facilitates achieving the certification goals. They also present a generic safety case for presentation and justification of formal analysis that shows feasibility of applying formal methods within a specific development. In contrast, our approach not only focuses on the use of formal methods in a safety case but also covers the design stage where the decisions how requirements can be implemented in a formal model are made.

5.2   Conclusions

In this paper, we have proposed the approach to support a system safety case with an evidence derived from a formal specification in Event-B. The safety case construction has been divided into two main parts: argumentation over safety requirements incorporation and argumentation over the whole model. To help the developers in the structured argumentation over safety requirements, we have provided the classification of safety requirements and have shown the link between informal requirements description and their formalisation within Event-B. We also defined mapping between the Event-B model and the elements of the safety case.

Obviously, the larger and more complex a safety-critical system, the larger and more complex its safety case. To increase effectiveness of safety case construction, availability of tools is essential. Therefore, as a part of our future work we plan to provide a tool support for automatic generation of safety cases as well as validate the proposed approach on large-scale case studies.

Acknowledgments. The authors would like to thank Linas Laibinis for fruitful discussions as well as Ilya Lopatkin, Alexei Iliasov and Alexander Romanovsky for their valuable feedback on the case study.

References

1. Habli, I., Kelly, T.: A Generic Goal-Based Certification Argument for the Justification of Formal Analysis. Electronic Notes in Theoretical Computer Science 238(4), 27–39 (2009)
2. Basir, N., Denney, E., Fischer, B.: Deriving Safety Cases from Machine-Generated Proofs. In: Proceedings of the Workshop on Proof-Carrying Code and Software Certification (PCC 2009), Los Angeles, California, USA (2009)
3. Méry, D., Singh, N.K.: Technical Report on Interpretation of the Electrocardiogram (ECG) Signal using Formal Methods. Technical Report inria-00584177 (2011)
4. Jastram, M., Hallerstede, S., Ladenberger, L.: Mixing Formal and Informal Model Elements for Tracing Requirements. ECEASST 46 (2011)
5. Yeganefard, S., Butler, M.: Structuring Functional Requirements of Control Systems to Facilitate Refinement-based Formalisation. ECEASST 46 (2011)
6. Event-B and the Rodin Platform (2012), http://www.event-b.org/
7. Abrial, J.-R.: Modeling in Event-B: System and Software Engineering. Cambridge University Press (2010)
8. Hawkins, R., Kelly, T.: A Structured Approach to Selecting and Justifying Software Safety Evidence. In: Proceedings of the 5th IET International Conference on System Safety, pp. 1–6 (2010)
9. UK Ministry of Defence. 00-56 Safety Management Requirements for Defence Systems (2007)

10. Bishop, P., Bloomfield, R.: A Methodology for Safety Case Development. In: Safety-Critical Systems Symposium. Springer, Birmingham (1998)
11. Kelly, T.P.: Arguing Safety – A Systematic Approach to Managing Safety Cases. Doctoral Thesis (1998)
12. Basir, N.: Safety Cases for the Formal Verification of Automatically Generated Code. University of Southampton, Dependable Systems and Software Engineering, ECS. Doctoral Thesis (2010)
13. Abrial, J.-R.: The B-Book: Assigning Programs to Meanings. Cambridge University Press (1996)
14. Metayer, C., Abrial, J.-R., Voisin, L.: Rigorous Open Development Environment for Complex Systems (RODIN). Event-B (2005),
    http://rodin.cs.ncl.ac.uk/deliverables/D7.pdf
15. Bitsch, F.: Safety Patterns - The Key to Formal Specification of Safety Requirements. In: Voges, U. (ed.) SAFECOMP 2001. LNCS, vol. 2187, pp. 176–189. Springer, Heidelberg (2001)
16. Iliasov, A.: Use Case Scenarios as Verification Conditions: Event-B/Flow Approach. In: Troubitsyna, E.A. (ed.) SERENE 2011. LNCS, vol. 6968, pp. 9–23. Springer, Heidelberg (2011)
17. Lopatkin, I., Prokhorova, Y., Troubitsyna, E., Iliasov, A., Romanovsky, A.: Patterns for Representing FMEA in Formal Specification of Control Systems. TUCS Technical Reports 1003, Turku Centre for Computer Science (2011)

Safety Lifecycle Development Process Modeling for Embedded Systems - Example of Railway Domain

Brahim Hamid[1], Jacob Geisel[1], Adel Ziani[1], and David Gonzalez[2]

[1] IRIT, University of Toulouse
118 Route de Narbonne, 31062 Toulouse Cedex 9, France
{brahim.hamid,jacob.geisel,adel.ziani}@irit.fr
[2] Ikerlan, Mandragon, Spain
DGonzalez@ikerlan.es

Abstract. Nowadays, many practitioners express their worries about current software engineering practices. New recommendations should be considered to ground software engineering on solid theory and on proven principles. We took such an approach towards software engineering process modeling for embedded system applications with security and dependability requirements, focusing on the problem of integrating safety during the process design to clarify assessment of this kind of applications.

In this paper, we propose a safety-oriented process metamodel to support all the requirements of safety processes. The resulting modeling framework serves primarily to capture the basic concepts of concerns related to safety development of embedded systems based on the clear separation between the development process, the system and their properties. Subsequently, the safety property model of the process is defined. The feasibility of the approach is evaluated with a case study from the railway domain.

Keywords: Safety Lifecycle, Development Process, Modeling, Process Metamodel, Repository.

1 Introduction

An embedded system is a system that is composed of two main parts, software and hardware, which evolves in a real world environment and fulfills a specific [8,12] function. Such systems come with a large number of common characteristics, including real-time and temperature constraints, dependability as well as efficiency requirements. They can be found in many application sectors such as automotive, aerospace and home control. Most of these systems are critical and require a high level of safety and integrity. Therefore, the generation of embedded systems involves specific software building processes. These processes are often error-prone, because they are not fully automated, even if some level of automatic code generation or even model driven engineering support

P. Avgeriou (Ed.): SERENE 2012, LNCS 7527, pp. 63–75, 2012.

is given. Furthermore, many critical embedded systems also have assurance requirements, ranging from very strong levels involving certification (e.g. DO178 and IEC-61508 for safety relevant embedded systems development) to lighter levels based on industry practices.

Over the last two decades, the need for formally defined safety lifecycle processes has emerged. This is because the inevitable requirement for better processes eventually pushed control systems to a level of complexity where sophisticated electronics and programmable systems have become the optimal solution for control and safety protection [17]. With these emergent requirements, many safety lifecycles have been proposed by different associations, like IEC or ANSI/ISA. These safety lifecycles are adopted by different domains or companies with some modifications to adapt different requirements (e.g. domain specific requirements). However, as the fundamental differences between a traditional development process and a safety lifecycle are huge, such as different kinds of safety checks and the safety relationships between these checks and phases, modeling these different safety lifecycles with traditional used process metamodel is not simple and direct.

A process metamodel supports the effort of creating flexible process models. The purpose of process models is to document and communicate processes and to enhance the reuse of processes. Thus, processes can be better taught and executed. Results of using a process metamodel are an increased productivity of process engineers and an improved quality of the models they produce. However, the most used metamodels such as SPEM [13], UMA [2], OPF [14], focus on modeling the process model with an activity-oriented viewpoint to accommodate a large range of development processes. Such orientation leads to lacks on the formalization of the required concepts of safety lifecycle, such as validation.

The goal of our work is to propose a model-based safety lifecycle development process technique in order to ease their use in a building process of system/software applications with safety support. The promoted vision reduces the cost of building a process for each application's properties and/or for each domain. The contribution of this paper is fourfold: (1) Modeling: we propose a metamodel to capture safety lifecycle concepts in process modeling; (2) Experimentation: some experiences are achieved to extend the V-Model to build safety oriented process models; 3) Tooling: we propose an EMF editor to create this modeling artifact with a repository interaction support to store them for reuse; 4) Validation: applied in practice to a resource constrained embedded system (RCES) in the context of TERESA project [5].

The remainder of this paper is organized as follows. Section 2 defines the context of the safety lifecycle followed by a motivating example. Section 3 outlines the Repository-Centric Process Metamodel (RCPM). Section 4 presents how the RCPM metamodel supports the safety lifecycle with its safety-related concepts. In Section 5, the supporting tool is highlighted, while Section 6 validates the RCPM metamodel by a railway process model example. Section 7 discusses the state of the art of process metamodels from the safety related viewpoint. Section 8 concludes and draws future work directions.

2 Development Context, Concepts and Definitions

2.1 Development Context

The work is conducted in the context of a project called SEMCO (System and software Engineering for embedded systems applications with Multi-COncerns). We build on a theory and novel methods based on a repository of modeling artifacts which (1) promote engineering separation of concerns, (2) support multiconcerns, (3) use patterns and model libraries to embed solutions of engineering concerns and (4) support multi-domain specific processes. This project is based on Domain-Specific Modeling (DSM) [4] and is threefold: providing a repository of modeling artifacts, tools to manage these artifacts and guidelines to build complete systems.

The SEMCO DSL process is divided into diverse kinds of activities: DSL (Domain-Specific Language) definition, transformation, coherence and relationships rules, design with DSL and qualification. The first three activities are achieved by the DSL designer and last two are used by final DSL user. There are several DSM environments available. In our context, we use the Eclipse Modeling Framework (EMF), an open-source platform. Note, however, that our vision is not limited to EMF.

In this paper, we follow the SEMCO DSL process to build the Repository Centric Process Modeling Framework: (1) we create the model's ecore file and then (2) we use the code generation techniques of EMF to create our modeling tools. The next sections detail these two steps. Now, we will introduce some definitions and concepts that might be useful for the understanding of our approach.

2.2 Safety Lifecycle: Definition and Concepts

Safety lifecycle can be defined as follows: an engineering process designed to achieve a risk-based level of safety with performance criteria that allow versatile technologies and optimal design solutions [3]. The risk-based levels are recognized as *System Integrity Levels* (SIL). SIL measures the confidence which can be attributed on the fact that the integrity of the system functions are conform with the requirements.

Many safety lifecycles are proposed, such as IEC 61508 [10], IEC 61511 [11], and ANSI/ISA S84.01 [16]. The differences between the safety lifecycle and a normal development process are not only the integration of safety related phases into the process, but also the special concepts used to verify whether the safety lifecycle and the SIL requirements are correctly implemented and satisfied. Generally, there are four kinds of checks employed to verify the safety lifecycle [10]:

- *Verification.* Confirmation by examination and provision of objective evidence that the intended functions have been correctly implemented and the requirements have been satisfied.
- *Validation.* The activity of demonstrating that the safety-related system under consideration, before or after installation, meets in all respects the safety requirements specification.

- *Functional safety audit.* Systematic and independent examination to determine whether the procedures specific to the functional safety requirements comply with the planned arrangements and are implemented effectively.
- *Functional safety assessment.* Investigation, based on evidence, to judge the functional safety achieved by one or more E/E/PE safety-related systems.

Beyond these checks, the interaction and influences between the process phases and activities should be considered.

2.3   Introduction to the Example

The domain specific requirements lead to different safety lifecycles [3], which are modified from the general or standard lifecycle to adapt their specific requirements. For example, the IEC (International Electrotechnical Commission) 61508 is today globally recognized and considered as the basic standard to evaluate the suppliers' products. IEC 61508 [10] recommends a V-model safety lifecycle. How to define this kind of safety lifecycle model, such as IEC 61508 V-model, is raised as a problem. As we shall see, in this paper we illustrate our study by using the example of an engineering process for building railway control systems. A summary of the actions that are performed in each phase of the process is shown in Fig. 1. These actions are very similar to those performed in a process designed to comply with IEC-61508 standard, but some particularities are introduced due to the differences between this standard and the CENELEC set of standards (EN-50126, EN-50128, etc.). Every phase receives some input documents; defines the set of activities to perform and the set of output documents to generate. The activities are assigned to roles, and may need specialized tools.

3   Repository-Centric Process Metamodel (RCPM)

Models are abstractions which are close to particular domain and are decoupled from implementation concepts. Model-Driven Engineering (MDE) is widely used in embedded systems where assurance requirements are important. This allows implementation independent validation of models, for instance, generally considered as an important assurance step. In the following, we highlight the sub-metamodels architecture of the Repository-Centric Process Metamodel (RCPM), while the next sections concentrate on presenting the safety-related part of the RCPM metamodel.

The solution we propose promotes the use of a model-based repository of modeling artifacts to foster reuse in domains where safety is one of the most important concerns. For instance, the repository provides the following kinds of artifacts [5]: (1) properties and constraints models, (2) security and dependability models, (3) resource models [19] and (4) patterns [6]. Once the repository is available, it must serve an underlying repository-centric engineering process that must be domain specific. To this end, we will also define a repository-centric engineering process metamodel called *RCPM* from which domain specific engineering models can be defined (see Fig. 2).

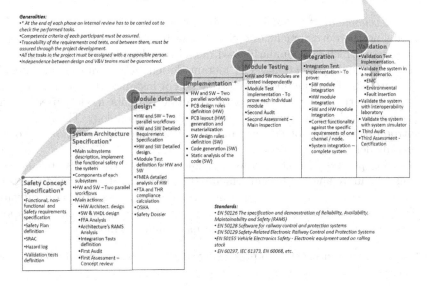

Fig. 1. Railway Engineering Process Lifecycle

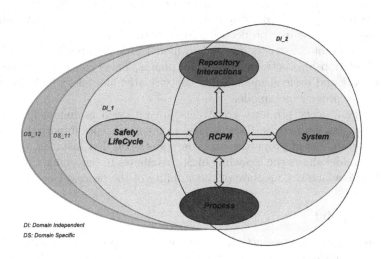

Fig. 2. Design principles of RCPM

The RCPM is a metamodel, which defines a new formalism for system development processes based on a repository of modeling artifacts. The RCPM metamodel contains different sub-metamodels, as shown in Fig. 2, which supply different capabilities. RCPM is oriented to support:

- *The development of embedded systems.* The metamodel focuses on facilitating modeling the development of embedded systems, including the concepts of partitions which are popularly used in embedded system development.
- *Reuse of existing solutions.* The metamodel enables to model the integration process of existing modeling artifacts. For instance, the metamodel supports patterns, as well as properties and constraints models used in the process model and a repository-centric design methodology. The metamodel introduces concepts of pattern and repository into the traditional process metamodel.
- *A safety process lifecycle.* As we can find in standards as IEC 61508 [10], there are more and more requirements transforming a traditional process to a safety process to meet specific safety requirements of systems or software. This metamodel adds the concepts used in the safety lifecycle to support this kind of process model, such as verification and validation.

In this paper, we concentrate on presenting the safety-related part of the RCPM metamodel.

4   Safety Concern of RCPM Metamodel

In this section, we present the safety-oriented process metamodel to extend the existing framework. Such a sub-metamodel captures all the required concepts to support natively safety of system development with S&D (Security and Dependability) and resource properties and constraints requirements. As shown in Fig. 3, we point constructs devoted to model SIL, checkpoints and different flows and relationships between checks and phases. These concepts are the minimum support and basic elements for a safety-related lifecycle, which should be modeled by a process metamodel.

In addition, safety property constructs are provided as model libraries to type the process' properties. Gray is used to label concepts imported from the common metamodel of properties and constraints [19]. For instance, the safety properties model allows the modeling of SIL attributes to determine the process' demand rate, which is a measure of the stability of the process (see Fig. 3).

4.1   Checkpoint

Checkpoint is defined as an activity or phase which represents the safety checks in different levels of the process. They are used to verify whether the safety requirements are correctly implemented. To reflect the requirements presented in Section 2.2, we specify four kinds of checkpoints: validation, verification, safety audit and safety assessment. The structure of the Checkpoint and related classes

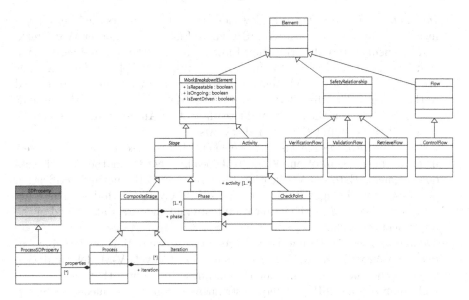

Fig. 3. The structure of RCPM from safety-related viewpoint

is depicted in the left part of Fig. 4. Furthermore, in order to facilitate the extension of the metamodel, the different kinds of Checkpoints are defined as CheckpointKind. With this class, the Checkpoint can be easily extended by different required types. The relationship in the right part of Fig. 4 shows the four kinds of Checkpoints used predefined in the RCPM metamodel and widely employed to verify the safety lifecycle.

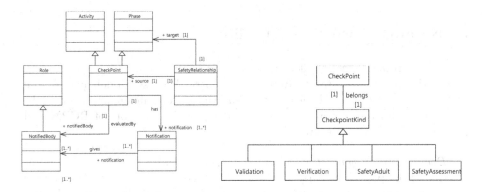

Fig. 4. Structure and Types of Checkpoint

4.2 Safety Relationships

There are four kinds of safety relationships: internal verification, external verification, validation and retrieve flow. We precise these different kinds of verification relationships in the RCPM metamodel.

– *Internal Verification Flow* is a Flow element that represents the internal verification relationship of one WorkBreakdownElement to another WorkBreakdownElement. Internal Verification Flow represents the internal verification that are performed before starting a new development phase. These actions are performed by a group independent to the design team and are restricted to the left branch of the safety lifecycle (V-Model). These verification actions are shared between the safety audit team (Safety Auditor) and the team in charge of carrying out the internal reviews.

– *External Verification Flow* is a Flow element that represents the external verification relationship of one WorkBreakdownElement to another WorkBreakdownElement. External Verification Flow represents the normal verification performed at the right branch of Safety Life Cycle (V-Model). These actions are performed by the verification team and they start at the end of the implementation phase.

– *Validation Flow* is a Flow that represents the validation relationship between two WorkBreakdownElements. In a safety lifecycle V-Model, validation holds at the end of the implementation phase to confirm that the installed and commissioned SIFs (Safety Instrumented Functions) meet the Safety Requirements Specification (SRS). In our metamodel, although it is a safety lifecycle concept, validation is kept general, meaning it can also concern different perspectives, for example dependability validation, security validation etc.

– *Retrieve Flow* is a Flow that represents the retrieve relationship from Checkpoints to Phases or Activities. The retrieve action will be proceeded when the Checkpoints don't pass the examination. The process will turn back to the previous WorkBreakdownElement to reexamine and/or redo the work.

5   Naravas Process Model Editor

Using the proposed metamodel, ongoing experimental work with the Naravas tool (IRIT Naravas Editor of Repository-Centric Process Model, part of the SEMCO tool suite) tests the features of Naravas for formalizing process models. The current release of Naravas supports most of the concepts of RCPM and provides the following features:

– *Documentation generation.* Documentation facilitates the dynamic verification of the process at early stages of design. For instance, a safety task may become invalid during activity execution due to some design error. This ability allows us to generate documentation (HTML, XML) to execute the process in a domain independent manner. Then the user can refine the guidelines for domain-specific application. In fact, there are some parts of the process which are automatically refined (mapped) to domain specific parts, but the programmer of the application does not need to be aware of this process.

– *Conformance validation.* Naravas includes a mechanism to validate the conformity of the process model to the RCPM.

- *Reuse.* Naravas provides mechanisms to create a library for the reusable objects, like WorkproductTypes, RoleTypes or Tasktypes.
- *Repository interaction.* Naravas supports the repository of the modeling artifacts API. For instance, using the Naravas features based on the RCPM presented above, the process model developer may use a subset of the Repository API to store/retrieve process model artifacts and required libraries.

The current release of Naravas uses an Eclipse EMF based ecore editor to model our Repository-Centric Process Metamodel (RCPM), creating ecore files containing the three packages needed for the process model, the SEMCO core package, the process package and the process type package. Minor modifications have been applied on the metamodel to support an EMF based editor and HTML documentation generation with Acceleo.

6   Case Study: Example of Engineering Process for Railway Domain

In this section, we illustrate the use of the modeling framework to represent the railway process introduced in Section 2.3, focusing in the safety concern. Fig. 5 depicts an example using the instantiation mechanisms of UML according to the process metamodel. The colored text indicates the following:

- The *green arrows* represent internal validation flows.
- The *magenta arrows* represent retrieve flows.
- The *red arrows* represent verification flows.
- The *blue arrows* represent external validation flows.
- The *magenta boxes* represent the safety audit checkpoints.

The Naravas editor is then used, as shown in Fig. 6, to model this process. From this illustration, we can easily demonstrate that it is more direct and precisely using the RCPM metamodel to define the different safety lifecycle models.

7   State of the Art

State-of-the-art of process metamodels have been analyzed from this perspective, trying to answer the following questions: (1) Do existing process metamodels support safety lifecycles?; (2) If so, can these metamodels can capture all required safety concepts mentioned above explicitly? Process metamodels can be modeled from different views: activity-oriented, product-oriented and decision-oriented views [15,9]. Most process metamodels adopt the activity-oriented views, such as SPEM, UMA and OPF.

SPEM (Software & Systems Process Engineering Metamodel) [13] is a *de facto*, high-level standard for processes used in object-oriented software development. The scope of SPEM is purposely limited to the minimal elements necessary to define any software and systems development process, without adding specific features for particular development domains or disciplines. The goal is to

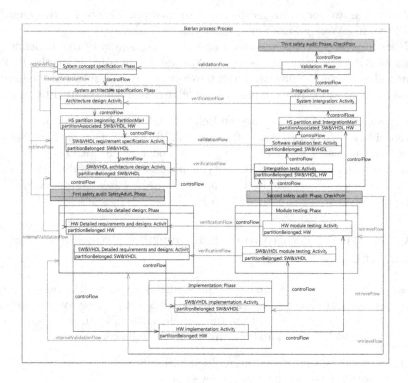

Fig. 5. RCPM Metamodel Instantiated by the Railway Lifecyle

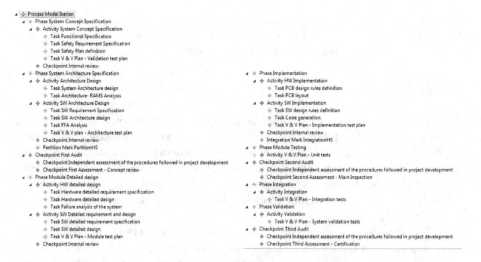

Fig. 6. Naravas in Action- Example of Railway Lifecyle

accommodate a large range of development methods and processes of different styles, cultural backgrounds, levels of formalism, lifecycle models, and communities. Thus, with SPEM, it is not easily to model all the specific concepts required by safety lifecycle.

The Unified Method Architecture (UMA)[1] [2] , which is mostly used in industry to support the most important standards. The metamodel of UMA is based on SPEM, thus it has the same weakness as SPEM. The OPEN Process Framework (OPF) is defined by OPEN [14]. Generally, it is a componentized OO development methodology underpinned by a full metamodel. The drawback of OPF is just like the above twos. We examine in the following Tables (1 and 2) the representative process metamodels to see whether safety related concepts are supported.

Table 1. Comparison of existing process metamodels in checkpoint

Metamodel	Validation	Verification	Safety audit	Safety assessment
SPEM	+	+	+	+
UMA	++	++	++	++
OPF	++	++	+++	+++

Table 2. Comparison of existing process metamodels in associations

Metamodel	Control Flow	Retrieve Flow	Validation Flow	Verification Flow
SPEM	++++	++	++	++
UMA	++++	++	++	++
OPF	++++	++	++	++

In addition to the above mentioned process metamodels, exist other activity-based metamodels like OOSPICE [7], SMSDM [18]. Other types of process metamodel such as decision based etc, do not orient to safety critical system development. As far as we know, the studied process metamodels unfortunately do not support safety related development processes explicitly or facilitate the modeling of safety lifecycles. Many safety critical systems use safety instrument systems (SIS) to manage the safety lifecycle, however, these SIS do not have process metamodels. Works like [1] propose to model different standards and try to give recommendations during the application development. In conclusion, this analysis results in requirements for the process metamodel presented in this paper with following characteristics: (1) Design with the viewpoint: safety-related; (2) Support safety-related development process with its necessary required concepts: SIL, checkpoints and safety control relationships; (3) Facilitate modeling the domain specific safety lifecycle using this metamodel.

---

[1] UMA has been developed in a collaborative effort by the architects of the IBM Rational Unified Process (RUP).

8 Conclusion

The proposed vision is to use modeling techniques to obtain a high level of abstractions in order to avoid the cost of building a process for each application property and/or for each domain. This metamodel is oriented to support different concerns, namely safety lifecycle, pattern, repository, embedded system and non- and extra-functional properties. This paper concentrates on the aspect of safety lifecycle with regard to the structural point of view. RCPM fulfills all the required characteristics mentioned. It permits (1) to design process models from the safety-related viewpoint, (2) to support safety-related development process with SIL (Safety Integrity Level), checkpoints and safety control relationships, (3) to facilitate modeling the domain specific safety lifecycle. The approach presented in this paper has been evaluated on a case study to build industry control systems: An adaptation of the safety lifecycle V-model standard from the railway domain. By this illustration, the feasibility and effectiveness of the RCPM metamodel can be validated. Furthermore, a prototype supporting the approach has been presented.

The presented process models are used by the industrial partners of the European FP7 TERESA project and are constantly tested, analyzed, evaluated and improved. First feedback on experiences from the project partners are promising (e.g. integrating domain standards and knowledge to the safety lifecycle V-Model standard, formalizing domain knowledge on validation and verification).

As future work, the metamodel will be extended to refine the specifications of safety lifecycle in order to support (i) design pattern solutions, (ii) additional non- and extra-functional requirements as system resilience and (iii) other system engineering case studies. With regard to tooling, a work on the development of a user-friendly editor based on Eclipse GMF is being carried out in order to support a set of diagrams (i.e. Process Diagram and Activity Diagram) targeting two levels of a process model: Domain Independent and Domain Specific levels.

Acknowledgments. This work is initiated in the context of SEMCO project. It is supported by the European FP7 TERESA project and by the French FUI 7 SIRSEC project.

References

1. Cheung, L.Y.C., Chung, P.W.H., Dawson, R.J.: Managing process compliance, pp. 48–62. IGI Publishing, Hershey (2003),
   http://portal.acm.org/citation.cfm?id=954321.954326
2. EPF: http://www.eclipse.org/epf
3. Exida: Iec 61508 overview report (version 2.0). Tech. rep. (January 2006)
4. Gray, J., Tolvanen, J.P., Kelly, S., Gokhale, A., Neema, S., Sprinkle, J.: Domain-Specific Modeling. Chapman & Hall/CRC (2007)
5. Hamid, B., Desnos, N., Grepet, C., Jouvray, C.: Model-based security and dependability patterns in RCES: the TERESA approach. In: 1st International Workshop on Security and Dependability for Resource Constrained Embedded Systems, SD4RCES (2010)

6. Hamid, B., Gürgens, S., Jouvray, C., Desnos, N.: Enforcing S&D Pattern Design in RCES with Modeling and Formal Approaches. In: Whittle, J., Clark, T., Kühne, T. (eds.) MODELS 2011. LNCS, vol. 6981, pp. 319–333. Springer, Heidelberg (2011)
7. Henderson-Sellers, B., Gonzalez-Perez, C.: A comparison of four process metamodels and the creation of a new generic standard. Information & Software Technology 47(1), 49–65 (2005)
8. Henzinger, T.: Two challenges in embedded systems design: Predictability and robustness. Philosophical Transactions of the Royal Society A 366, 3727–3736 (2008)
9. Hug, C., Front, A., Rieu, D., Henderson-Sellers, B.: A method to build information systems engineering process metamodels. J. Syst. Softw. 82, 1730–1742 (2009)
10. IEC 61508, I.S.: Functional safety of electrical/ electronic/programmable electronic safetyrelated systems (2000)
11. IEC 61511, I.S.: Functional safety - safety instrumented systems for the process industry sector (2003)
12. Kopetz, H.: The complexity challenge in embedded system design. In: ISORC, pp. 3–12 (2008)
13. OMG: Software & Systems Process Engineering Meta-Model Specification (2008)
14. (OPF), O.P.F. http://www.opfro.org/
15. Rolland, C.: A Comprehensive View of Process Engineering. In: Pernici, B., Thanos, C. (eds.) CAiSE 1998. LNCS, vol. 1413, pp. 1–24. Springer, Heidelberg (1998)
16. S84.01, A.S.: Application of safety instrumented systems for the process industry (1996)
17. Smith, D.J., Simpson, K.G.L.: Functional Safety: A straightforward guide to applying IEC 61508 and related standards, 2nd edn. Elsevier, Butterworth Heinemann (2004)
18. Standards Australia: Standard Metamodel for Software Development Methodologies (2004)
19. Ziani, A., Hamid, B., Trujillo, S.: Towards a unified meta-model for resources-constrained embedded systems. In: 37th EUROMICRO Conference on Software Engineering and Advanced Applications, pp. 485–492. IEEE (2011)

Language Enrichment for Resilient MDE

Yasir Imtiaz Khan and Matteo Risoldi

University of Luxembourg, Laboratory of Advanced Software Systems
6, rue Richard Coudenhove-Khalergi – L-1359 Luxembourg
{yasir.khan,matteo.risoldi}@uni.lu

Abstract. In Model-Driven Engineering, as in many engineering approaches, it is desireable to be able to assess the quality of a system or model as it evolves. A resilient engineering practice systematically assesses whether evolutions improve on the capabilities of a system. We argue that to achieve a systematic resilient model-driven engineering practice, resilience concepts should be first-class citizens in models. This article discusses how DREF, a formal framework defining resilience concepts, can be integrated with other modeling languages in order to pursue a resilient development process.

Keywords: resilience, language, metamodel, composition, enrichment.

1 Introduction

Many current development methodologies for software systems support iterative refinements and/or incremental developments. This is well suited to respond to needs such as changing requirements, optimization of development resources and early detection of problems. This has typically been true for techniques known as "agile", but trends are developing in order to bring these qualities to approaches that have traditionally a reputation of being less flexible, like Model-Driven Engineering (MDE) [14,2]. Iterations and incremental development have thus acquired the status of current practices in MDE. In most cases it is desirable for the developers to be able to assess the quality of the system as it evolves. In particular, it is interesting to know whether each new version of the system satisfies the requirements better than the previous one. We will call a system evolution process that improves quality with each new version a *resilient evolution process*. A resilient evolution process is especially desirable for dependable systems, where keeping or improving the satisfaction of properties is highly critical.

Achieving a resilient evolution process requires having quality metrics of the system, and assessing their variation during evolution. While this could in principle be done informally, we argue that a systematic practice of resilience calls for a well-defined set of concepts such as required and achieved satisfiability, failures or tolerance levels. Moreover, we argue that development and quality assurance would benefit from resilience concerns being "natively" included in languages and tools.

P. Avgeriou (Ed.): SERENE 2012, LNCS 7527, pp. 76–90, 2012.

DREF [7] is a formal framework that precisely defines the fundamental concepts underlying dependability and resilience of ICT systems. It is oriented to describe how the satisfaction of properties of a system changes over a system evolution axis. The evolution axis can represent different types of evolutions, e.g., different versions of a system, different products in a product line, or even different states in the runtime evolution of a system. DREF proposes measures of satisfiability at various granularity levels, including concepts like different observers, property and/or observer weights, and tolerance thresholds. It defines the concept of *resilient evolution process* as an evolution process of a system that improves its capabilities, increasing overall satisfiability and reducing failures. DREF is rather generic and leaves the definition of details like the exact nature of the system under study, of its properties or of the methods used to assess satisfiability to the user. Therefore it can be applied to a wide range of systems and evolution processes.

The formal definition of DREF has been given [7]. A prototype metamodel for a DREF Domain-Specific Language (DSL) has been defined [7,16] in order to tailor DREF to the Model-driven engineering methodology. In this article, we discuss how the DREF metamodel can be used with other existing modeling languages in order to enrich them with resilience concerns. We will discuss a few approaches to associate a model with a DREF specification, and discuss their advantages and disadvantages. We will also show a simple case study where a model expressed in Algebraic Petri Nets (APNs) undergoes a number of evolutions, with DREF being used to assess the resilience of the evolution process. The goal of this article is not to introduce new language composition techniques. It is rather to give practical advice on the advantages and disadvantages of some existing composition techniques in systematic DSL enrichment, required for pursuing a resilient model-driven development practice.

2   Background and Previous Work

Resilience is a concept that is strictly related to evolution. According to [13], resilience is defined as *"[t]he persistence of service delivery [...] when facing changes"*. These *changes* can be environmental or intrinsic. Some of these changes are part of the planned behavior, while others are not and may be regarded as faults.

Generally speaking, the term *resilient* is frequently intended as the system being good at remaining – or returning – in an acceptable range of operation despite disruptive changes during its evolution at runtime. This view of resilience is somewhat akin to fault tolerance.

However, systems and models are also subject to evolution during their development phase, where an initial version goes through a series of evolutions generally aimed at improving its capabilities – among other things, the satisfaction of its requirements and properties. But it is often not trivial to understand whether or not an evolution has actually brought an improvement in requirement satisfaction. Behaviors may be so complex that a modification may potentially have a positive impact on some properties and a negative impact on others, and the net result may be difficult to quantify objectively. In this respect, we argue that it is desirable to speak about the *resilience of the evolution process itself* that takes place during the development phase. This "view" of resilience is tantamount to measuring whether the evolution process aims in the direction of a general improvement, defined in terms of how well the system is satisfying required properties.

One might imagine going about assessing the resilience of an evolution process by ad-hoc techniques where some metrics are identified and repeatedly used to calculate property satisfaction during evolution. We argue however that for the model-driven engineering community, requirement satisfaction and resilience are attributes that should be first-class citizens in a model, and thus they should appear as part of a specification: i) in an explicit way and ii) with a precise definition. The formal definition of DREF [7] tackles point ii); in the context of model-driven engineering, we propose to tackle point i) by composing modeling languages with DREF, creating models that explicitly include resilience concepts.

2.1 The DREF Metamodel

DREF (Dependability and Resilience Engineering Framework) [7] is a formal framework that precisely defines the fundamental concepts underlying dependability and resilience of ICT systems. It allows to quantify variations in the level of property satisfaction over an evolution axis. DREF is based on the following core concepts.

– An **entity** is anything of interest that is considered. An entity could be, for example, a program, a database, a person, a hardware device, or a development process.
– A **property** is a basic concept used to characterize an entity. It can be, for example, an informal requirement or a logic formula.
– An **evolution axis** is a set of values that are used to index a set of entities and/or a set of properties. Each index corresponds to a "version", or a stage in the evolution of entities and properties.
– An entity will generally have to satisfy some property. This fact is expressed with a **satisfiability function**, defined as follows. Let Ent be a set of entities and $Prop$ a set of properties. The satisfiability of properties by entities is a function $sat : Prop \times Ent \to \mathbb{R} \cup \{\bot\}$. The sat function can be defined arbitrarily depending on the application. For example, if a property can only be "satisfied or unsatisfied" (like, e.g., in model checking), the codomain of sat might be $\{0, 1\}$; whereas if the satisfiability is a more nuanced concept (like, e.g., in a performance measurement), it could assume any value in $\mathbb{R}$, or a subset thereof. Semantically, sat quantifies how much an entity satisfies (or not) a property. The satisfiability function sat is a partial function, and can be defined only for a subset of $Prop \times Ent$, meaning that for some entity/property pairs a satisfaction value could be not expected (in other

words, some properties might be applicable only to some entities and not others). Moreover, the ⊥ value accounts for the cases where the satisfiability value is not computable.

Using the above concepts in the engineering process, it is possible to get an assessment not only of the extent to which an entity satisfies its properties, but also of how this satisfiability changes during subsequent evolutions of the entity.

The DREF framework also defines a number of other concepts which are useful for dependability and resilience. We will not give a complete definition for them all as this is not the goal of this paper, they are fully defined in [7]. They include *nominal satisfiability* (a satisfiability level that has to be reached for an entity to be considered dependable), *tolerance thresholds* (a satisfiability level below nominal satisfiability but still within operational limits) and *failures* (the difference between the measured satisfiability of an entity and its nominal satisfiability).

In order to use the DREF framework in an MDE context, a metamodel has been given for DREF concepts. This metamodel defines the abstract syntax of a DREF DSL, and can be used to create a DREF specification referring to a model expressed in some other language. This raises the question of how a DREF specification integrates with a model in a different language. In particular, the entities and properties of the DREF framework should be somehow expressed in the other language, so that the concepts of entity and property should bridge the two languages.

A fragment of the class diagram for the DREF metamodel is shown in Figure 1. This fragment focuses on the DrefEntity and DrefProperty metaclasses that are – if we may borrow the aspect-oriented terminology – the "join points" between DREF and other languages. A complete description of the metamodel and its associated constraints is given in [16].

Remark that DrefEntity contains an abstract ModelEntity metaclass. The latter represents the actual entity in the model expressed in the other language. We will see that there are three ways in which we can link this metaclass to the other language. A similar structure is present for the DrefProperty metaclass, that contains the abstract ModelProperty metaclass.

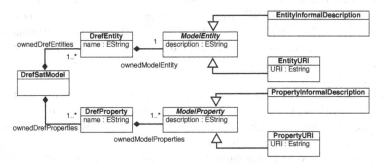

Fig. 1. A fragment of the DREF metamodel

3 Related Work

Enriching languages with new concerns has been done in a number of ways. In Aspect-Oriented Programming [12] (AOP), languages are extended with cross-cutting concerns given in a separate modular specification. AOP can be seen as a generic composition mechanism where a concern can be added to a model. It needs compilers and platforms that support aspect execution, and is appropriate for general purpose languages where the necessary constructs to weave aspects in a model can be added to the language once and used for different concerns. A popular example of AOP language is AspectJ [1].

Another approach to extending languages is by embedding a (generally small) sublanguage in a host language. The sublanguage will typically treat a specific concern, and may therefore be considered a Domain-Specific Language (DSL). Approaches exist that embed DSLs in host languages using, among others, keyword extension [3], role bindings [4] and term representation composition [8]. Embedded DSLs may be used in conjunction with AOP for the generation of code [4].

In the field of DSLs, language composition is mostly sought for modularity and reuse. DSLs bring usability by defining small, dedicated sets of concepts, but tend to have a moderate to high cost of development and deployment. This effort can be minimized by reusing predefined DSLs for the definition of more complex ones. This is particularly useful when families of languages need to be developed. Techniques to specify the composition include ad-hoc techniques based on metamodel [15,5] and domain [6,10] composition, or more systematic techniques for DSL reuse in families of languages [19,18].

This paper is based on DSL-oriented approaches, in particular on metamodel-based techniques, as they best suit our current applications and goals. It must be noted that DSL embedding or AOP composition could be pursued, provided that the DREF DSL is specified with an appropriate syntax and semantics.

4 Composing DREF with other Languages

We will discuss three ways in which DREF and another language can be used together. The first is using DREF stand-alone on the side of the modeling language. The second is composing DREF with a modeling language through metamodel parameterization. The third (which can actually be done in two different ways) is composing with metamodel interfacing. Note that the second and third techniques imply that a metamodel is available for both languages, and that they are homogeneous.

Also remark that DREF does not have an executable semantics; it is a conceptual framework designed to describe sets of organized data, with no concept of execution. Furthermore, the semantics of its concepts is intentionally very abstract, to allow the user to define it appropriately in the context of language composition. Thus we will limit ourselves to consider the composition of DREF with other languages on a syntactical plan (i.e., by integrating metamodels) as the semantic aspects are difficult to foresee in a general way.

4.1   Approach 1: Using DREF Stand-Alone

This strategy keeps the DREF specification and the model separate. The model is created using its own modeling language, and the properties are written in an appropriate property specification language. Then, the DREF specification is created on the side. The link between DREF and the model is done using the metaclasses in the DREF metamodel that inherit the ModelEntity and Model-Property metaclasses (Figure 1). For the entity, there are two possibilities. Either the entity has been saved in a file, and thus an instance of EntityURI is created in the DREF specification pointing to said file (via the URI attribute); or if no such file exists (for example, if the entity is an hardware device), an instance of EntityInformalDescription is created that simply describes textually (via the inherited description attribute) what the entity is. Likewise for properties, either a property file is pointed to by a PropertyURI instance, or an informal description is given by a PropertyInformalDescription instance. Subsequent evolutions of the entity and properties will be linked to further instances of said metaclasses.

This strategy requires no language engineering effort; the DREF metamodel can be used as-is, and the modeling language must not undergo any modifications. Another advantage is that editors for the modeling language will require no re-engineering to read the models, as these continue to be expressed in their supported modeling language. However, there is no proper integration here. The resilience specification is separate from the model, and its consistency with the model has to be ensured manually. Also, if the goal is to enrich a language to natively support resilient engineering, this approach does not achieve it.

4.2   Approach 2: Metamodel Parameterization

Real integration between DREF and another modeling language can instead be achieved through metamodel composition. The general idea is that, instead of creating instances of ModelEntity and ModelProperty in the DREF specification, it should be possible to create instances of the appropriate metaclasses coming from the modeling language.

One way to achieve this composition is through *metamodel parameterization*. This strategy takes two metamodels as inputs for a metamodel transformation, producing a third metamodel which is the composition of the two. This typically involves building and executing the transformation with a suitable language transformation framework such as ATL.

An example of this type of composition has been defined formally in [15]. In it, a part of a metamodel is marked as a *formal parameter*, and it is replaced by an *effective parameter* which redefines the elements in the formal parameter. More precisely, simplifying a bit the definitions in [15]: let MM be the universe of metamodels; $mm \in MM$ a metamodel; we can define a *formal parameter* $fp \in MM$ in mm ($fp \subseteq mm$) acting as a template for possible replacements. In our case, fp is made of ModelEntity and ModelProperty.

Let us now consider a metamodel $ep \in MM$, called *effective parameter* that redefines at least the elements in fp. The parameterization is then defined as:

$$mm' = mm[fp \xleftarrow{\varphi} ep]$$

where $\varphi : fp \to ep$ is a total mapping function between fp and ep, and mm' is the metamodel resulting from the parameterization. In our case, ep is made of the metaclasses from the modeling language that model entities and properties, and mm' will be the composed metamodel of DREF plus the modeling language.

This approach offers a fine granularity of control over the detailed definition of the mapping function φ, and has the advantage of treating several possible cases of composition (e.g. solving possible ambiguities with respect to attribute composition, containment relationships, constraint violation etc.). However, it requires a high level of language engineering effort in order to define the composition. Also, the approach would likely break compatibility of the resulting metamodel with the editors for the modeling language. It is worth following this type of approach when some degree of generality is desired with respect of possible types of composition. In the case of DREF, however, the simplicity of composition rather suggests adopting the *metamodel interfacing* composition strategy, described in the following paragraphs.

4.3   Approach 3: Metamodel Interfacing

In the case of DREF, there is a very simple type of composition, where one metaclass must replace an abstract metaclass that only participates in a containment relationship as the containee. Under this assumption, we don't need to treat all possible composition problems and we can choose a strategy that is restricted to this very particular type of composition. Metamodel interfacing [5] proposes to interface two metamodels by creating a third metamodel called *interfacing metamodel* that contains references to elements in both metamodels, and establishes the desired relationships.

There are two ways we can interface the DREF metamodel with another metamodel: through reference, or through inheritance.

In Metamodel Interfacing through Reference, metaclasses in the interfacing metamodel inherit from one metamodel and reference the other. A generic example is represented in Figure 2 and defined as follows. Let:

- mm_{dref} be the DREF metamodel we showed in Figure 1;
- $mm_{ent} \in MM$ the metamodel of the modeling language which contains the definition of the entities;
- $mm_{prop} \in MM$ the metamodel of the property language which contains the definition of the properties.

Let Entity $\subseteq mm_{ent}$ be the metaclass modeling entities, and Property $\subseteq mm_{prop}$ the metaclass modeling properties. The interfacing metamodel $mm_{int} \in MM$ contains:

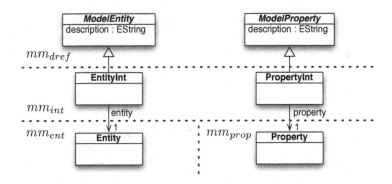

Fig. 2. Example of interfacing metamodel through reference

- a metaclass EntityInt that inherits from ModelEntity in mm_{dref} and has a reference to Entity in mm_{ent};
- a metaclass PropertyInt that inherits from ModelProperty in mm_{dref} and has a reference to Property in mm_{prop};

When modeling, it will be possible to create instances of EntityInt (resp. PropertyInt) as part of the DREF model and to reference existing instances of Entity (resp. Property).

With this technique, the focus of the model stays on DREF. It is recommended to use it when the models for entities and properties already exist. It has the advantage of not modifying the metamodel for entities and properties, thus not breaking compatibility with existing tools and not requiring a big language engineering effort (only mm_{int} has to be created). Moreover, the references between the two models are actually stored in the DREF model.

In Metamodel Interfacing through Inheritance, instead, the metaclasses in the interfacing metamodel inherit from both metamodels, using multiple inheritance. A generic example is represented in Figure 3 and defined as follows.

Given the same definitions as in the previous paragraph for mm_{dref}, mm_{ent}, mm_{prop}, *Entity* and *Property*; the interfacing metamodel $mm_{int} \in MM$ contains:

- a metaclass EntityInt that inherits both from ModelEntity in mm_{dref} and from Entity in mm_{ent};
- a metaclass PropertyInt that inherits both from ModelProperty in mm_{dref} and from Property in mm_{prop};

When modeling, it will be possible to create instances of EntityInt (resp. PropertyInt) that are at the same time part of the DREF model and of the entity (resp. property) model, enabling the specification of resilience and entities (resp. properties) directly in the same model.

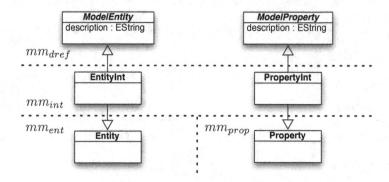

Fig. 3. Example of interfacing metamodel through inheritance

With this technique the same integrated model will contain the entity/property model and the DREF specification. Moreover, a single model will be able to contain all evolutions of entities and properties, indexed by the evolution axis of the DREF specification. This approach achieves full integration, and is better used when designing a language from scratch or if the goal is to enrich a DSL with native support for resilient engineering concepts. However, the inconvenient is that the resulting models will likely not be compatible with tools made to interpret stand-alone entity or property models. Also, care has to be taken if there are syntactic or semantic conflicts between the metaclasses (e.g. if the ModelEntity and the Entity metaclasses have conflicting attributes).

5   Composition Example: DREF + APN

We will now show an example of how we used the metamodel interfacing technique to compose DREF with algebraic Petri nets (APNs), using the APN metamodel from the AlPiNA model checker [9].

Composition through Reference: Figure 4(a) shows the interfacing metamodel composing DREF with APNs through reference, creating a new metamodel that we will call DREFAPN$_r$ (r for *reference*). This metamodel references elements in three other metamodels:

- The DREF metamodel (drefv2 in Figure 4)
- The APN metamodel (apnmm in Figure 4)
- The AlPiNA property language metamodel [9] (propertymm in Figure 4)

The APNModelEntity metaclass inherits from ModelEntity in the DREF metamodel, and references the APN metaclass in the APN metamodel (representing an algebraic Petri net).

The APNProperty metaclass inherits from ModelProperty in DREF and references the PropertiesDeclaration metaclass in the AlPiNA property language metamodel (representing a property declaration).

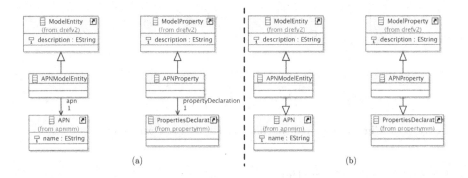

Fig. 4. Interfacing metamodel between DREF and APNs: (a) through reference, and (b) through inheritance

Composition through Inheritance: Figure 4(b) shows the interfacing metamodel that interfaces DREF with APNs through inheritance, creating a new composed metamodel that we will call DREFAPN$_i$ (i for *inheritance*). This metamodel references elements from the same three metamodels as the interfacing through reference approach.

The APNModelEntity metaclass inherits from ModelEntity in the DREF metamodel *and* from the APN metaclass in the APN metamodel (representing an APN). Instances of APNModelEntity will be at the same time a part of the DREF model and the root of an APN specification.

The APNProperty metaclass inherits from ModelProperty in DREF and from the PropertiesDeclaration metaclass in the AlPiNA property language metamodel (representing a property declaration). Instances of APNProperty will be at the same time a part of the DREF model and the root of a property declaration.

6   Case Study: Resilient Evolution of a Car Crash System

We experimented using the discussed integration approaches for the resilient evolution of a car crash emergency management system modeled using APNs [11]. In this system, reports on a car crash are received and validated, and a *super-observer* (i.e. an emergency response team) is assigned to manage each crash.

Three versions of the car crash system have been modeled, with different levels of satisfaction of provided properties. In this example, rather than developing a language from scratch, we took an existing language (with existing tool support), which are APNs, and enriched it with DREF. Therefore, we tried the stand-alone (Section 4.1) and metamodel interfacing (Section 4.3) approaches. We used the Eclipse Modeling Framework (EMF) [17] for metamodel creation and editor generation. This example does not use all of DREF concepts and features, and is intentionally very simple so as to clearly focus on the language composition rather than on a complex resilience specification.

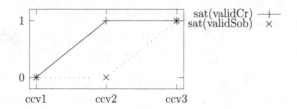

Fig. 5. Measured satisfiability for the car crash system

6.1   Entities and Properties

The set of entities *Ent* is comprised of the three versions of the car crash system (three APNs) named as follows:

$$Ent = \{\mathsf{ccv1}, \mathsf{ccv2}, \mathsf{ccv3}\}$$

The set of properties *Prop* $\subset$ *PROPERTY* is comprised of two properties:

$$Prop = \{\mathsf{validCr}, \mathsf{validSob}\}$$

that are informally specified as follows (see [11] for terminology):

- *validCr*: A crisis can only be assigned to a superobserver if its report has been validated
- *validSob*: A crisis can only be assigned to a superobserver that is capable to handle it

and that have a formal specification in the AlPiNA property language.

The system evolves over an evolution axis where guards are added with each version to improve property satisfaction. The first version, *ccv1*, has no guards; *ccv2* has a guard ensuring the satisfaction of *validCr*; *ccv3* has guards for both properties. There are thus three index points on the evolution axis, corresponding respectively to *ccv1*, *ccv2* and *ccv3*.

The properties being boolean expressions, their satisfiability is a boolean function *sat* : *Ent* $\times$ *Prop* $\rightarrow$ $\{0, 1\}$ that was evaluated using the AlPiNA model checker. Figure 5 shows the satisfiability values calculated by AlPiNA for the three versions.

6.2   DREF Model without Composition (Stand-Alone)

Using EMF to create a stand-alone DREF specification for the car crash system is straightforward. As we said, no intervention on the language metamodels is needed. The APN models can be created using the AlPiNA built-in editor. For the DREF specification, EMF can generate an editor from the DREF metamodel. Using this editor, we could create a DREF specification that references the entities and properties of the APN models, indexes them on an evolution axis,

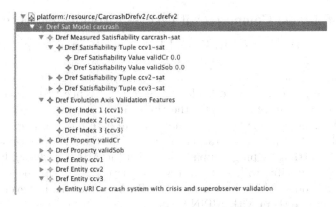

Fig. 6. Car Crash DREF satisfiability model in Eclipse, using only the DREF meta-model (no composition)

and associates them to their satisfiability values. Figure 6 shows a screenshot of the DREF editor. It is possible to see the entities definition (at the bottom), their indexing (in the middle) and some of the satisfiability values (at the top). Clicking on the Entity URI instances reveals the URI of the corresponding file.

The result of this approach is a set of APN files containing the models and the properties, and a DREF file containing the resilience specification. The association between the two is not immediately apparent, relying on the Entity URI attributes. The compatibility of the APN models with AlPiNA is full (they are original AlPiNA models).

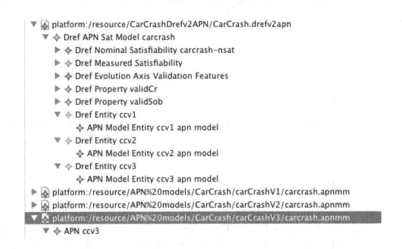

Fig. 7. Car Crash DREF satisfiability model in Eclipse, using the DREFAPN$_r$ metamodel

6.3   DREF Model Composed with APNs through Reference

Figure 7 shows the same DREF model, but made using the DREFAPN$_r$ metamodel.

It is almost identical to the previous one, except for the fact that, instead of simply having a reference to a file, we have a reference to the actual APN model. At the bottom of the figure, the three APNs (previously created using the AlPiNA editor) are loaded in the model as an external resource.

The result of this approach is rather interesting, as the APNs continue to exist as separate files (thus keeping compatibility with the AlPiNA editor), but at the same time it is possible to load them together with the DREF specification in an integrated model. This editor is able to edit APN models, however it is still necessary to create them with AlPiNA first.

6.4   DREF Model Composed with APNs through Inheritance

Figure 8 shows a fragment of the editor obtained from the DREFAPN$_i$ meta-model. In this case, this editor is able to create both the DREF specification and the APN (APN editing is shown in the popup menu). We thus have a fully integrated language and editor; the result of this approach is a single model containing the APNs and the DREF specification. However, the resulting models are not compatible with AlPiNA out of the box. In principle this compatibility could be achieved through model transformations, however the added effort of writing the transformations would be considerable.

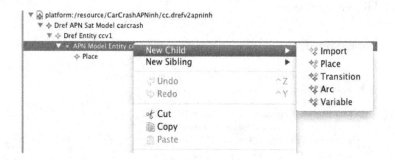

Fig. 8. Car Crash DREF satisfiability model in Eclipse, using the DREFAPN$_i$ metamodel

7   Conclusion

We have discussed a few techniques to enrich languages with resilience concepts by integrating them with DREF. Three approaches have been discussed and two of them have been experimented. We can draw the following conclusions and recommendations concerning the amount of effort, compatibility with pre-existing tools, and the circumstances when the approach is appropriated.

The stand-alone approach (Section 4.1) does not require any metamodel editing effort, and can simply reference existing models using files or informal descriptions. It does not introduce compatibility issues, but requires effort in keeping specifications consistent. It is useful for occasional, non-systematic assessments of resilience.

The metamodel interfacing through reference approach (first part of Section 4.3) brings limited integration of DREF with other languages, by allowing a DREF model to reference actual models expressed in other languages, while maintaining separate models. This has the advantage of building a comprehensive model, keeping track of the association between the DREF specification and the entities and properties. At the same time it leaves untouched the entity/property metamodels, thus preserving compatibility with existing tools. It requires some effort in editing an interface metamodel. It is the best compromise when wanting to introduce resilience in a modeling chain without breaking the compatibility with existing toolkits.

The metamodel interfacing through inheritance approach (second part of Section 4.3) is an actual full integration of DREF with another language, where the constructs of the different metamodels coexist in the same space. This allows actual enrichment of a DSL with resilience constructs, at the cost of creating a metamodel which may be incompatible with previously existing tools. It is better suited when wanting to design a language with resilience support from scratch, or when a major language revision is foreseen anyway.

Finally, we think that the metamodel parameterization approach (Section 4.2) requires too much effort to be useful in this type of language composition, and is better suited to cases in which the other approaches fall short (i.e., when the nature of the composition presents a risk of conflicts and calls for a finer control over the composition semantics).

The metamodels discussed in this document are available for download at
http://wiki.lassy.uni.lu/@api/deki/files/499/=drefv2metamodels.zip

Acknowledgement. This work has been supported by the National Research Fund, Luxembourg, project MOVERE C09/IS/02.

References

1. AspectJ team. The AspectJ project, http://www.eclipse.org/aspectj/ (visited on May 9, 2012)
2. Atkinson, C., Kuhne, T.: Model-driven development: a metamodeling foundation. IEEE Software 20(5), 36–41 (2003)
3. Cuadrado, J., Molina, J.: A model-based approach to families of embedded domain-specific languages. IEEE Transactions on Software Engineering 35(6), 825–840 (2009)
4. Dinkelaker, T., Wende, C., Lochmann, H.: Implementing and Composing MDSD-Typical DSLs. Technical Report TUD-CS-2009-0156, Technische Universität Darmstadt (October 2009)

5. Emerson, M., Sztipanovits, J.: Techniques for Metamodel Composition. In: OOP-SLA 6th Workshop on Domain Specific Modeling, pp. 123–139 (2006)
6. Estublier, J., Vega, G., Ionita, A.: Composing Domain-Specific Languages for Wide-Scope Software Engineering Applications. In: Briand, L.C., Williams, C. (eds.) MoDELS 2005. LNCS, vol. 3713, pp. 69–83. Springer, Heidelberg (2005)
7. Guelfi, N.: A formal framework for dependability and resilience from a software engineering perspective. Central European Journal of Computer Science 1, 294–328 (2011), doi:10.2478/s13537-011-0025-x
8. Hofer, C., Ostermann, K.: Modular domain-specific language components in scala. In: Proceedings of the Ninth International Conference on Generative Programming and Component Engineering, GPCE 2010, pp. 83–92. ACM, New York (2010)
9. Hostettler, S., Marechal, A., Linard, A., Risoldi, M., Buchs, D.: High-Level Petri Net Model Checking with AlPiNA. Fundamenta Informaticae 113(3-4), 229–264 (2011)
10. Ionita, A.D., Estublier, J., Leveque, T., Nguyen, T.: Bi-dimensional composition with domain specific languages. e-Informatica Software Engineering Journal 3(1) (2009)
11. Khan, Y.: A formal approach for engineering resilient car crash management system. Technical Report TR-LASSY-12-05, University of Luxembourg (2012)
12. Kiczales, G., Lamping, J., Mendhekar, A., Maeda, C., Lopes, C., Loingtier, J.-M., Irwin, J.: Aspect-Oriented Programming. In: Aksit, M., Auletta, V. (eds.) ECOOP 1997. LNCS, vol. 1241, pp. 220–242. Springer, Heidelberg (1997)
13. Laprie, J.-C.: From dependability to resilience. In: Proceedings of the 38th Annual IEEE/IFIP International Conference on Dependable Systems and Networks (DSN), page Fast Abstracts, Anchorage, USA (2008)
14. Ludewig, J.: Models in software engineering – an introduction. Software and Systems Modeling 2, 5–14 (2003), doi:10.1007/s10270-003-0020-3
15. Pedro, L.: A Systematic Language Engineering Approach for Prototyping Domain Specific Languages. PhD thesis, Université de Genève, Thesis # 4068 (2009)
16. Risoldi, M.: A metamodel for a DREF DSL. Technical Report TR-LASSY-12-03, University of Luxembourg (2012),
    http://wiki.lassy.uni.lu/Special:LassyBibDownload?id=3169
17. The Eclipse Foundation. The Eclipse Modeling Framework Project (2012),
    http://www.eclipse.org/modeling/emf/ (visited on May 16, 2012)
18. Voelter, M.: A family of languages for architecture description. In: 8th OOPSLA Workshop on Domain-Specific Modeling, DSM 2008 (2008)
19. White, J., Hill, J.H., Gray, J., Tambe, S., Gokhale, A.S., Schmidt, D.C.: Improving domain-specific language reuse with software product line techniques. IEEE Softw. 26(4), 47–53 (2009)

Assume-Guarantee Testing of Evolving Software Product Line Architectures

Maurice H. ter Beek[1], Henry Muccini[2], and Patrizio Pelliccione[2]

[1] ISTI–CNR, Pisa, Italy
maurice.terbeek@isti.cnr.it
[2] Dipartimento di Ingegneria e Scienze dell'Informazione e Matematica
Università dell'Aquila, Italy
{henry.muccini,patrizio.pelliccione}@univaq.it

Abstract. Despite some work on testing software product lines, maintaining the quality of products when a software product line evolves is still an open problem. In this paper, we propose a novel assume-guarantee testing approach as a solution to the following research question: *how can we verify the correct functioning of products of an software product line when core components evolve?* The underlying idea is to retest only some of the products that conform to the software product line architecture and to infer, using assume-guarantee reasoning, the correctness of the other products. Assume-guarantee reasoning moreover permits the retesting of only those components that are affected by the changes.

Keywords: Assume-guarantee testing, Evolving software product lines, Software testing, Compositional verification.

1 Introduction

Software product line engineering makes use of different components to describe and realize families of systems, such as requirements, architectural and design models, and implementation components [1, 2]. The architecture of a software product line is typically referred to as a software product line architecture and it is meant to define the common reference architecture for the products that are related to a specific family. Variability is achieved by identifying variation points as places in the product line architecture where specific decisions are reduced to a choice among several *features*, but the feature to be chosen for a particular product variant is left open (due to optional, mandatory or alternative features).

For enterprises from safety-critical domains, such as avionics, the application of software product line engineering technology is often problematic because of the high costs of certification efforts. In such domains, every product has to pass a costly certification stage, even if it belongs to an established family of products for which certification efforts have already been performed. It is therefore important to reduce the effort needed to retest modified products. By predicting the impact of evolution of an software product line, we might be able to avoid re-certification of certified products that have evolved. This cannot

P. Avgeriou (Ed.): SERENE 2012, LNCS 7527, pp. 91–105, 2012.

solve the issue of repeated certification in a product line altogether, since testing one product of a family in general does not provide any guarantee for another product of the family. A possible solution, however, is to investigate how testing and variability can be combined to selectively test only components actually affected by the evolution.

In [3], we proposed a first step towards a solution to this problem by reusing, adapting and combining state-of-the-art techniques. We found assume-guarantee reasoning well suited for evolving systems. The environment of a component is seen as a set of properties, called *assumptions*, that should be satisfied for it to function. If these assumptions are satisfied by the environment, then components in this environment will typically satisfy other properties, called *guarantees*. By appropriately combining the assume and guarantee properties, it is possible to prove the correctness of an entire system before actually constructing it.

The idea we presented was thus to annotate components of a product line architecture with pairs of assume-guarantee properties, considering a component's environment as the composition of the remaining components. In this way, we enabled compositional verification based on assume-guarantee reasoning to deal with evolution in product line architectures. The underlying idea is to decompose a system specification into (asssume-guarantee) properties that describe the behavior of a system's subset, to model check these properties locally, and to deduce from the local checks that the complete system satisfies the overall specification. The main advantage is that one never has to compose all subsystems, thus avoiding the state explosion problem. On the downside, assume-guarantee verification by means of model checking cannot scale to the size of industrial systems (as remarked in [4]).

For this reason, we envision the use of software testing for verifying evolving product line architectures. While many approaches to validate software product lines and their products in a cost effective way by exploiting similarities among products and using proper variability management have been proposed [5–15], we know of only a few approaches that investigate how to retest the resilience of products when a software product line evolves [16, 17].

After analyzing state-of-the-art techniques for verifying and validating software product lines, in this paper we present a preliminary approach to retest the resilience of products of a software product line by properly extending and adapting assume-guarantee reasoning to evolving software product lines. The main goal is to permit selective (re)testing of assume-guarantee properties on only those components and products of the software product line that are actually affected by the evolution.

Section 2 recalls the problem that drives our research effort. Section 3 presents background information on assume-guarantee reasoning and assume-guarantee testing. Section 4 presents our proposed solution for assume-guarantee testing of evolving software product lines. Section 5 briefly reports on related work on regression testing of software product lines, while Section 6 concludes the paper outlining some future work on our wish list.

2   Problem Setup

We recall the research problem that we set up in [3]: how to guarantee the correct evolution of a software product line upon changes in components of its underlying product line architecture. We illustrate the problem in Fig. 1, based on the following example that is originally due to Paul Clements et al. at the Software Engineering Institute:

> *"I run the same software in different kinds of helicopters. When the software in a helicopter powers up, it checks a hardware register to see what kind of helicopter it is and starts behaving appropriately for that kind of helicopter. When I make a change to the software, I would like to flight test it only on one helicopter, and prove or (more likely, assert with high confidence) that it will run correctly on the other helicopters. I know I can't achieve this for all changes, but I would like to do it where possible."*

In a software product line context, this example can be re-phrased as: assuming various products (helicopters) have been derived from a software product line, which have moreover been formally certified, what can be concluded for new products obtained from the software product line by modifying one or more core components?

We assume that all products of the product line must be guaranteed to conform to a specific standard. Furthermore, we assume that there is a policy according to which any change to a core component requires all products containing that core component to be rebuilt. The question is whether it is necessary to re-validate all the products of the software product line or whether a subset can suffice. For instance, in the aforementioned example, when we change the software of the helicopter line, such as installing a new kind of radio across the fleet, we would like to flight test it only on one helicopter and assert with high confidence that it will run correctly on the other helicopters. In this paper we concentrate on modifications that are the result of changing, adding or removing components, but not their connections.

3   Assume-Guarantee Reasoning and Testing

Compositional verification is thus based on decomposing the system specification into a set of properties each of which describing the behavior of a system's subset. In general, checking local properties over subsystems does not imply the correctness of the entire system. This is due to the existence of mutual dependencies among components. More precisely, each single component cannot be considered in isolation but must be considered as behaving and interacting with its environment (i.e., the rest of the system).

Assume-guarantee reasoning is one of the most promising approaches proposed for compositional reasoning. It was originally introduced in the Ph.D. thesis of Cliff Jones [18] and in the context of temporal logic by Amir Pnueli [19]. Assume-guarantee reasoning considers both components and the environment

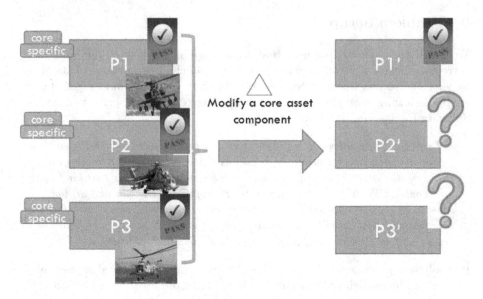

Fig. 1. The helicopter certification problem

they interact with. The environment is described a set of properties that should be satisfied for it to correctly interact with the components. These properties are the *assumptions* that the component makes on the environment. If they are satisfied by the environment, then the component behaving in this environment usually satisfies other properties, the *guarantees*. As said before, a system can sometimes be proved correct without actually constructing it through the appropriate combination of assume and guarantee properties.

We use Pnueli's notation to state that if the environment of component M satisfies logic formula φ (i.e., φ is the *assumption* that M makes about the components it interacts with), then in that environment M satisfies ψ (i.e., M *guarantees* ψ):

$$\langle \varphi \rangle \ M \ \langle \psi \rangle$$

Pnueli's classical reasoning chain then becomes:

$$\frac{\langle \ \rangle \ M \ \langle \varphi \rangle \qquad \langle \varphi \rangle \ M' \ \langle \psi \rangle}{\langle \ \rangle \ M \cdot M' \ \langle \psi \rangle}$$

in which '·' is a suitable composition operator. This reasoning chain should be interpreted as follows: if M, with no assumption on its environment, satisfies φ, and M', over an environment that satisfies φ, satisfies ψ, then without any assumption on its environment $M \cdot M'$ satisfies ψ. In this paper, we consider M and M' to model component behaviors and φ and ψ to be formulae expressed in Linear Temporal Logic.

As witnessed by [20], the main difficulties of applying assume-guarantee reasoning are (i) *generating* the assumptions and (ii) *decomposing* a system into subsystems with the purpose of efficiently verifying general system properties. Therefore, in [21] three main dimensions to be considered when dealing with assume-guarantee reasoning were identified:

1. The *composition operator* should be carefully selected and has to be associative. It defines a *system and properties decomposition* and this is fundamental in order to correctly work with the reasoning chain;
2. The *assumptions generation* technique is fundamental for assuring effective assume-guarantee reasoning;
3. The language used to specify the system and that used to specify the assume-guarantee properties are crucial. Semantic relationships between these two languages (if they differ) are fundamental to make the assumption generation process fully automatic.

The authors of [22] introduce a framework for performing assume-guarantee reasoning in an incremental and fully automatic fashion. More specifically, the approach automatically generates via a learning algorithm assumptions that the environment needs to satisfy for the property to hold. These assumptions are initially approximate, but become gradually more precise by means of counterexamples obtained by model checking the component and its environment. In [23], the authors observe that in reality a component is only required to satisfy properties in specific environments. Inspired by these motivations, they generate assumptions that characterize exactly those environments in which the component satisfies its required property.

Assume-guarantee testing has been proposed as a technique to complement assume-guarantee model checking, to be used for the verification of components' implementations [4]. While formal verification with assume-guarantee testing increases scalability when compared to traditional formal verification techniques such as model checking, it may still be unfeasible when applied to the implementation of large-scale industrial systems. For this reason, Giannakopoulou et al. proposed in [4] an approach that, after applying assume-guarantee formal verification at the design level, uses assume-guarantee information to test whether the components' implementations continue to satisfy the assumptions. In affirmative cases, this will show that there is no incompatibility between the design models and their implementations. The main advantages of assume-guarantee testing rely on the possibility of detecting violations with a higher probability than in the case of traditional testing, avoiding state explosion problems that typically arise when combining components, and with the same coverage as that of traditional systems — but with fewer tests.

More formally, consider a system S in a possibly empty context E. Let S be composed of n components $C_1, C_2, \ldots, C_n$[1]. The idea is to produce for each C_i, with $1 < i < n$, both G_i and A_i, representing respectively the local requirements that C_i has to guarantee and the assumptions that characterize the context

---

[1] Here the term component is used as a synonym of part.

in that point. In other words, each component C_i will guarantee property G_i whenever its context satisfies assumption A_i.

Next consider two components C_1 and C_2 (but the reasoning can straightfor-wardly be extended to a multitude of components) and two implementations I_1 and I_2 of these components, respectively. After having validated with assume-guarantee model checking that $C_1 \cdot C_2$ satisfies a property ψ, we subsequently want to test whether $I_1 \cdot I_2$ still satisfies ψ. The idea for doing so is to check this separately, via unit testing, for the two component implementations $\langle \varphi \rangle I_1 \langle \psi \rangle$ and $\langle \ \rangle I_2 \langle \varphi \rangle$. Assume-guarantee testing is then run according to the following three steps:

1. The assumption φ is used to restrict the execution of the component I_1 when producing test traces. This means that sets of test traces T_1 and T_2 are pro-duced from I_1 composed with an implementation of φ, and from I_2 composed with an implementation of the universal environment, respectively;
2. The resulting traces are individually checked against the appropriate assume-guarantee premise. Thus, each trace in T_1 is checked against ψ, and each trace in T_2 is checked against φ, individually, without requiring the construction of all the interleavings of the two components' implementations;
3. If either of these above checks fails, then there is an incompatibility between the components' models and their implementations that needs to be fixed. Otherwise, $I_1 \cdot I_2 \models \psi$.

Assume-guarantee testing is still testing, i.e. it lacks exhaustive coverage. How-ever, as said before, assume-guarantee testing has the potential of checking more system behaviors with the same amount of coverage as traditional testing.

4   Assume-Guarantee Testing of Evolving Software Product Line Architectures

While we have seen that a lot of research efforts have been devoted to software product line testing [17, 24–26, 13], limited research has been conducted on how to test evolving software product lines (some research that has been carried out is discussed in Section 5). The solution we propose below combines the principles of traditional regression testing, in the context of evolving software product line architectures, with the use of assume-guarantee reasoning. As the architecture of the software product line plays a central role in our approach, the latter can thus be considered architecture-centric.

Figure 2 contextualizes our work: all components used in the original prod-uct line architecture of the software product line of interest (i.e., A, B, C, D and E) are enriched with assume and guarantee properties. These assumptions can automatically be calculated by extending the approach presented in [23] to software product line architectures.

The configuration of the product line architecture (i.e., the way components are instantiated, selected, and connected) provides context to the assumptions

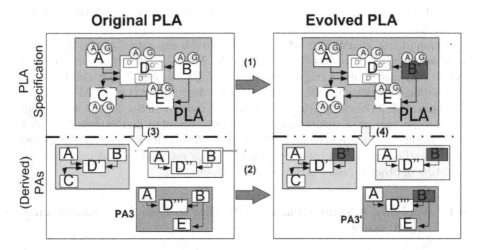

Fig. 2. The original software product line architecture (PLA) and the evolved one, including the product architectures (PAs) of their derived products

and guarantees: given a component C with its assume-guarantee pair, its environment becomes the subarchitecture connected with C. What is challenging in assume-guarantee reasoning in the context of product line architectures is that the reasoning is performed on the product line architecture, including all variation points, rather than on each single concrete product — or better, on the architecture of each single product. This means that the assumptions will have to be calculated in a smart way, taking into account the commonalities and variability among the components.

Once a component evolves, this modification is expected to have an impact on a number of product architectures, namely each one that contains the modified component. For instance, consider that component B evolves into B' (cf. Fig. 2). Then the assume-guarantee pairs of both B and B' will have to be checked.

In such a context, our solution envisions a combination of regression testing and assume-guarantee testing in the context of evolving product line architectures. Conceptually, this requires us to better understand two issues.

First, we need to understand how to extend the assume-guarantee testing approach proposed in [4] to evolving (product line) architectures. In [4], in fact, the assume-guarantee pair associated to each component in the architecture is used to generate component-specific testing traces. These traces, when adequately evaluated against the appropriate assume-guarantee premise, can demonstrate whether the composition of components can produce failures. Assuming that a product (line) architecture has been tested, the challenge becomes how to apply assume-guarantee reasoning for regression testing of the modified product (line) architecture (cf. (1) and (2) in Fig. 2).

Second, we need to understand how to use the relationships between a product line architecture and its derived product architectures (cf. (3) in Fig. 2) in order to be able to apply regression testing to the evolved product architectures (cf. (4) in Fig. 2).

Summarizing, we envision what we call a *double regression testing* approach, in which an evolved product (e.g., PA3′ in Fig. 2) can be tested not only based on how it regressed from an original product (i.e., PA3 in Fig. 2) but also based on its relationship with the architecture of its product family (i.e., PLA′ in Fig. 2).

The remainder of this section is organized as follows. In Section 4.1, we present the assume-guarantee testing approach from [4] adapted and extended to work with product line architectures, while Section 4.2 describes the strategy followed to select the product architectures that — once retested — can minimize the retesting of other product architectures.

4.1 Applying Assume-Guarantee Testing to Evolving Product Line Architectures

In this section, we describe how to adapt the assume-guarantee testing approach presented in [4] (and recalled in Section 3) to evolving product line architectures. We initially explain how to adapt the assume-guarantee testing approach to evolving architectures, and subsequently how this approach can be extended to evolving product line architectures.

Assume-Guarantee Testing Applied to Evolving Systems

Consider a system S that is decomposed into n components $C_1, C_2, \ldots, C_n$. Assume that for each C_i, with $1 < i < n$, a pair of assumptions A_i and guarantees G_i is available. As said before, the assumptions can automatically be calculated by a suitable assumption generation function defined over the considered language (e.g., the $\mathcal{L}^*$ learning algorithm defined in [23]).

Now set C_i as the component that is affected by a change and that is substituted by C_x. According to the approach presented in [21], the changes' correctness can be checked locally over the changed component(s). In case component C_x can substitute C_i without consequences (i.e., the assume-guarantee pairs A_x, G_x and A_i, G_i match), then the properties guaranteed by C_i are also guaranteed by C_x and no retesting is needed. This case provides an extraordinary advantage with respect to traditional (non compositional) verification approaches, where local changes have to be checked against the entire system. On the other hand, when component C_x cannot substitute C_i without consequences (i.e., the assume-guarantee pairs A_x, G_x and A_i, G_i do not match), then the assume-guarantee reasoning chain my help understand the effect of a change.

In fact, since the components composing the system S are organized as a chain of assumptions and guarantees (through which the composition of the system is realized), assume-guarantee reasoning enables an immediate understanding of how local changes affect the entire system, without applying traditional impact analysis approaches. Again, this facilitates (and potentially automates) the regression testing analysis of evolving systems.

Assume-Guarantee Testing Applied to Evolving Product Line Architectures

In order to extend the assume-guarantee regression testing approach outlined in Section 4.1 to product line architectures, it becomes particularly important to consider the commonalities and variability in product line architectures and, more specifically, normal, optional and variant components. Below we present in detail the way in which the approach of Section 4.1 has to be reconsidered in the case of such components.

Normal or Optional Component. When a component C has to be substituted with a component C', there are two possible cases:

1. The pair of assumptions and guarantees of C' matches the assumptions and guarantees of C and thus no re-verification is needed.
2. The pair of assumptions and guarantees of C' does not match that of C. This may impact only a part or, in the worst case, the entire chain. To measure the impact, we check whether an environment exists for C' such that the guarantee of C can be satisfied. If it does, then the chain allows to check if the component that should match this assumption with its guarantee is analyzed. This reasoning is iterated until each incongruence in the assume-guarantee chain has been resolved. If, on the other hand, no such environment exists for C', then we have to also analyze the right side of the chain.

Variant Component. Let D be an abstract variant component with n variants $D_1, D_2, \ldots, D_n$. When a variant D_i evolves in D_i', a reasoning similar to the one made for normal and optional components must be performed. In addition, however, we have to consider that D_i was a variant of D and therefore also D_i' should be a variant of D. This means that the pair of assumptions and guarantees of D should hold also for D_i'. If this is indeed the case, then the chain in which D is involved does not require changes. Otherwise, even the assumptions and guarantees of D have to be updated and the changes must be propagated by suitably recalculating all involved assume and guarantee properties in the chain.

Adding or removing a component in a product line architecture requires a reasoning similar to the one we just outlined for substitution. We can have an optimal integration or removal, meaning that no assumptions and guarantees must be recalculated (such as the removal of an optional component). In general, however, assumptions and guarantees must be recalculated (and in the worst case, the entire chain must be recalculated).

The next step is to apply the assume-guarantee testing approach. When applying assume-guarantee testing in the context of evolving product line architectures, the assume-guarantee testing process presented in [4] has to be applied as follows: we initially apply assume-guarantee reasoning at the level of the product line architecture in order to analyze the conformance of product architectures to assume-guarantee properties. Successively, we apply assume-guarantee testing to check the conformance of the implementation of the product architecture with respect to the its specification (exactly as proposed in [4]).

When the product line architecture evolves, we first need to identify the product architectures that should be retested. As we will explain in Section 4.2, it is important to appropriately select the product architectures to be retested since the selection strategy can impact the number of tests to be performed on other product architectures. Once the product architectures to be retested have been selected, we have to apply the assume-guarantee strategy described above to reassure the conformance of each such product architecture to the modified product line architecture (or to evolve the product architecture in accordance to the changes). Subsequently, we again apply assume-guarantee testing to check the conformance of the implementation of the product architecture with respect to its specification (exactly as proposed in [4]). Finally, we need to reselect a subset of test traces for those components that need to be retested. Existing test traces for the component implementation have to be modified only when the assume-guarantee properties of its component specification C have changed. New test traces have to be added for all the new components added to the product architecture.

As far as automation is concerned, in this paper we consider both the architectural models and the implementations to be represented (at different levels of abstraction) by labeled transition systems. As a result, the Labelled Transition System Analyser[2] as described in [23] becomes an ideal candidate tool to be extended in order to cope with test traces generation. Such a setting is inherited from [4] and can be applied when detailed models are constructed through the refinement of more abstract models.

4.2 Testing Strategy: Selection of Products to Retest

The main strategic decision we need to make in order to apply the proposed double regression testing approach is the choice of the products that need to be retested and the test sets. The apparently most useful information we have at hand is the so-called feature model of the software product line, the original product (line) architecture and the previous tests. By making intelligent use of the commonalities and variability inherent to the software product line, we can select both the products that need retesting and a set of test cases from the existing ones. Ideally, this allows us to avoid having to retest all products and to rerun all test cases.

A *feature model* has become the de facto standard variability model in software product line engineering. It provides a compact representation of all products of a product family in terms of their features, and additional constraints among them. Graphically, features are represented as the nodes of a tree, with the family as its root and relations between these features representing constraints. The first three relations below form the tree, while the latter two model additional constraints:

---

[2] http://www.doc.ic.ac.uk/ltsa/

Optional features may (but need not) be present only if their parent is present;

Mandatory features are (have to be) present if and only if their parent is present;

Alternative features are such that only one is present if their parent is present;

Requires is a unidirectional relation indicating that the presence of one feature requires that of the other;

Excludes is a bidirectional relation indicating the presence of two features to be mutually exclusive.

From a feature model we can thus extract all necessary information on the relationships between features, such as which features exclude each other and which are optional. By analyzing the features that are involved in the component that has evolved, we can obtain useful information on the impact on other features. From the product line architecture we know which product architecture contains the component that has evolved. Combining this information, we can thus select the product architecture that needs to be retested and appropriately adjust the test sets. In a similar way, in [27] it is shown that the addition/modification of so-called *conservative* and *regulative* features in a software product line requires only a subset of the new products to be model checked.

To make this more concrete, consider once more Fig. 2. Component B has evolved in component B' and this component is part of three product architectures, among which PA3. Now we inspect the feature model regarding the features that are present in B and B', and in particular regarding their difference. If, for instance, B' contains a feature f that B did not, then we need to inspect the feature model for the features that are related with f. If the feature model states that the inclusion of f in a product *excludes* the presence of a feature g, for instance, then we need to inspect the product architectures of which B' is part to see whether or not the other components contain g. Moreover, we need to add the exclusion of g to the assumptions that B' makes on the environment (in addition to the assumptions inherited from B). Similar reasonings can easily be imagined in case B' contains less features than B or exactly the same features as B. Likewise, a related reasoning applies to the cases in which the feature model states that f *requires* a feature g and/or other relationships.

5   Related Work

Software product line testing consists of using product line artifacts (e.g., requirements, architectures, code with variability) or artifacts of products derived from a software product line, to select test suites enabling the validation of a software product line and of its derivable products. During software product line testing at least two main (and opposite) dimensions need to be considered: testing the core components present at the domain engineering level (i.e., testing the software product line artifacts) and testing the products derivable from the product line during application engineering (i.e., testing the product that is part of a software product line).

Testing product lines during domain engineering means testing the software product line based on all the artifacts common to the product line (e.g., software product line testing based on domain-level requirements, design, and realized components). The opposite dimension means testing the single products that can be obtained during application engineering. At this stage, the main goal is to test the variety of products obtained by assembling core and domain-specific components, possibly written in different programming languages, distributed across the network and executed in various platforms. Other techniques use a mix of product and product line information in order to derive a testing campaign (as discussed in the systematic study in [17]).

Several software product line testing approaches have been proposed so far in the literature, many of which use software product line requirements (with explicit variability modeling) for selecting requirements-based test suites, while most of the approaches use models (of the requirements or of the architecture) defined formally or semi-formally for the derivation of test cases. A problem common to all approaches is the number of test cases to consider, which obviously increases exponentially with the number of features of the software product line (cf. [13] for an overview and comparison of several scalable testing techniques that aim at reducing the number of products to be tested, among which so-called combinatorial interaction testing).

Since the focus of this paper is on evolving software product lines, the work most closely related to our research is that on software product line regression testing, which aims to minimize the effort to retest a software product line when components change. The most advanced regression testing approach for software product line architectures can be found in [16], in which three different software product line evolution scenarios and a regression testing approach for software product lines are described. By considering a regression testing strategy RT that takes as input two versions of the same component, three scenarios can be defined, as follows:

1. Given a reference architecture RA, once a core component in RA is changed, a strategy RT(RA,RA') is needed for retesting the reference architecture;
2. Given a reference architecture RA and a product P derived from it, a strategy RT(RA,P) can be used to test P under the assumption that RA has already been tested, taking advantage of the similarities between the RA and P;
3. Given two products P1 and P2, both derived from the same reference architecture RA, a strategy RT(P1,P2) can be applied to test P2 under the assumption that P1 has already been tested, taking advantage of the similarities among products derived from the same RA.

By taking the two versions (the original and its modified one) as the main input of the RT regression testing approach, a 4-step approach (from regression testing planning to test reporting) is proposed. Architectural specifications, feature models, the product map, and the feature dependency diagram can be used to identify portions that need retesting.

The preliminary work of Engström in [28] presents observations coming from two systematic reviews of the relevant literature; one deals with regression test selection and the other one with software product line testing. As future work, Engström plans to investigate (among others) how to perform regression testing in software product lines.

6   Conclusions and Future Work

The most important concepts characterizing software product line engineering as a discipline for the development of a diversity of software products or systems based on the underlying architecture of the product platform, are a product line's commonalities and variability (often defined in terms of features whose relations are expressed in a feature model). Commonalities define what different software products or systems have in common and guides the production of domain-specific core components. Variability defines the ability to change or customize a software product or system (i.e., to distinguish one product from another in the software product line).

In this paper, we define a testing approach to exploit the commonalities and variability of the products of a software product line when the software product line (architecture) is subject to evolution. The idea is to retest only selected products while inferring the "correct" functioning of other products conforming to the software product line. Our approach, heavily based on that of [4], makes use of assume-guarantee reasoning, which is used both to verify the (underlying architectural) design of the product or system and to drive the testing phase.

While we are obviously aware that this work is quite preliminary, we believe it can trigger interesting discussions, and for this purpose we are submitting it to this workshop. As a consequence, there is a long list of future work we would like to accomplish in the near future.

First, we plan to apply the presented approach to the Arcade Game Maker Pedagogical Product Line whose specification and code are available online[3].

Second, we want to experiment with the presented approach also on other industrial case studies, like the one presented in Section 2.

Some further real-world industrial case studies can be found through the Architecture Support for Testing initiative[4] which this research is part of.

Finally, we ideally would like to automate our approach. As said before, labeled transition systems are currently used for describing the components' behavior as well as the assume and guarantee properties of a given software product or system, while in the approach of [4] the aforementioned Labelled Transition System Analyser is used for automatically generating assumptions. Our approach, however, would require an extension in order to be able to deal with product line architectures, for which we intend to move from labeled transition systems to so-called modal transition systems, which were recognized in [11] as a useful formal model for describing in a compact way the possible operational behavior of all products of a product line. As a result, we foresee the need for an appropriate extension of the Modal Transition System Analyser [29] (a tool

---

[3] http://www.sei.cmu.edu/productlines/ppl/
[4] http://www.henrymuccini.com/index.php?pageId=AST

built on top of the Labelled Transition System Analyser in order to deal with limited variability) for automatically generating assumptions for product line architectures, and for coping with test traces generation.

References

1. Clements, P., Northrop, L.: Software Product Lines: Practices and Patterns. Addison-Wesley (2002)
2. Pohl, K., Böckle, G., van der Linden, F.: Software Product Line Engineering: Foundations, Principles, and Techniques. Springer (2005)
3. ter Beek, M.H., Muccini, H., Pelliccione, P.: Guaranteeing Correct Evolution of Software Product Lines: Setting up the Problem. In: Troubitsyna, E.A. (ed.) SERENE 2011. LNCS, vol. 6968, pp. 100–105. Springer, Heidelberg (2011)
4. Giannakopoulou, D., Pasareanu, C., Blundell, C.: Assume-guarantee testing for software components. IET Softw. 2(6), 547–562 (2008)
5. Asirelli, P., ter Beek, M.H., Fantechi, A., Gnesi, S.: Formal Description of Variability in Product Families. In: SPLC 2011 Conference Proceedings, pp. 130–139. IEEE Press (2011)
6. Asirelli, P., ter Beek, M.H., Fantechi, A., Gnesi, S., Mazzanti, F.: Design and Validation of Variability in Product Lines. In: PLEASE 2011 Workshop Proceedings, pp. 25–30. ACM Press (2011)
7. ter Beek, M.H., Mazzanti, F., Sulova, A.: VMC: A Tool for Product Variability Analysis. In: Giannakopoulou, D., Méry, D. (eds.) FM 2012. LNCS, vol. 7436, pp. 450–454. Springer, Heidelberg (2012)
8. Classen, A., Cordy, M., Heymans, P., Legay, A., Schobbens, P.Y.: Model Checking Software Product Lines with SNIP. To appear in Int. J. Softw. Tools Technol. Transfer (2012)
9. Classen, A., Heymans, P., Schobbens, P.Y., Legay, A.: Symbolic model checking of software product lines. In: ICSE 2011 Conference Proceedings, pp. 321–330. ACM Press (2011)
10. Classen, A., Heymans, P., Schobbens, P.Y., Legay, A., Raskin, J.F.: Model checking lots of systems: efficient verification of temporal properties in software product lines. In: ICSE 2010 Conference Proceedings, pp. 335–344. ACM Press (2010)
11. Fischbein, D., Uchitel, S., Braberman, V.A.: A foundation for behavioural conformance in software product line architectures. In: ROSATEA 2006 Workshop Proceedings, pp. 39–48. ACM Press (2006)
12. Lauenroth, K., Pohl, K., Toehning, S.: Model Checking of Domain Artifacts in Product Line Engineering. In: ASE 2009 Conference Proceedings, pp. 269–280. IEEE Press (2009)
13. Perrouin, G., Oster, S., Sen, S., Klein, J., Baudry, B., le Traon, Y.: Pairwise Testing for Software Product Lines: Comparison of Two Approaches. To appear in Software Qual. J. (2012)
14. Schaefer, I., Gurov, D., Soleimanifard, S.: Compositional Algorithmic Verification of Software Product Lines. In: Aichernig, B.K., de Boer, F.S., Bonsangue, M.M. (eds.) FMCO 2010. LNCS, vol. 6957, pp. 184–203. Springer, Heidelberg (2011)
15. Thüm, T., Schaefer, I., Kuhlemann, M., Apel, S.: Proof Composition for Deductive Verification of Software Product Lines. In: ICSTW 2011 Conference Proceedings, pp. 270–277. IEEE Press (2011)

16. da Mota Silveira Neto, P.A.: A Regression Testing Approach for Software Product Lines Architectures: Selecting an efficient and effective set of test cases. LAP (2010)
17. da Mota Silveira Neto, P.A., do Carmo Machado, I., McGregor, J.D., de Almeida, E.S., de Lemos Meira, S.R.: A systematic mapping study of software product lines testing. Inf. Softw. Technol. 53(5), 407–423 (2011)
18. Jones, C.B.: Development Methods for Computer Programs including a Notion of Interference. PhD thesis, Oxford University (1981)
19. Pnueli, A.: In Transition from Global to Modular Temporal Reasoning about Programs. In: Logics and Models of Concurrent Systems, pp. 123–144. Springer (1985)
20. Cobleigh, J.M., Avrunin, G.S., Clarke, L.A.: Breaking up is hard to do: An evaluation of automated assume-guarantee reasoning. ACM Trans. Softw. Eng. Methodol. 17(2), 1–52 (2008)
21. Inverardi, P., Pelliccione, P., Tivoli, M.: Towards an assume-guarantee theory for adaptable systems. In: SEAMS 2009 Workshop Proceedings, pp. 106–115 (2009)
22. Cobleigh, J.M., Giannakopoulou, D., Pǎsǎreanu, C.S.: Learning Assumptions for Compositional Verification. In: Garavel, H., Hatcliff, J. (eds.) TACAS 2003. LNCS, vol. 2619, pp. 331–346. Springer, Heidelberg (2003)
23. Giannakopoulou, D., Pasareanu, C.S., Barringer, H.: Component Verification with Automatically Generated Assumptions. Autom. Softw. Eng. 12(3), 297–320 (2005)
24. Engström, E., Runeson, P.: Software product line testing: A systematic mapping study. Inf. Softw. Technol. 53(1), 2–13 (2011)
25. Kim, C.H.P., Batory, D.S., Khurshid, S.: Reducing combinatorics in testing product lines. In: AOSD 2011 Conference Proceedings, pp. 57–68. ACM Press (2011)
26. Kim, C.H.P., Bodden, E., Batory, D., Khurshid, S.: Reducing Configurations to Monitor in a Software Product Line. In: Barringer, H., Falcone, Y., Finkbeiner, B., Havelund, K., Lee, I., Pace, G., Roşu, G., Sokolsky, O., Tillmann, N. (eds.) RV 2010. LNCS, vol. 6418, pp. 285–299. Springer, Heidelberg (2010)
27. Cordy, M., Classen, A., Schobbens, P.Y., Heymans, P., Legay, A.: Managing evolution in software product lines: a model-checking perspective. In: VaMoS 2012 Workshop Proceedings, pp. 183–191. ACM Press (2012)
28. Engström, E.: Regression Test Selection and Product Line System Testing. In: ICST 2010 Conference Proceedings, pp. 512–515. IEEE Press (2010)
29. D'Ippolito, N., Fischbein, D., Chechik, M., Uchitel, S.: MTSA: The modal transition system analyser. In: ASE 2008 Conference Proceedings, pp. 475–476. IEEE Press (2008)

FAS: Introducing a Service
for Avoiding Faults in Composite Services

Koray Gülcü[1], Hasan Sözer[2], and Barış Aktemur[2]

[1] Vestel Electronics, Manisa, Turkey
koray.gulcu@vestel.com.tr
[2] Özyeğin University, İstanbul, Turkey
{hasan.sozer,baris.aktemur}@ozyegin.edu.tr

Abstract. In service-oriented architectures, composite services depend on a set of partner services to perform the required tasks. These partner services may become unavailable due to system and/or network faults, leading to an increased error rate for the composite service. In this paper, we propose an approach to prevent the occurrence of errors that result from the unavailability of partner services. We introduce an external Web service, FAS (Fault Avoidance Service), to which composite services can register at will. After registration, FAS periodically checks the partner links, detects unavailable partner services, and updates the composite service with available alternatives. Thus, in case of a partner service error, the composite service will have been updated before invoking the partner service. We provide mathematical analysis regarding the error rate and the ratio of false positives with respect to the monitoring frequency of FAS for different partner service availabilities. We also provide empirical results regarding these metrics based on several tests we performed using the Amazon Elastic Compute Cloud.

1 Introduction

In service-oriented architectures [14], composite services depend on a set of partner services to perform the required tasks. Some of the partner services can cease to be available due to system and/or network faults, which have been shown in recent experimental studies [28] to be very common. These faults result in an error and possibly a failure of the composite service that relies on the availability of its partner services. Preferably, the composite service should discover and utilize alternative services to tolerate such external faults. As such, there have been several service fault tolerance approaches proposed in the literature [25,27,17]. However, fault tolerance increases the response time due to the additional time it takes to detect errors and recover from them[1]. The consequential

---

[1] If the composite service employs the *Active* fault tolerance strategy (i.e., connects to all of the partner services in parallel and proceeds immediately after receiving a response from a partner), occurrence of a fault in a partner service would not affect the composite service. However, this is not possible in many cases due to constraints imposed by unavailable resources or the problem domain.

P. Avgeriou (Ed.): SERENE 2012, LNCS 7527, pp. 106–120, 2012.

delay can be very significant especially for composite services that utilize many other services [4]. Therefore, external faults should be avoided (if possible) to improve the dependability and performance of service-oriented systems. One way to avoid partner service faults is to execute the service selection process per each request [3,7] or per each flow of requests [2]. However, a partner service might be accessed multiple times during the processing of a request and it can cease to be available at any time. Moreover, executing the service selection process per each request/flow also introduces an overhead, just like the overhead of error detection and recovery.

Research efforts so far have mainly focused on providing service brokers [6,7], middleware [26,13,27] and framework support [10,12,5,17] to compose dependable services. In this paper, we propose *fault avoidance as a service*, whose utilization does not require a particular composite service model. We introduce an external Web service, FAS(Fault Avoidance Service), to which a composite service registers the set of its partner services. FAS periodically checks the availability of the registered partner services and locates the alternatives when they are unavailable. Here, our goal is not to provide health monitoring or fault tolerance, for which many approaches have already been proposed [28,27,17]. Instead, FAS aims at proactively updating composite services and as such, *avoiding* faults. Faults are avoided by updating the links for unavailable partner services with available alternatives *before* they are invoked by the composite service. This reduces the error-rate.

We studied the impact of the *monitoring frequency* of FAS on the effectiveness of our approach. In particular, we defined analytical metrics regarding the error rate and the false positive rate for different monitoring frequencies and partner service availabilities. We performed several tests using a prototype implementation deployed on the Amazon Elastic Compute Cloud (EC2) [1]. Our measurements confirmed the accuracy of our analytical metrics, which can be used for determining an optimal monitoring frequency depending on varying partner service availabilities.

Contributions of this paper are twofold. First, we propose the implementation of forecasting, detection and the handling of external faults as external services. In this way, a set of services can provide dependability support for other services, i.e., Dependability as a Service (DaaS). To our knowledge, so far this concept has only been realized in the context of software/service testing (Testing as a Service - TaaS). Second, we provide analytical metrics regarding the impact of monitoring frequency on the error rate and the false positive rate. We also validate these metrics with empirical results for various partner service availabilities. We have not encountered such an analysis in the literature although service monitoring has been employed in many studies.

Organization: Section 2 presents the problem statement. Section 3 introduces our solution approach. In Section 4, we introduce analytical metrics and related mathematical analysis. In Section 5, we present our experimental setup, results and evaluation. In Section 6, related previous studies are summarized. Finally, in Section 7 we discuss some future work issues and provide the conclusions.

2   Background and the Problem Statement

A typical process in service-oriented systems involves a service requester and a service provider, which communicate with each other through service requests [14]. Usually a service provider registers its services at a service broker that maintains a registry of "available" services [14]; a service requester can look up and discover these services through the service broker. For instance, a UDDI [23] service registry is a specialized type of service broker [14]. The service requester can select any service provider among the ones that are discovered from a registry service. In some cases, a service provider can request services of several other service providers to perform a task. Such services are called composite services. Usually, they are defined by service aggregators as a composition of a number of partner services. Composition languages (e.g., WS-BPEL [16]) introduce special structures called partner links, through which partner services can be accessed.

After registering itself to the service registry, or after being discovered by the composite service, or even after being successfully invoked several times, a partner service can become unavailable due to system and/or network faults. In fact, recent experimental studies [28] show that the majority of service invocation failures are caused by these types of faults (connection timeout, service unavailablity, etc.). As a result, the invocation attempt leads to an error. In turn, the composite service can *i)* report a failure to its service requester, or *ii)* discover and utilize alternative services to recover from the error. Figure 1 presents a scenario for the second case. In this scenario, the previously designated partner service fails and becomes unavailable. Hereby, $MTTF$ and $MTTR$ correspond to the *mean time to failure* and the *mean time to recover* for this service, respectively. After the failure and before the recovery of the partner service, the composite service makes an invocation without success. The composite service waits for a timeout duration ($t_{timeout}$) to decide whether the partner service is available or not. Once it is deemed to be unavailable, the composite service discovers an alternative service from the service registry. The duration of this discovery is t_{lookup}. In case there is already a designated alternative service (might be hardcoded in the source code or the WS-BPEL description, or it might be stored in an external cache), t_{lookup} will be negligibly small. In any case, a new invocation has to be made to the designated/discovered alternative service. The total time that is necessary to recover from the error is $t_{overhead}$.

Failure of a partner service is an external fault from the perspective of the composite service that tries to utilize the failed service. A composite service can be exposed to many such external faults and for each of these faults, $t_{overhead}$ will be added to its overall response time as a cost of fault tolerance. The consequential delay can be significant especially for composite services that utilize many other services [4] to perform their tasks. In the following, we introduce an approach, where these external faults are avoided to improve the dependability and performance of composite services.

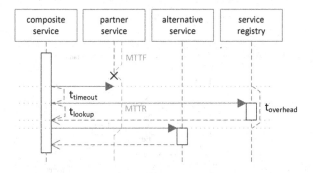

Fig. 1. An error recovery scenario

3 The Solution Approach

In our approach, we introduce a Web service for avoiding faults. We name this service as *Fault Avoidance Service (FAS)*. A composite service first determines the list of partner services that are going to be utilized, and registers this list of services to FAS. FAS periodically checks the availability of these services. In case a partner service becomes unavailable, FAS locates alternatives and updates the associated partner link of the composite service accordingly. When needed, the composite service uses the updated partner links during invocation. This prevents composite service from trying to reach unavailable partner services, as such reduces the error rate and the overall response time of the process. To be able to incorporate partner link updates, a registered composite service exposes a callback method to receive updates from FAS.

Figure 2 depicts our overall approach. FAS stores a *partner service list* that is provided by the composite service as the list of services to be monitored. This list is used by the *error detection* module to check if the invocation of these services can cause an error due to system/network faults that make the services unavailable. The detected errors are reported to the *fault handling* module. This module is responsible for preventing the detected errors at the composite service by updating its partner links associated with the unavailable partner services. As such, the composite service becomes oblivious to the faults rooted at its partner services. The *fault handling* module may make use of a *service cache* and occasionally the *service registry* to locate alternative and available services. If a faulty service becomes available again, FAS updates the composite service's partner link back to its original setting. FAS checks the availability of the registered partner links periodically. In the following section, we analyze the effect of FAS checking frequency on the error rate and the false positive rate.

4 Mathematical Analysis

In an ideal situation, FAS will immediately detect whenever the partner service becomes unavailable or available. This way, the composite service can be notified

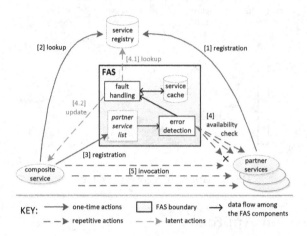

Fig. 2. The overall approach

right away so that no request from the composite service will fail (i.e., no errors) and no request will be unnecessarily forwarded to the secondary service (i.e., no false positives). However, in real life, there will be cases where the composite service sends its request to the partner service before FAS notices that the service is down, or the cases where the composite service still uses the secondary service because FAS did not notice yet that the partner service is back in life. The error rate and the number of false positives depend on the frequency of requests sent from the composite service, the frequency of FAS checks, and the chance of a FAS check occurring right after a partner service status change. Increasing the frequency of FAS checks would obviously decrease the error rate and false positives, however, an increased frequency means more load and resource usage. Being aware of this trade-off is vital for system administrators in adjusting the checking period for FAS. In this section we provide the mathematical analysis of the expected values of the error rate and the false positive rate.

Figure 3 shows the important events in a system using FAS. In this scenario, we assume that the composite service (CS) periodically sends requests at some frequency C, FAS checks availability of the partner service at a frequency F, and the partner service becomes unavailable for a certain period of its lifetime T_U. For simplicity, we assume that the requests, checks and partner service up/down events are instantaneous. The duration between the moment the partner service becomes unavailable and the time FAS detects this, is the *period of errors*, because any request sent from the CS during this period will fail. Similarly, the duration between the moment the partner service becomes available again and the time FAS detects this, is the *period of false positives*, because any request sent from the CS during this period will unnecessarily be forwarded to the secondary service. For example, the third CS request in Figure 3 fails because FAS has not notified the CS for the unavailability of the partner service yet. After the third FAS check, FAS notifies the CS, the fourth CS request is succesfully forwarded

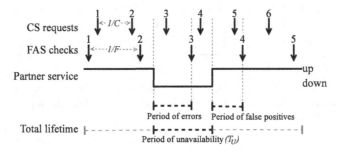

Fig. 3. A scenario showing the important events in a system that uses FAS. This scenario also illustrates the case where $1/F \leq T_U$.

to the secondary service and the potential error is avoided. However, the fifth request will still be forwarded even though the partner service is back to life, resulting in a false positive. This is because the fourth FAS check occurs after the fifth CS request.

The question we look into at this moment is the expected rate of errors that are not avoided and the false positive rate. The smaller these values are, the more useful FAS is. To calculate these values, we first list the metrics and units we use.

- A (%): Availability of the partner service.
- F (1/s): Frequency of FAS checks.
- C (1/s): Frequency of CS requests.
- T (s): Total lifetime of the system.
- T_U: Period of unavailability of the partner service, i.e., $T_U = (1 - A)T$.
- T_E (s): Period of errors.
- T_F (s): Period of false positives.
- ER: Error rate, calculated as the ratio of the number of errors to the total number of requests.
- FP: False positive rate, calculated as the ratio of the number of false positives to the total number of requests.

Based on these terms, the expected error rate is calculated using the following formulae:

$$E[ER] = \frac{Expected\ number\ of\ errors}{Total\ number\ of\ requests} = \frac{\frac{Expected\ length\ of\ T_E}{Duration\ between\ two\ CS\ checks}}{\frac{Total\ lifetime}{Duration\ between\ two\ CS\ checks}} = E[T_E]/T$$

Similarly,

$$E[FP] = E[T_F]/T$$

$E[T_E]$ and $E[T_F]$ are calculated according to a case analysis as follows.

- *Case 1:* $1/F \leq T_U$. In this case there is at least one FAS check that occurs during the period of unavailability; Figure 3 is a depiction of this case. In

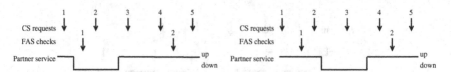

Fig. 4. Two scenarios for when the duration between two FAS checks is larger than the period of unavailability (i.e., $1/F > T_U$). In this case, a FAS check may or may not occur during unavailability.

this scenario, the minimum value of T_E can be 0 (if a FAS check occurs immediately after the partner service goes down), the maximum value can be $1/F$ (if a FAS check occurs immediately before the partner service goes down). Assuming that the starting time of FAS is uniformly distributed,

$$E[T_E] = (1/F)/2 = \frac{1}{2F}$$

Similarly, the minimum value of T_F can be 0, the maximum value can be $1/F$. Assuming uniform distribution,

$$E[T_F] = (1/F)/2 = \frac{1}{2F}$$

– *Case 2*: $1/F > T_U$. In this case, a FAS check may or may not occur during the period of unavailability. Illustration of both cases is given in Figure 4.

   • *Case 2.1*: A FAS check occurs. In this case, the value of T_E is between 0 and T_U; the value of T_F is between $1/F - T_U$ and $1/F$. Hence, assuming uniform distribution,

$$E[T_E] = (T_U - 0)/2 = T_U/2$$

$$E[T_F] = (1/F - (1/F - T_U))/2 = T_U/2$$

   • *Case 2.2*: A FAS check does *not* occur. In this scenario, FAS misses the unavailability of the partner service; CS is never notified by FAS. Hence, there are no false positives and all the requests that occur during T_U result in error:

$$E[T_E] = T_U \qquad E[T_F] = 0$$

Again assuming uniform distribution, *Case 2.1* may occur with probability $P_{2.1} = T_U/(1/F) = F T_U$; *Case 2.2* may occur with probability $P_{2.2} = 1 - F T_U$. Thus, the expected values in *Case 2* are calculated as below:

$$\begin{aligned} E[T_E] &= P_{2.1} \times T_U/2 + P_{2.2} \times T_U \\ &= F T_U^2/2 + T_U - F T_U^2 \\ &= T_U - F T_U^2/2 \end{aligned}$$

$$\begin{aligned} E[T_F] &= P_{2.1} \times T_U/2 + P_{2.2} \times 0 \\ &= F T_U^2/2 \end{aligned}$$

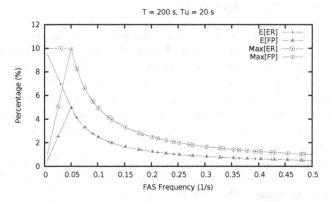

Fig. 5. Change of expected and maximum values of error and false positive rates with respect to FAS frequency

Putting the cases together, we have

$$E[ER] = \begin{cases} 1/(2FT), & \text{if } 1/F \leq T_U \\ (T_U - F T_U^2/2)/T, & \text{otherwise} \end{cases}$$

$$E[FP] = \begin{cases} 1/(2FT), & \text{if } 1/F \leq T_U \\ F T_U^2/(2T), & \text{otherwise} \end{cases}$$

Note that the expected error and false positive rates are inversely proportional to T. This means, the advantage of using FAS will be higher in longer-running systems.

Following a similar case analysis, below are the upperbounds to ER and FP. The plots of the expected and maximum values are given in Figure 5 for when $T = 200$ s and $T_U = 20$ s (i.e., $A = 90\%$).

$$Max[ER] = \begin{cases} 1/(FT), & \text{if } 1/F \leq T_U \\ T_U/T, & \text{otherwise} \end{cases}$$

$$Max[FP] = \begin{cases} 1/(FT), & \text{if } 1/F \leq T_U \\ F T_U^2/T, & \text{otherwise} \end{cases}$$

5 Evaluation

We performed several tests to evaluate our approach and analysis. In the following subsections, we discuss the realization of our approach, the experimental setup and the results.

5.1   Realization of the Approach

We developed FAS in Java as a Web service that provides an interface to composite services for registration at start-up. During registration, composite services convey two types of information: *i)* a callback method to be used by FAS to perform partner link updates, and *ii)* a list of partner services and methods to be monitored. FAS uses high-level (service-level) transactions to monitor the partner services. This is to guarantee that the target Web service is functional and reachable. Other, low-level mechanisms (e.g., ping requests) can be used for confirming the availability of a system, however, this does not necessarily imply the functional availability of services. For sending updates, FAS uses nonblocking Web service invocation. Hence, in principle, FAS should be able to handle multiple clients simultaneously without significant delay.

The utilization of FAS does not require the use of a platform/middleware or any composite service model. However, composite services should have *i)* a FAS registration process as part of their initialization, and *ii)* an interface implemented for receiving partner link updates. In accordance with these two requirements, we developed a composite service in Java. We did not use WS-BPEL because it does not directly support stateful (i.e., persistent and global) data. Therefore, partner link updates in a FAS instance cannot be reflected to the other, subsequently created instances. In principle, our approach is agnostic to the composite service implementation and the employed composition language. It is also possible to utilize WS-BPEL, for instance, using the extension proposed by Wu et al. [24].

We also implemented a partner service and replicated it. If FAS updates the partner link before the (unavailable) first replica is invoked, composite service sends the request directly to the second replica. If not, the composite service tries to invoke the first replica. In case of an error, the second replica is invoked and the received response is returned to the client.

5.2   Experimental Setup

We used Axis v2.0 [20] and Tomcat v7.0 [22] to develop and deploy Web services in our experiments. We globally distributed these services using the Amazon EC2 [1]. We utilized *micro instances* [1] and used identical machines, each of which has one CPU core with one *EC2 Compute Unit* [1], 613 MB memory and 8 GB of storage. All instances were running 32-bit Linux operating system. We deployed a composite service and two replicas of our partner service. Partner service replicas were deployed in Ireland and Tokyo, while composite service was in North California and FAS was in Sao Paulo, Brazil. Tests were conducted and controlled with a PC located in Istanbul, Turkey. The PC had Intel(R) Core 2 Duo P8600 at 2.40 Ghz with 4G RAM. As the client to the composite service, JMeter v2.4 [21] was used for executing different test scenarios and collecting measurements automatically.

Throughout our tests, we varied availability (A) only for the first replica of the partner service. The second replica is configured to be 100% available for all tests. Hence, it is assumed that an available replica always exists in the environment.

We varied A between 60% and 95%, whereas F was varied between 0.02 ($1/s$) and 0.5 ($1/s$). We performed tests for combinations of these parameters. For each combination, the tests were repeated 20 times; ER and FP were calculated by taking the average of measurements made over these repetitions. During a test, the client sends 100 requests to the composite service at a frequency of 0.25 ($1/s$). Hence, for each parameter combination, 2000 requests were sent in total for calculating the ER and FP. The results are presented in the following subsection.

5.3   Results and Discussion

In this subsection, we present and discuss the results of our tests for different parameter settings. In Figure 6, $E[ER]$ and $Max[ER]$ are plotted together with the measured error rate ($Measured[ER]$) with respect to F. Results are shown when A is 60%, 70%, 80%, 85%, 90%, 92%, 94% and 95%. Figure 7 shows $E[FP]$, $Max[FP]$, and the measured false positive rate ($Measured[FP]$) for the same range and settings of F and A.

It can be seen from the figures that $E[ER]$ and $Max[ER]$ values are consistent with respect to the measured error rates. Likewise, the measured false positive rates confirm the accuracy of our mathematical analysis regarding $E[FP]$ and $Max[FP]$. We could also observe the difference in the change of ER and FP depending on if $1/F \leq T_U$ as shown in Figure 5. See for instance the change of $Measured[FP]$ in Figure 7(h) when F is just less than 0.05. As an interesting observation, we noticed that in many cases $Measured[ER]$ converges to $Max[ER]$ as F increases. We could not observe the same trend consistently for $Measured[FP]$.

The rate of change of ER and FP with respect to F provides us a trade-off curve, which can be utilized for selecting an (pareto-)optimal F for FAS. For our experimental setup and parameter settings for instance, $F = 0.1$ could be a reasonable trade-off point. In general, we can calculate F depending on the value of A and how much we decide to compromise between ER and the load on FAS. The partial derivative of the $E[ER]$ function with respect to F defines the rate of change of $E[ER]$ with respect to F. If we want to balance the objectives of minimizing ER and minimizing the load on FAS for instance, we can find the value of F for which this rate of change (i.e., slope) is -1, e.g., for $1/F \leq T_U$, $E[ER] = 1/2FT \Rightarrow \partial(1/2FT)/\partial F = -1/2TF^2 = -1 \Rightarrow F = \sqrt{1/2T}$.

5.4   Threats to Validity

In our approach, we assume the availability of at least one replica of the partner service. Accordingly, we deployed a partner service replica with 100% availability in our experimental setup. There might be cases where *i)* there is no alternative partner service, *ii)* the alternative service is also unavailable, or *iii)* the

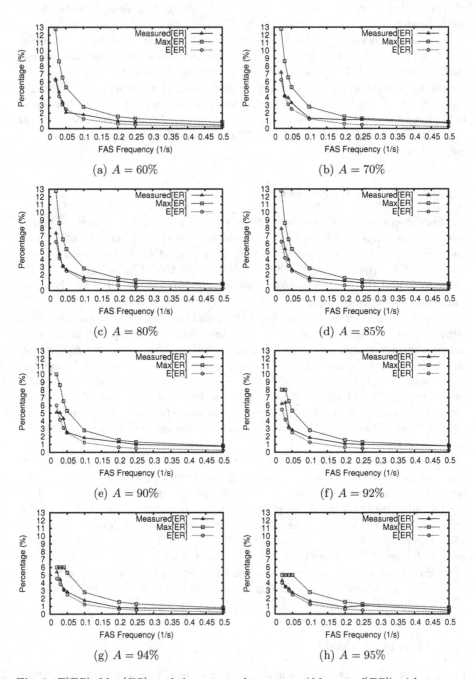

Fig. 6. $E[ER]$, $Max[ER]$, and the measured error rate ($Measured[ER]$) with respect to F, when A is 60%, 70%, 80%, 85%, 90%, 92%, 94% and 95%

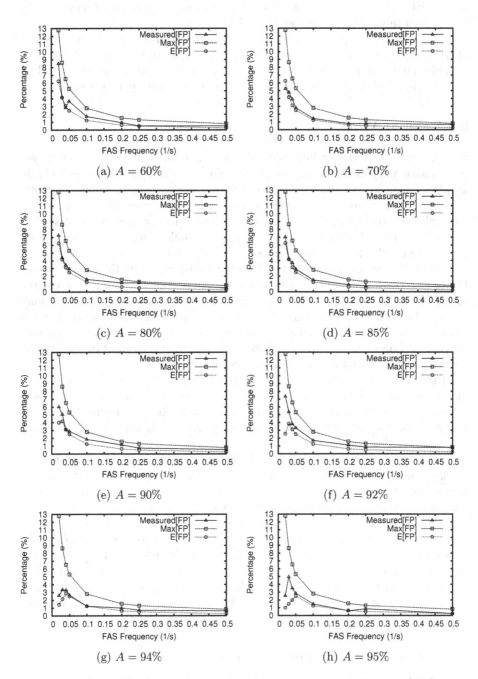

Fig. 7. $E[FP]$, $Max[FP]$, and the measured false positive rate ($Measured[FP]$) with respect to F, when A is 60%, 70%, 80%, 85%, 90%, 92%, 94% and 95%

alternative service cannot be directly substituted due to stateful properties [13]. We ignored these cases in this work.

The availability of partner services are being monitored from the perspective of FAS, which might possibly mismatch the experience of the composite service. Complementary mediators [9] can be incorporated to monitor the dependability characteristics of partner services from composite services' perspectives.

6   Related Work

So far, research efforts for improving the dependability of service-oriented systems have mainly focused on service fault tolerance [17,12,10]. We focus on fault avoidance instead. An analysis of the literature also reveals that dependability improvement has been mainly facilitated by means of frameworks [15,12], architectural methods [8,4], reliable service connectors [18], proxies [11] and service dispatchers [19]. We propose implementing a standalone service to which other services can register for improving their dependability.

There exist service brokers and architectural frameworks [6] that are responsible for the creation/composition as well as the adaptation of a composite service. As an advantage of this approach, structural changes (i.e., architecture selection) can also be applied to the composite service [6]. However, such approaches are inherently coupled with the adapted composite service based on a composite service model. FAS does not change the structure and the behavior of the composite service and it does not assume any composite service model.

In this work, we assumed the existence of alternative services that can be directly substituted with unavailable services. However, dynamic service substitution can be problematic in case of stateful services. As a complementary work, SIROCO middleware [13] was introduced to tackle this problem by enabling semantic-based service substitution.

Zheng and Lyu [27] introduce a middleware for composite services to keep track of the QoS information regarding the utilized services. This information is updated at each use of a service and sent occasionally to a common server. The collected QoS information is used for dynamically selecting the most appropriate fault tolerance strategy in case of an error. Empirical results show that their dynamic selection approach performs better than sticking to a statically determined strategy. The differences with their approach to ours are: *i)* They use a middleware; we propose implementing a standalone service to which other services can register. *ii)* Our service actively monitors the replicas. Their monitor is passive; it only stores data. *iii)* We update the user's list of preferred replicas, whereas they update the user's preferred fault tolerance strategy.

7   Conclusions and Future Work

We introduced an approach for avoiding faults during the invocation of partner services and as such, preventing errors in composite services. We developed FAS, an external fault avoidance service that periodically checks the availability of a set of partner services that are registered by a composite service. If one of the partner services ceases to be available, FAS locates alternative services and sends an update to the corresponding composite service, before the faulty partner service is invoked.

We defined analytical metrics for the error rate and the ratio of false positives for different monitoring frequencies of FAS and partner service availabilities. We performed several tests using a prototype implementation deployed on the Amazon EC2. Our measurements confirmed the accuracy of our analytical metrics, which can be used for configuring FAS based on varying partner service availabilities. Our analysis also revealed that FAS is expected to be more effective in reducing the error rate for long-running systems.

In the future, we are planning to enhance FAS so that it can adapt the service checking period at runtime, based on the monitored failure/usage frequencies and response times. We will evaluate the effectiveness of adaptive FAS in the context of an industrial case study for improving the dependability of Smart TVs that utilize many external services.

Acknowledgments. This work is supported by the joint grant of Vestel Electronics and the Turkish Ministry of Science, Industry and Technology (00995.STZ.2011-2). The authors also thank Dr. Ali Özer Ercan for his help in the derivation of analytical metrics.

References

1. Amazon.com: Elastic Compute Cloud (EC2) (2012), http://aws.amazon.com/ec2
2. Ardagna, D., Mirandola, R.: Per-flow optimal service selection for web services based processes. Journal of Systems and Software 83(8), 1512–1523 (2010)
3. Ardagna, D., Pernici, B.: Adaptive service composition in flexible processes. IEEE Transactions on Software Engineering 33, 369–384 (2007)
4. Baresi, L., Ghezzi, C.: Towards self-healing service compositions. In: Proceedings of the 1st Conference on the Principles of Software Engineering, pp. 27–46 (2004)
5. Canfora, G., Penta, M.D., Esposito, R., Villani, M.: A framework for QoS-aware binding and re-binding of composite web services. Journal of Systems and Software 81(10), 1754–1769 (2008)
6. Cardellini, V., Casalicchio, E., Grassi, V., Lo Presti, F., Mirandola, R.: Towards Self-adaptation for Dependable Service-Oriented Systems. In: de Lemos, R., Fabre, J.-C., Gacek, C., Gadducci, F., ter Beek, M. (eds.) Architecting Dependable Systems VI. LNCS, vol. 5835, pp. 24–48. Springer, Heidelberg (2009)
7. Cardellini, V., Valerio, V.D., Grassi, V., Iannucci, S., Presti, F.L.: A new approach to QoS driven service selection in service oriented architectures. In: Proceedings of the 6th IEEE International Symposium on Service Oriented System Engineering, pp. 102–113 (2011)
8. Chen, I., Ni, G., Kuo, C., Lin, C.Y.: A BPEL-Based fault-handling architecture for telecom operation support systems. Journal of Advanced Computational Intelligence and Intelligent Informatics 14(5), 523–530 (2010)
9. Chen, Y., Romanovsky, A.: WS-Mediator for improving the dependability of web services integration. Journal of IT Professionals 10(3), 29–35 (2008)

10. Dobson, G.: Using WS-BPEL to implement software fault tolerance for Web services. In: Proceedings of the 32nd EUROMICRO Conference on Software Engineering and Advanced Applications, pp. 126–133 (2006)
11. Ezenwoye, O., Sadjadi, S.: A proxy-based approach to enhancing the autonomic behavior in composite services. Journal of Networks 3(5), 42–53 (2008)
12. Fang, C.L., Liang, D., Lin, F., Lin, C.C.: Fault tolerant Web services. Journal of System Architure 53(1), 21–38 (2007)
13. Fredj, M., Georgantas, N., Issarny, V., Zarras, A.: Dynamic service substitution in service-oriented architectures. In: Proceedings of the IEEE Congress on Services, pp. 101–104 (2008)
14. Georgakopoulos, D., Papazoglu, M. (eds.): Service-Oriented Computing. MIT Press (2009)
15. Gorbenko, A., Iraj, E.K., Kharchenko, V.S., Mikhaylichenko, A.: Exception analysis in service-oriented architecture. In: Information Systems Technology and its Applications, pp. 228–233 (2007)
16. Jordan, D., Evdemon, J.: Web services business process execution language version 2.0 (2009), http://docs.oasis-open.org/wsbpel/2.0/serviceref, OASIS Standard
17. Liu, A., Li, Q., Huang, L., Xiao, M.: FACTS: A framework for fault-tolerant composition of transactional web services. IEEE Transactions on Services Computing 3(1), 46–59 (2010)
18. Salatge, N., Fabre, N., Fault, J.C.: Fault tolerance connectors for unreliable Web services. In: Proceedings of the 37th Annual IEEE/IFIP International Conference on Dependable Systems and Networks, pp. 51–60 (2007)
19. Santos, G., Lung, L., Montez, C.: FTWeb: A fault tolerant infrastructure for Web services. In: Proceedings of the 9th IEEE International Conference on Enterprise Computing, pp. 95–105 (2005)
20. The Apache Software Foundation: Axis (2012), http://axis.apache.org/
21. The Apache Software Foundation: JMeter (2012), http://jmeter.apache.org/
22. The Apache Software Foundation: Tomcat (2012), http://tomcat.apache.org/
23. Tsalgatidou, A., Pilioura, T.: An overview of standards and related technology in Web services. Distributed Parallel Databases 12(2), 135–162 (2002)
24. Wu, G., Wei, J., Huang, T.: Flexible pattern monitoring for WS-BPEL through stateful aspect extension. In: Proceedings of the IEEE International Conference on Web Services, pp. 577–584 (2008)
25. Zarras, A., Fredj, M., Georgantas, N., Issarny, V.: Engineering Reconfigurable Distributed Software Systems: Issues Arising for Pervasive Computing. In: Butler, M., Jones, C.B., Romanovsky, A., Troubitsyna, E. (eds.) Fault-Tolerant Systems. LNCS, vol. 4157, pp. 364–386. Springer, Heidelberg (2006)
26. Zeng, L., Benatallah, B., Ngu, A., Dumas, M., Kalagnanam, J., Chang, H.: QoS-aware middleware for web services composition. IEEE Transactions on Software Engineering 30(5), 311–327 (2004)
27. Zheng, Z., Lyu, M.: An adaptive QoS aware fault tolerance strategy for web services. Journal of Empirical Software Engineering 15(4), 323–345 (2010)
28. Zheng, Z., Zhang, Y., Lyu, M.: Distributed QoS evaluation for real-world web services. In: Proceedings of the IEEE International Conference on Web Services, pp. 83–90 (2010)

Dependability of Service-Oriented Computing: Time-Probabilistic Failure Modelling

Anatoliy Gorbenko[1], Alexander Romanovsky[2]
Vyacheslav Kharchenko[1], and Olga Tarasyuk[1]

[1] Department of Computer Systems and Networks (503),
National Aerospace University, Kharkiv, Ukraine
{A.Gorbenko,O.Tarasyuk}@csac.khai.edu,
V.Kharchenko@khai.edu,
[2] School of Computing Science, Newcastle University, Newcastle upon Tyne, UK
Alexander.Romanovsky@ncl.ac.uk

Abstract. In the paper we discuss a failure and servicing model of software applications that employ the service-oriented paradigm for defining cooperation with clients. The model takes into account a time-probabilistic relationship between different servicing outcomes and failures modes. We put forward a set of measures for estimating dependability of service provisioning from the client's viewpoint and present analytical models to be used for the assessment of the mean servicing and waiting times depending on client's timeout settings.

Keywords: Service oriented computing, dependability, failure modelling, servicing time, optimal timeout settings.

1 Introduction

The Service-Oriented Architecture (SOA) supports rapid, low-cost and seamless composition of globally distributed applications, and enables effective interoperability in a loosely-coupled heterogeneous environment. Services are autonomous, platform-independent computational entities that can be dynamically discovered and integrated into a single service to be offered to the users or, in turn, used as a building block in further composition. The essential principles of SOA and services provisioning form the foundation for various modern and emerging IT technologies, such as service-oriented and cloud computing, SaaS (software as a service), etc.

The service-oriented paradigm of cooperation between clients and providers is now widely used in e-science, critical infrastructures and business-critical systems. Failures of such applications can affect people's lives and businesses (see, for example, the well-known incident at the London Stock Exchange on 8 Sept. 2008 or a spate of recent service outages on the Amazon S3 and Google cloud platforms). Thus, ensuring dependability of SOA-based systems is a must, as well as a challenge.

P. Avgeriou (Ed.): SERENE 2012, LNCS 7527, pp. 121–133, 2012.

Although the SOA and web services technologies have seen significantly improved in recent times, we believe that they have not yet revealed their full potential. In particular, SOA is still in its infancy when it comes to ensuring dependability of large-scale dynamically composed service-oriented systems involving multiple independent web services. Dependability enhancing technologies will thus be essential in supporting mission and business critical application, for personal use or in enterprise, government or military.

There is significant on-going research devoted to dependability and performance in service-oriented computing [1]. Recent related work (e.g. [2, 3, 4]) introduced several approaches to incorporating fault tolerance techniques (including voting, backward and forward error recovery mechanisms and replication techniques) into the web service architectures. There has been work on fault analysis, dependability and performance evaluation and experimental measurements, e.g. [5, 6, 7]. However, coming from dispersed areas of research, the work addresses individual issues but do not yet advance them in unison or offer general solutions. Very often the researchers use simple and, hence, not realistic failure models or do not take into account the interdependency between dependability and performance of service-oriented solutions that is in the very nature of such distributed interacting systems.

To be more effective fault-tolerant techniques incorporated into the service-oriented architecture should distinguish between evident failures of different types, like application exceptions, communication errors or timeouts and should be capable to minimize the probability of non-evident application errors.

Experimental studies [10, 12] show that response time of web services very often can exceed ones minimal value in more than 10 or even 20 times. Moreover, sometimes clients await for the response from a web service for more than two hours instead of reporting an exception or resending a request. Therefore, right timeout setting is a key means improving performance of many distributed systems including web services.

Besides most of the fault tolerance and error recovery mechanisms at the application level also depend on timeout settings [1-4]. However, the existing work mainly focuses on optimizing timeouts used by communication protocols like TCP and HTTP without examining how timeout settings at the application level affect both performance and dependability of web services.

This is why the purpose of the paper is (i) to develop an advanced failure model for the service-oriented architecture taking into account a time-probabilistic interconnection between different servicing outcomes and (ii) to investigate analytical models assessing the average servicing and waiting times under certain timeout in case of probabilistic uncertainty of web services performance characteristics.

The rest of the paper is organised as follows. In Section 2 we describe the proposed failure and servicing model capturing the fundamental principles of the service-oriented architecture from the client's point of view. Section 3 proposes analytical models aimed at estimation of average servicing and waiting time depending on timeout settings in case of known response time probability density function. In Section 4 we present a numeric example of using the proposed analytical solution.

2   SOA Failure and Servicing Model

2.1   Servicing Outcomes and Web Services Failures

Web services as any other complex software may contain faults which may manifest themselves in operation. On every request the web service may succeed, i.e. return a correct response, or fail, i.e. return an incorrect response or not return any response at all within waiting time. Such failure behaviour of the web services is characterised by the probability of failure on demand (*pfd*). This probability can be statistically measured as a ratio between r failures observed in n demands [8]. It can vary between the environments and the contexts (operational profiles) in which a web service is used.

The various factors, which affect the *pfd* may be unknown with certainty, thus the value of *pfd* may be uncertain as well. This uncertainty can be captured by a probability density series or probability distribution, built by aggregating usage experience of different clients. The response returned to the client by a web service may be of several types:

1. *correct result*;
2. *evident error* – an error that needs no special means to be detected. It concerns exception messages of different types reported to the client and notifying him about denial of the requested service for some reason;
3. *non-evident (hidden) error* – an error that can be detected only by using a multiversioning at the application level (e.g. diversity of web services used).

However, the distributed nature of the service-oriented architectural model does not guarantee that the client receives a response from the web service within the finite time. If this happens we face so-called timing failures when the response is received too late or is not received at all (see Table 1). Thus, the known dependability definition [9] should be extended for service oriented systems as the "ability to deliver service *within the expected time* that can justifiably be trusted".

Table 1. Description of possible servicing outcomes

Result's correctness	Time of receiving	Servicing outcome	Symbolic notation
Correct result		Correct servicing	OK
Non-evident (hidden) error	Until timeout	Hidden error	HE
Exception message		Evident error	EX
Correct result			
Non-evident (hidden) error	After timeout	No response during timeout (silence)	TO
Exception message			

In the Figure 1 we adopt the failure model introduced by Avizienis, et al. in [9] to the distributed nature of service-oriented systems. The model distinguishes between the two main failure domains: (i) *timing failures* when the duration of the response delivered to the client exceeds the specified waiting time – the application timeout (i.e. the service is delivered too late), and (ii) *content failures* when the content (value) of the response delivered to the client deviates from implementing the system function.

Probabilities p^{ok}, p^{he} and p^{ex} are conditional probabilities. They are conditioned on the arrival of some response within the timeout. Probabilities p^{ex} and p^{he} refer to failure modes that in the Avizienis's classification correspond to the *detectability* viewpoint, where they are classified as: *signaled* and *unsignaled* failures, respectively.

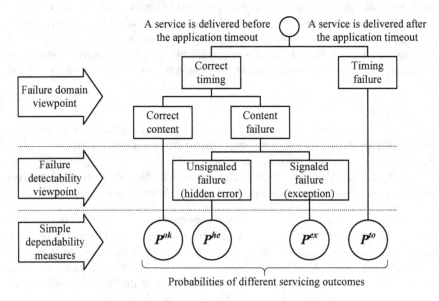

Fig. 1. Service failure modes from the failure domain viewpoint

2.2   Simple and Complex Dependability Measures

Four servicing outcomes form the set of collectively exhaustive events characterized by probabilities:

- p^{ok} – probability of correct servicing within the specified waiting time (i.e. timeout);
- p^{he} – probability of non-evident incorrect servicing within the waiting time;
- p^{ex} – probability of evident incorrect servicing (i.e. exception message reporting) within the specified waiting time;
- p^{to} – probability of timeout.

These probabilities can be combined together to form complex dependability measures characterizing different dependability attributes of a web service or service-oriented system from the client's point of view (see Table 2).

We also introduce the following two measures to estimate the performance of a web service:

- t^{av_srv} – average servicing time (average time estimated for those invocations when a response of any type (OK, HE or EX) was received by a client until the timeout);
- t^{av_wait} – average waiting time (average time estimated for all invocations including those when the timeouts were triggered). It is obvious that $t^{av\_srv} \leq t^{av\_wait}$.

Table 2. Complex dependability measures for SOA and Web Services

Dependability attribute	Measure
Accessibility (readiness for the response within the waiting time)	$1 - (p^{ex\text{-}con} + p^{to})$, where $p^{ex\text{-}con}$ is the probability of getting an exception message like "TCP connection times out" testifying to inability to establish a network connection with the remote host on the specified TCP port ($p^{ex\text{-}con}$ is a part of p^{ex}); the closer to 1 the better
Availability (readiness for the servicing within the waiting time)	$1 - \dfrac{p^{ex}}{p^{ok} + p^{he} + p^{ex}} = 1 - \dfrac{p^{ex}}{1 - p^{to}}$, i.e. the probability of getting a response until timeout excluding evident errors, i.e. {OK, HE}; the closer to 1 the better
Trustworthiness (assurance of a correct service within the waiting time)	$1 - \dfrac{p^{he}}{p^{ok} + p^{he} + p^{ex}} = 1 - \dfrac{p^{he}}{1 - p^{to}}$ or $1 - \dfrac{p^{he}}{p^{ok} + p^{he}}$, i.e. the probability that a web service returns a correct or evident incorrect response (i.e. a signalled failure), given that a response was received before the timeout; the closer to 1 the better

Usually, clients of a remote service have limited possibility to measure its dependability attributes. Most of the time it is only possible to count how many times a response from a web service is not received before the application timeout or how many times exceptional messages of different type are returned instead of the awaited response.

However, as it was shown in [13], typically the exception message does not provide enough information to understand what exactly happened and to distinguish for sure between numerous client, network or service failures. In table 2 we discuss several dependability attributes that can be practically used by a client of a service-oriented systems among those, provided in [9]:

- *Accessibility* – readiness of a service for the response of any type, i.e. {OK, HE, EX}, given that a response is received by a client before the timeout. To account the accessibility attribute client should take out the consideration a client-side exception caused by inability to establish a connection with a web service.

- *Availability* – readiness for the servicing within the waiting time. In the contrast to the classical definition of availability [9] we count here both correct and incorrect servicing (i.e. unsignalled failures) as a client usually cannot distinguish between them without applying application-specific failure detection techniques.
- *Trustworthiness* – assurance of a correct service within the waiting time. This attribute can be measured by applying the voting procedure making use of the redundancy of functionally-equivalent diverse web services provided by different vendors. A more sensitive measure that can be used in addition to the one already presented in Table 2 is the probability of getting an incorrect unsignaled response, given that a response was received (the closer to 0 the better).

2.3   Failure Model Assumptions and Properties

Probabilities p^{ok}, p^{he}, p^{ex} and p^{to} are interconnected and their values depend on the time-out settings used by a client. In our failure model we use the following assumption capturing the time-probabilistic dependence between different servicing outcomes.

Assumption 1. The sum of probabilities of all servicing outcomes {OK, HE, EX, TO} is equal to one as they form the set of collectively exhaustive events: $p^{ok} + p^{he} + p^{ex} + p^{to} = 1$

Assumption 2. Servicing time is a random variable with the known probability distribution function $f_t(t)$ and certain parameters. This function and values of its parameters can be determined by hypothesis checking using experimental data in a way, described in [10].

Assumption 3. Time during which a client waits for the response is limited by the *timeout* parameter.

Assumption 3. Probabilities of the correct (OK), evident and non-evident incorrect (EX and HE) servicing does not depend on the time when the response was received by a client. This assumption can be used if we take out of consideration some specific exceptions mainly caused by networking errors and failures. For example, usually exceptions arisen 21 seconds after a web service has been invoked by a Windows client are caused by inability of client software to establish a TCP connection with the remote host. This time depends on client's OS settings. For example, for Linux it is set at about 180 seconds by default.

The interdependency between probabilities of different servicing outcomes under the specified assumptions is shown in Fig. 2. Based on the analysis of Fig. 1 and taking into account the assumptions used we can formulate the set of properties of the proposed web services failure model.

Property 1. Value of the probability of timeout depends on the application timeout used by a client: $p^{to} = f(timeout)$. The bigger timeout value the bigger the probability of getting a response (the less the probability of timeout):

$$\forall\ timeout_1,\ timeout_2:\ timeout_1 > timeout_2 \Rightarrow \int_0^{timeout_1} f_t(t)dt > \int_0^{timeout_2} f_t(t)dt\ .$$

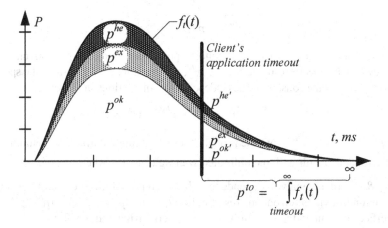

Fig. 2. Time-probabilistic interconnection between different servicing outcomes

Property 2. Changing of timeout value causes changing the probability of timeout and, hence changing (redistribution) values of p^{ok}, p^{he}, p^{ex} as long as the sum of all probabilities must be equal to one. Hence, p^{ok}, p^{he}, p^{ex} are functions of a *timeout* value.

Property 3. Probability of timeout is equal to the integral of $f_t(t)$ over the interval [timeout...∞]:

$$p^{to} = \int\limits_{timeout}^{\infty} f_t(t)dt = 1 - \int\limits_{0}^{timeout} f_t(t)dt . \tag{1}$$

Property 4. The sum of probabilities of getting a correct, evident and non-evident erroneous result $p^{ok'}$, $p^{he'}$, $p^{ex'}$ after a timeout is equal to the probability of a timeout p^{to}:

$$p^{ok'} + p^{he'} + p^{ex'} = p^{to} .$$

Property 5. The sum of probabilities of getting a correct, evident and non-evident erroneous result before (p^{ok}, p^{he}, p^{ex}) and after ($p^{ok'}$, $p^{he'}$, $p^{ex'}$) the specified timeout is equal to 1:

$$(p^{ok} + p^{ok'}) + (p^{he} + p^{he'}) + (p^{ex} + p^{ex'}) = 1 .$$

We hold properties 4 and 5 under the hypothesis that each computation eventually terminates. In practice, the client can face rare cases of a never-ending computation due to some network or service failures. If we use the TCP 'keep-alive' option these connections will be automatically terminate after two hours with the exceptional message "Connection timed out" returned to the client.

Property 6. There is a constant ratio between the corresponding probabilities of getting a correct, evident and non-evident erroneous result before (p^{ok}, p^{he}, p^{ex}) and after ($p^{ok'}$, $p^{he'}$, $p^{ex'}$) the specified timeout:

$$\frac{p^{ok}}{p^{ok'}} = \frac{p^{he}}{p^{he'}} = \frac{p^{ex}}{p^{ex'}}.$$

Property 7. Pairwise sums of the corresponding probabilities of getting a correct, evident and non-evident erroneous result before (p^{ok}, p^{he}, p^{ex}) and after $(p^{ok'}, p^{he'}, p^{ex'})$ the specified timeout are equal to the constant values independently of the timeout value:

$$(p^{ok} + p^{ok'}) = p^{ok\infty}, \quad (p^{he} + p^{he'}) = p^{he\infty}, \quad (p^{ex} + p^{ex'}) = p^{ex\infty},$$

where $p^{ok\infty}$, $p^{ex\infty}$, $p^{he\infty}$ are the probabilities of getting a correct, evident and non-evident erroneous result with the unlimited waiting time, i.e. when $timeout \to \infty$.

Property 8. There are analytic dependencies between probabilities of getting a correct, evident and non-evident erroneous result before (p^{ok}, p^{he}, p^{ex}) and after $(p^{ok'}, p^{he'}, p^{ex'})$ the specified timeout and a probability of this timeout triggered, i.e. p^{to}:

$$p^{ok} = (1 - p^{to}) \cdot p^{ok\infty}, \quad p^{he} = (1 - p^{to}) \cdot p^{he\infty}, \quad p^{ex} = (1 - p^{to}) \cdot p^{ex\infty}.$$

Taking into account the third property we can define:

$$p^{ok} = p^{ok\infty} \cdot \int_0^{timeout} f_t(t) dt \tag{2}$$

$$p^{he} = p^{he\infty} \cdot \int_0^{timeout} f_t(t) dt \tag{3}$$

$$p^{ex} = p^{ex\infty} \cdot \int_0^{timeout} f_t(t) dt \tag{4}$$

3 Average Servicing and Waiting Time Assessment Models

The average servicing time can be estimated by using a well-known equation for the mean value of the independent variable defined by its probability density function:

$$t^{av} = E[T] = \int_0^\infty t \cdot f_t(t) dt.$$

The expectation of a probability density function $f_t(t)$ truncated from the right by a *timeout* can be defined as [11]:

$$t^{av\_srv} = E^{trunc\_srv}[T] = \frac{\int_0^{timeout} t \cdot f_t(t) dt}{\int_0^{timeout} f_t(t) dt} = \frac{\int_0^{timeout} t \cdot f_t(t) dt}{F_t(t \le timeout)}. \tag{5}$$

However, equation (5) is correct only if we are interested in the average servicing time t^{av_srv} of those invocations in which a response of any type (OK, HE or EX) is received by a client before the specified timeout.

The average waiting time t^{av_wait} estimated for all invocations including those when a timeout is triggered can be defined as a sum of the average servicing time t^{av_srv} under the specified timeout and a product of the timeout value and the probability of timeout:

$$t^{av\_wait} = E^{trunc\_wait}[T] = \int_0^{timeout} t \cdot f_t(t)dt + timeout \cdot \int_{timeout}^{\infty} f_t(t)dt =$$

$$= \int_0^{timeout} t \cdot f_t(t)dt + timeout \cdot (1 - F_t(t \le timeout)). \tag{6}$$

This is due to the fact that the waiting time for those invocations for which a timeout is triggered is equal to the timeout value. Hence, the weight of a tail of the probability density function $f_t(t)$ truncated by the timeout is concentrated at the truncation border (see Fig. 3).

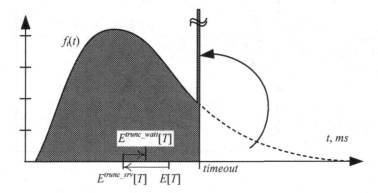

Fig. 3. Concentration of the mass of a probability of a timeout at the truncation border

4 An Example of Average Servicing and Waiting Times Estimation

This section presents an example of estimating the average servicing time t^{av_srv} and the average waiting time t^{av_wait} in case of the exponential distribution of a web service response time. By applying equations (4) and (5) we have:

$$t^{av\_srv}(timeout) = \frac{\int_0^{timeout} t \cdot \mu \cdot e^{-\mu \cdot t}}{1 - e^{-\mu \cdot timeout}} = -\frac{e^{-\mu \cdot timeout} + \mu \cdot timeout \cdot e^{\mu \cdot timeout} - 1}{\mu \cdot (1 - e^{-\mu \cdot timeout})}, \tag{7}$$

$$t^{av-wait}(timeout) = \int_{0}^{timeout} t \cdot \mu \cdot e^{-\mu \cdot t} + timeout \cdot e^{-\mu \cdot timeout} = -\frac{e^{-\mu \cdot timeout} - 1}{\mu}. \tag{8}$$

Corresponding curves of t^{av_wait} and t^{av_srv}, as well as p^{to} depending on the timeout value are shown on Fig. 4 and Fig. 5. The curves were plot using parameter μ which is equal to 0.01 that corresponds to 100 ms of average response time in case of the unlimited waiting time. Figures 4 and 5 show that, actually, there is no point in waiting for a response from a web service for more than 600 *ms* as the probability of timeouting by that time is less than $2{,}47 \cdot 10^{-3}$. At the same time an average servicing time in this case is equal to 98.5 *ms*. If the response time of a web service is subject to one of the heavy-tailed distributions, which is more realistic in practice, the profit will be more significant.

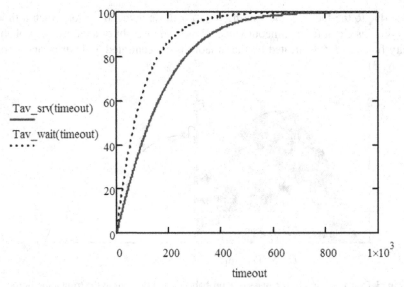

Fig. 4. Curves of the average servicing time t^{av_srv} and average waiting time t^{av_wait} depending on timeout value in case of the exponential distribution of the random response time with the parameter $\mu=0.01$

Finally, we can solve the equation (1) relatively to *timeout* and then put the result into (5) and (6). This will allow us to resolve a trade-off problem between the dependability and performance of a particular Web service. In our example (in case of exponential distribution of the Web service response time) the *timeout* can be expressed by the formula:

$$p^{to}(timeout) = \int_{timeout}^{\infty} \mu \, e^{-\mu \cdot t} dt = e^{-\mu \cdot timeout} \Rightarrow timeout(p^{to}) = -\frac{ln(p^{to})}{\mu}. \tag{9}$$

Putting it into (7) and (8) we can get equations estimating t^{av_wait} and t^{av_srv} depending on specified probability of timeout p^{to}. This dependency, shown in Fig. 6, can be used to setup application timeout and to assess performance of a web-service (using t^{av_wait} and t^{av_srv} measures) with regards to dependability requirements expressed in form of maximal allowed value of p^{to}.

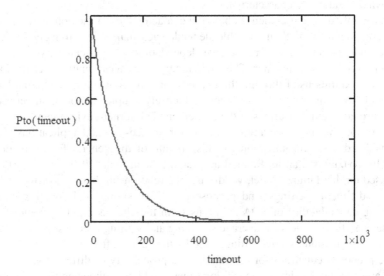

Fig. 5. Curve of the probability of timeout p^{to} depending on timeout value in case of the exponential distribution of the random response time with the parameter $\mu=0.01$

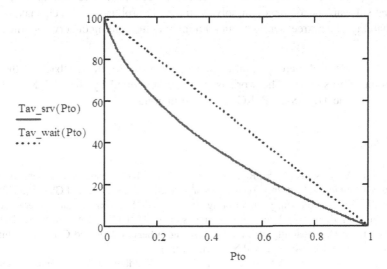

Fig. 6. Curves of the average servicing time t^{av_srv} and average waiting time t^{av_wait} depending on the probability of timeouting p^{to} in case of the exponential distribution of the random response time with the parameter $\mu=0.01$

5   Conclusions

Ensuring and assessing dependability of complex service-oriented systems are complicated when these systems are dynamically built or when their components (i.e. web services) are dynamically replaced by the new ones with the similar functionality but unknown dependability characteristics.

The lack of sufficient evidence about the characteristics of the communication medium, components and their possible dependencies makes it extremely difficult to achieve and predict (composite) service dependability which can vary over a wide range in a very random manner. This uncertainty of services running over the Internet and clouds exhibits itself through the unpredictable response times and complex failure model, resulting from the distributed and loosely-coupled cooperation between the service provider and consumers in the unpredictable Internet-environment.

In the paper we introduce a failure model for service-oriented applications, that can be considered as a specialization for this domain of the general failure model presented by Avizienis, Laprie, Randell and Landwehr in their IEEE TDSC 2004 paper [9]. Based on this failure model, we discuss the relationship between different failure modes and timeout settings, and propose the set of simple and complex measures estimating dependability of SOA solutions from the client's point of view. We also propose analytical models for average servicing and waiting times estimation depending on the application timeout settings used by the client software.

The proposed equations for estimation of a probability of different servicing outcomes and average servicing and waiting times can help in choosing the right application timeouts which are the fundamental part of all fault-tolerant mechanisms working over the Internet used as the main error detection mechanism here. Making use these equations software developers can solve a trade-off problems between maximizing the probability of a correct servicing and minimizing the waiting or servicing time.

Acknowledgement. We are grateful to Aad van Moorsel for his feedback on the earlier version of this work. The work is partially supported by the FP7 KhAI-ERA project and by the TrAmS-2 EPSRC/UK platform grant.

References

1. Cardellini, V., Casalicchio, E., Regina, K., et al. (eds.): Performance and Dependability in Service Computing: Concepts, Techniques and Research Directions. IGI Global (2012)
2. Lyu, M.: Service Reliability Engineering: Performance Evaluation, Fault Tolerance, and Reliability Prediction. In: International Symposium on High Confidence Software (2011)
3. Sargeant, A.: Dependability of Dynamic Binding in Service-Oriented Computing. In: Int. Conf. on Dependable Systems and Networks (2011)
4. Zheng, Z., Lyu, M.A.: QoS-Aware Fault Tolerant Middleware for Dependable Service Composition. In: Int. Conf. On Dependable Systems and Networks, pp. 239–248 (2009)
5. Zheng, Z., Lyu, M.: A Runtime Dependability Evaluation Framework for Fault Tolerant Web Services. In: Int. Conf. On Dependable Systems and Networks (2009)

6. Fahad, A., Saurabh, A., Saurabh, B.: Dangers and Joys of Stock Trading on the Web: Failure Characterization of a Three-Tier Web Service. In: 30th International Symposium on Reliable Distributed Systems (2011)
7. Mendes, N., Duraes, J., Madeira, H.: Evaluating and comparing the impact of software faults on web servers. In: 9th European Dependable Computing Conference (2010)
8. Smith, D., Simpson, K.: Safety Critical Systems Handbook: A Straightforward Guide to Functional Safety, IEC 61508 and Related Standards, 3rd edn. Butterworth-Heinemann, Oxford (2004)
9. Avizienis, A., Laprie, J.-C., Randell, B., Landwehr, C.: Basic Concepts and Taxonomy of Dependable and Secure Computing. IEEE Transactions on Dependable and Secure Computing 1(1), 11–33 (2004)
10. Gorbenko, A., Romanovsky, A., Mamutov, S., et al.: Real Distribution of Response Time Instability in Service-Oriented Architecture. In: 29th IEEE International Symposium on Reliable Distributed Systems, pp. 92–99 (2010)
11. Olive, D.J.: Applied Robust Statistics. Southern Illinois University Press, Illinois (2008)
12. Reinecke, P., van Moorsel, A., Wolter, K.: Experimental Analysis of the Correlation of HTTP GET Invocations. In: Horváth, A., Telek, M. (eds.) EPEW 2006. LNCS, vol. 4054, pp. 226–237. Springer, Heidelberg (2006)
13. Gorbenko, A., Kharchenko, V., Romanovsky, A., Mikhaylichenko, A.: Experimenting with exception propagation mechanisms in service-oriented architecture. In: 4th Int. Workshop on Exception Handling, pp. 1–7 (2008)

Monitoring Service Choreographies
from Multiple Sources

Amira Ben Hamida[2], Antonia Bertolino[1], Antonello Calabrò[1],
Guglielmo De Angelis[1], Nelson Lago[3], and Julien Lesbegueries[2]

[1] CNR–ISTI, Italy
{antonia.bertolino,antonello.calabro,guglielmo.deangelis}@isti.cnr.it
[2] Linagora R&D Toulouse, France
{amira.benhamida,julien.lesbegueries}@linagora.com
[3] University of São Paulo, Brazil
lago@ime.usp.br

Abstract. Modern software applications are more and more conceived
as distributed service compositions deployed over Grid and Cloud technologies. Choreographies provide abstract specifications of such compositions, by modeling message-based multi-party interactions without
assuming any central coordination. To enable the management and dynamic adaptation of choreographies, it is essential to keep track of events
and exchanged messages and to monitor the status of the underlying
platform, and combine these different levels of information into complex events meaningful at the application level. Towards this goal, we
propose a Multi-source Monitoring Framework that we are developing
within the EU Project CHOReOS, which can correlate the messages
passed at business-service level with observations relative to the infrastructure resources. We present the monitor architecture and illustrate it
on a use-case excerpted from the CHOReOS project.

Keywords: Monitoring, Choreographies, Complex Event Processing,
SOA, SLA, QoS.

1 Introduction

The Future Internet (FI) context envisions a global environment that expands
itself along two key dimensions, the Internet of Services and the Internet of
Things. Among the others, a key feature offered by these dimensions concerns the
availability of loosely-coupled methods for the management of remote resources
allowing the execution of distributed and composite service-based applications.

In this vision, black-box entities (i.e., either the services, or the things) are
discovered, chosen and bound at run-time. Specifically, this run-time binding
can take place based on the functional interface each entity exports, or on the
Quality of Service (QoS) levels they manifest. Both negotiations and run-time
bindings leave space to unexpected events or scenarios that were not considered
when designing either the single services or the whole composition.

P. Avgeriou (Ed.): SERENE 2012, LNCS 7527, pp. 134–149, 2012.
© Springer-Verlag Berlin Heidelberg 2012

Because of this inherent nondeterminism and dynamism, system *adaptation* is the key feature to pursue: paraphrasing Darwin, the applications that are going to survive in the fight for survival among the plethora of arising services, will be the ones that are the most adaptable to change. At the basis of adaption is awareness: systems must be enhanced with the capability to monitor the behaviour resulting from the composition of services and things and trigger adaption as failures occur.

We investigate such concern in the context of service choreography. Choreographies are conceived as abstract specifications, typically defined and managed by third party organizations, aimed at modeling dynamic and flexible composition of services into complex business workflows [1]. Specifically, a service choreography is a description of the *peer-to-peer* externally observable interactions that cooperating services should put in place. Such multi-party collaboration model focuses on message exchange, and no central coordination can be assumed.

The EU Project CHOReOS[1] addresses the challenges posed by the development, management and assessment of choreography-centric distributed applications, advocating a highly dynamic and user-centric model-driven approach. The project is developing an Integrated Development and Runtime Environment (IDRE), as well as an associated development process. Part of the IDRE is a framework for testing and monitoring the developed and enacted choreographies. Here, comprehensive testing techniques such as [2,3,4], have to be necessarily complemented with run-time monitoring approaches that are essential to support adaptation as well as informed run-time management activities [5].

Monitoring consists in collecting data from a running application so that they can be analyzed to either notify, or predict run-time anomalies. Several works in the literature deal with run-time software monitoring [6,7,8,9,10]. Nevertheless, the emphasis of the service-oriented paradigm natively drives the building of software systems as multi-layered [11]. Consequently, monitoring is often dealing with layer-specific events, and addressing layer-specific issues.

The main contribution of this paper is to propose a Multi-source Monitoring Framework that we are investigating within the CHOReOS project, and that can correlate the messages monitored at business-service level, with the observations captured by the infrastructure monitoring the low level resources.

The rest of the paper is organized as follows: Section 2 presents the overall architecture of our multi-source monitoring approach; then the next three sections detail the features of each specific source. Section 5 illustrates a case study while in Section 6 we contrast our results against related work. Finally, Section 7 closes the paper drawing conclusions and future work.

2   Proposed Approach

Figure 1 depicts the high-level architecture of our Multi-source Monitoring Framework. Specifically, the architecture relies on the Distributed Service Bus

---

[1] http://www.choreos.eu

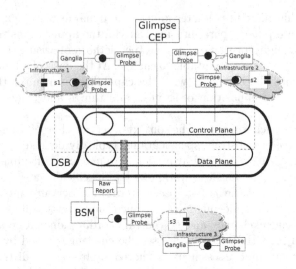

Fig. 1. Multi-source Monitoring

(DSB) component, a shared and distributed communication channel for the monitored events. The DSB distinguishes between a set of channels dedicated to the monitoring activities (i.e., `Control Plane`), and other channels where both coordination and application messages can flow (i.e. `Data Plane`). The data passing through the `Control Plane` can be correlated and analyzed by means of a Complex Event Processor (CEP).

The Multi-source Monitoring Framework integrates three different solutions by means of the DSB. Each solution provides monitoring facilities for a specific kind of source, specifically:

Infrastructure Monitoring: The monitoring elements belonging to this kind of source are focused on the knowledge of the status of the environment where both services and things are running. In this sense, these sources provide support for the monitoring of resources, both in terms of utilization and health status. As detailed in Section 3, among others approaches on resource monitoring, we will mainly implement such sources by means of Ganglia [12].

Business Service Oriented Monitoring: This kind of source is responsible for monitoring messages exchanged among services cooperating within either a workflow or a choreography by means of the DSB. Specifically, distributed interceptors are deployed in the DSB in order to capture the messages that services exchange. As reported in Section 3.1, the goal of this source is to analyze the temporal sequence of messages passing through the bus and look for violations of the choreography specification with respect to functional, QoS, or Service Level Agreement (SLA) violations.

Event Monitoring: This kind of source belongs to a generic event-based monitoring infrastructure able to bridge the notifications coming from the other two sources. As detailed in Section 4, such sources are based on Glimpse[2], which can include a coherent set of domain-specific languages, expressed as meta-models. In this way, we can exploit the support for automation offered by model-driven engineering techniques [13].

3   Infrastructure-Oriented Monitoring

Any large scale cloud-based system needs to support the monitoring of resources, both in terms of utilization and health status. This is what allows the system to perform corrective actions in order to maintain optimal resource usage (avoiding both overloading and wasting resources) and to handle failures such as crashed or overloaded nodes. A lot of sophisticated monitoring systems dedicated to resource monitoring in large-scale computing environments such as grids already exist (see Section 6); in our work, we leverage previous works by borrowing heavily from Ganglia [12]. Ganglia is one of the most successful grid monitoring systems, offering good performance, low overhead, and flexibility, which explains why it is used in several high-performance computing clusters.

The resource monitor subsystem has two main components:

1. A set of data collectors that gather local information such as load average, I/O rates, and network utilization. These collectors run on every active node of the cloud. Data for each node is both made available on demand over TCP/IP and, at the same time, periodically pushed over UDP to be replicated in nearby nodes.
2. A notification mechanism that detects potentially relevant events, such as exceptional load average or too little available disk space, and generates a corresponding notification that is forwarded to the event monitoring subsystem so that this will trigger some corrective action. This might be replicating an overloaded service, migrating services that communicate a lot to be closer together etc.

For data collection, we simply reuse the *gmond* component of Ganglia, since it offers rich functionality, low overhead, and depends on almost no configuration to work. However, *gmond* depends on static pre-configuration to identify peers for data replication, which is not adequate for a highly dynamic cloud environment. In order to tackle this configuration problem, the notification daemon running on each machine also continuously refines the list of replication peers and modifies the configuration of *gmond* accordingly.

The notification mechanism simply polls *gmond* periodically and identifies eventual relevant events according to some hard-coded rules, such as "load average above 3" or "free disk space less than 10%". Such events are forwarded to the higher-level event monitor system described in Section 4 for further analysis. It should be noted that those constitute *potentially* relevant events; it is up to the event monitor to make more refined decisions regarding what is and is not

---

[2] See at http://labse.isti.cnr.it/tools/glimpse

significant and what party to notify, according to the parameters defined by the clients of the monitoring system. Therefore, these local rules do not need to be reconfigured at run-time, which alleviates the need for communication from the CEP (to deploy configuration rules on each node); instead, they just provide "hints" about suspected problems. Accordingly, the provided information may be either used or ignored according to the more dynamic monitoring rules that are active in the CEP at each moment.

Beyond detecting problems, this monitoring subsystem may also be used to detect under-used virtual nodes, which may in turn guide the deployment of new services to reuse such nodes or trigger their removal altogether. Some of this may be accomplished by rules that provide notifications if some resource utilization is *below* some predefined rule. However, inspecting the recent history of each node's resource utilization is much more useful in this regard. We are currently working on a layer dedicated to the collection and usage of such data by making use of Ganglia's *gmetad*, but that is not yet integrated with the rest of the system in the current implementation.

3.1 Business Service Monitoring

The Business Service Monitoring (BSM) [14] is responsible for providing the monitoring functionality that relates to business services and choreographies. It ensures a multilevel service supervision, from the QoS of a service to the global business workflow control, realizing an incremental supervision from a finer to a coarse-grained level.

Basically, we take benefit from the Enterprise Service Bus (ESB) technology to build the BSM architecture on a distributed topology of bus nodes. A BSM node is considered as a bus node, onto which a particular "profile" is added in order to fulfill the requirements of the monitoring of Service Oriented Architecture (SOA). This profile provides an additional administration service, and deploys monitoring components specific for QoS and SLA management as well as for Choreographies.

Figure 2 depicts the overall architecture of the BSM. Specifically, it is composed of a Service Level Monitoring, a Choreography Level Monitoring and a Data Collector components. The BSM is exclusively based on the WS-Notifications standard that brings loosely coupled and event-driven capabilities. We assume that business services are exposed thanks to a middleware, for our case, we rely on the Petals Distributed Service Bus (DSB). The BSM can also be applied to other kinds of middleware, provided that they expose a WS-Notification producer interface.

More precisely, we implement specific interceptors that are able to send reports summarizing the message exchanges between services. We design and implement a report model for formalizing the exchange information. These reports are named Raw Reports, we detail them in Section 3.2.

Furthermore, we rely on the Data Collector that is in charge of the subscription to the middleware. For instance, when a connection to this node is requested,

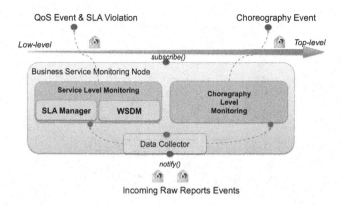

Fig. 2. Business Service Monitoring Architecture

it acts as a WS-Notifications broker. Then, Components that are interested in specific topics subscribe on its events.

In the following, the internal mechanisms of the BSM are detailed. Specifically, Section 3.2 details the interception mechanisms enabling the monitoring when deployed on the middleware. Then, Section 3.3 presents the Runtime Quality Assessment. Finally, Section 3.4 describes the choreography monitoring.

3.2   Interception Mechanisms

Targeting ultra-large scaled environments, the monitoring mechanisms needs to be as transparent and non intrusive as possible. Adopting lightweight and decoupled architectures enhances the ability of the system to be maintained in a flexible way. To that purpose, we adopt an interception mechanism that we deploy in the middleware automatically for enabling services monitoring when activated. Each time an endpoint to a service is created into the middleware, we assign to it an interceptor that will listen to the calls from and to the service.

In each exchange a set of basic information can be extracted. In order to formalize this information, we create a dedicated model that we call Raw Report. Raw Reports contain useful data such as the identifiers for the consumer and the provider, the monitored exchange id, the called operation, a date, the size of the message, and informs if the response is a fault or not. It is important to notice each Raw Report contains two reports, corresponding to the different places the interception is made. Indeed, the interception mechanism allows to perform interceptions at 4 different time stamps (see Figure 3), at the following steps: (i) T1, before the request goes from the client to the provider, (ii) T2, after the request reaches the provider, (iii) T3, before the response goes from the provider to the client, and (iv) at T4, after the response reaches the consumer.

We exploit these Raw Reports in order to assess the services are behaving as contracted in the SLA. In the following section, we detail the operated QoS run-time assessment.

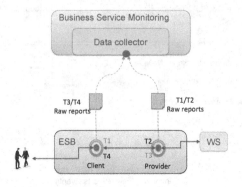

Fig. 3. Raw Reports time stamps illustration

3.3   Runtime Quality Assessment

We rely on a standard based mechanism for ensuring the services run-time quality monitoring and assessment. The use of standards increases the compliance with a wider range of services. We implement standards coming from the Web Services domain, namely, the Web Services Distributed Management (WS-DM[3]) and the Web Services Agreement[4].

We adopt the following process. At the beginning, services contract service level agreements that describe their performances (time, security, etc.). Once deployed, services face the run-time conditions and their real performances may be different from the ones stated in the SLA. More precisely and referring to the BSM architecture in Figure 2, the WSDM Manager receives the Raw Reports from the DataCollector and computes QoS metrics for each service. A prior subscription-based mechanism (with *CreationResource* topic) triggers the creation of a non-functional endpoint in the BSM, for each functional endpoint deployed, then a notification is sent to the BSM when a connected DSB declares a new endpoint. This non-functional endpoint stores current metrics, computed thanks to the gathered Raw Reports. These metrics are updated each time the monitored service is invoked.

The second component dedicated to the Service Level Monitoring is the SLA Manager which is in charge to check if the SLA metrics are being violated. To fulfill this, the SLA component receives the Raw Reports from the DataCollector and checks if a particular exchange is violating an agreement (Service Level Agreement). When an agreement is loaded in the SLA Manager, we define a consumer. Then, an SLA alert can potentially be sent as an upper level monitoring notification. We apply the Common Alerting Protocol (CAP[5]) to formalize the alert.

---

[3] http://www.oasis-open.org/committees/wsdm

[4] http://www.ogf.org/documents/GFD.107.pdf

[5] http://docs.oasis-open.org/emergency/cap/v1.2/CAP-v1.2-os.html

In addition to the performances and QoS verification, the BSM is also able to detect if a service deployed on a remote machine is answering or not thanks to the interceptions that we realize at 2 times. Indeed, once the T1/T2 report is received by the SLA Manager, a timer is started (provided the agreement is about latency) and if the time waiting the T3/T4 report is higher than the latency defined in the SLA, a first potential alert is sent. If the T3/T4 report is finally received and the effective latency is really violating the SLA, then a confirmation alert is sent. The alert can also be invalidated and the confirmation alert is canceled. The latency computed is the difference between T3 and T2 dates values. This calculus represents the time taken by the service request and response outside the DSB. The times taken between T1 and T2, and T3 and T4 are considered as negligible. However, if a problem occurring in the middleware provokes the violation of the SLA, the service is not considered as the origin of the violation. The collected events are sent to the CEP that identifies the nature of the violation and forwards an alert to a governing decision entity (e.g. a Choreography Governing Board) that would trigger when needed the reconfiguration of the choreography by the replacement of the failed services. Meanwhile, detailing the applied decision mechanism is beyond of the scope of this paper.

3.4   Choreography Level Monitoring

In addition to the Runtime Quality Assessment, the BSM dedicates a component for the monitoring of the choreographies, the Choreography Level Monitoring Manager. It is responsible for the communication level and gathers the messages exchanged within services collaborations and interactions. The main functionality of this component is to ensure that the choreographies are behaving according to the specification policies.

The Choreography Level Monitoring Manager takes as input the choreography specification written in BPMN 2.0 and put interceptors on the services involved in the choreography and exposed thanks to the middleware. The services are event producers that trigger Raw Report as described in Section 3.2.

We realize a correspondence between the choreography model and the monitoring activities generated from the model. A specific structure called MEMB (for Message Exchange Monitoring Behavior) is implemented for this sake. Each MEMB subscribes to Raw Reports, related to the choreography coordination logic. Then, it waits for the expected notifications and checks the several timestamps validity. In case of timeout or not acceptable timestamps, alerts are sent to the CEP 4.

4   Event-Oriented Monitoring

In [13], the authors proposed a distributed event-based monitoring infrastructure called Glimpse, developed with the goal of decoupling the event specification from the analysis mechanism. We reuse Glimpse as a component of the Multi-source Monitoring framework.

Glimpse (see Figure 4) collects a representative set of raw observation data, and then needs to interpret such raw information in order to recognize composite events that may be relevant at higher abstraction levels. The proper combination and correlation of such raw events make it possible either to timely detect unexpected behaviors of the systems, or to predict failures for enhancing system resilience.

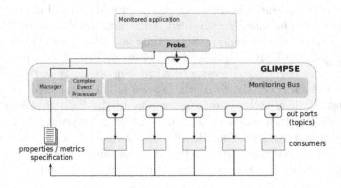

Fig. 4. Glimpse: high-level architecture

Probes are in charge to collect and/or send raw data deriving from the execution of a process within a choreography. Any instance of a Glimpse probe can implement a component in execution at a given observation layer of the software, for example at the infrastructure level (i.e. interacting with Ganglia – see Section 3), or at business level (i.e. interacting with the BSM – see Section 3.1). These two kind of probes can provide data that Glimpse can use to infer complex pattern of events. A detailed description about the communication interfaces defined by a Glimpse probe can be found in [15].

Glimpse implements the data transmission layer by means a publish-subscribe bus, that constitutes the communication backbone conveying all information (events, requests, notifications) flowing among all components. With respect to our Multi-source Monitoring architecture depicted in Figure 1, this bus is implemented by the DSB, as anticipated in Section 2.

The core of the event-oriented monitoring system offered by Glimpse is the CEP. Specifically, the CEP is a rule engine which analyzes the raw events, generated from the probes belonging to all sources (i.e. infrastructure, business service message), and infers complex events matching a set of rules that can be dynamically loaded. In this sense the resilience of the monitored system is enhanced by dynamically adapting to the evolving criticalities of the system. As detailed in [13], the current implementation of the CEP is based on the Drools Fusion rule language[6].

---

[6] See http://www.jboss.org/drools/drools-fusion.html

Finally, the Manager component is the orchestrator of the Glimpse architecture. It manages all communications between the various instances of the Glimpse components. Specifically, the Manager fetches requests received from consumer, analyzes them and instructs the CEP. It then creates a dedicated channel on which it will provide the results produced by the CEP.

5 Case Study

We present one of the use-cases developed within the CHOReOS project. Specifically, it is based on the "Passenger-friendly Airport" [16] scenario, modeling the interactions that take place among different actors (i.e. both services and things) in an airport by means of a set of choreographies. In particular, this case study refers to the monitoring of non-functional properties during the interactions between a Weather Forecast Service (i.e. WF) and a smart-device referred to as Mobile Internet Device (i.e. MID).

In the following we describe how an SLA violation can be due to two possible issues that our Multi-source Monitoring framework contributes to analyze and discover. Specifically, we assume that monitoring the interactions between the WF and the MID as described in Section 3.1, an SLA violation is revealed. Such violation could be due to either the current status of the infrastructure hosting WF, or the implementation of the service WF.

In the former case, the monitoring system reveals that the SLA is going to be violated due either an overload, or a crash of the machine hosting the service. Thus, the rule can suggest a migration of the service on another (more powerful, more reliable) machine in the infrastructure. While in the latter, the monitoring system reveals that the SLA is going to be violated even though the machine is available and is not overloaded. Here, the CEP can notify the redeployment of an updated version of the service WF.

Configuration of the Infrastructure Monitoring: On each created node, we set up the DSB server, deploy the Ganglia *gmond* daemon and the notification mechanism, and inject the address for the Glimpse CEP onto its configuration file. Finally, we deploy the actual services we are interested in. The notification mechanism periodically sends an "alive" message to the Glimpse CEP; this allows Glimpse to detect node failures. Other than that, we set it to notify the CEP whenever the load average of any node goes above 3[7]. While the typical load average on a production system may vary a lot depending on the application, such a value is a common indicator that the machine is overloaded either because of too much I/O or too much CPU utilization. More sophisticated information might be used, but we leave these out of scope for this example.

Configuration of the BSM Mechanism: First, the BSM receives raw reports giving information about each service exchange, in particular involving the WF

---

[7] On Unix-like systems, the load average is the average number of processes in the queue waiting for processor time in the last minute.

service. This is done thanks to a prior subscription to the ESB middleware on
Raw Report topic. In addition, a SLA between the WF and the MID services
is loaded. This action launches a routine that uses raw reports notifications to
check for possible violations. When a violation occurs, the BSM sends a SLA
alert to the CEP.

Presentation of the Rules for the CEP: The CEP must be instructed with
a set of rules matching the event set that satisfies the monitoring request.

```
1   <ComplexEventRuleActionList ... >
2     <Insert RuleType="drools">
3     <RuleName>Machine Overloaded</RuleName>
4     <RuleBody>
5     ...
6       rule "Check for overloads"
7       ...
8         when
9           $aEvent : GlimpseBaseEventImpl(this.serviceID == "WF", this.serviceInstanceID == "
              WF1234", this.getConsumed == false, this.isException == false);
10          $bEvent : GlimpseBaseEventImpl(this.machineID == "hubble.eclipse.ime.usp.br", this
              .data == "Machine overload", this.isException == false, this.getConsumed == false,
              this after $aEvent);
11        then
12          $aEvent.setConsumed(true);
13          update( $aEvent );
14          retract( $aEvent );
15          ResponseDispatcher.NotifyMeValue(... ...);
16        end
17    </RuleBody>
18    </Insert>
19  </ComplexEventRuleActionList>
```

Listing 1. Check for machine overload rule

```
1   <ComplexEventRuleActionList ... >
2     <Insert RuleType="drools">
3       <RuleName>Machine Overloaded No Ganglia Notification</RuleName>
4         <RuleBody>
5     ...
6         rule "Machine Overloaded No Ganglia Notification"
7         ...
8           when
9             $aEvent : GlimpseBaseEventImpl(this.serviceID == "WF", this.serviceInstanceID ==
                  "WF1234", this.getConsumed == false, this.isException == false)
10                not (GlimpseBaseEventImpl(this.machineID == "hubble.eclipse.ime.usp.br"
                      , this.isException == false, this.getConsumed == false, this after
                      [0s, 30s] $aEvent))
11          then
12            $aEvent.setConsumed(true);
13            update( $aEvent );
14            retract( $aEvent );
15            ResponseDispatcher.NotifyMeValue( ... ... );
16          end
17        </RuleBody>
18    </Insert>
19  </ComplexEventRuleActionList>
```

Listing 2. SLA Violation and machine is not answering

```
1   <ComplexEventRuleActionList ... >
2   <Insert RuleType="drools">
3     <RuleName>SLAViolation</RuleName>
4       <RuleBody>
5       ...
6       rule "SLAViolation"
7       ...
8       when
9         $aEvent : GlimpseBaseEventImpl(this.serviceID == "WF", this.serviceInstanceID == "
          WF1234", this.getConsumed == false, this.isException == false);
10        $bEvent : GlimpseBaseEventImpl(this.machineID == "hubble.eclipse.ime.usp.br", this
          after $aEvent, this.data == "ALIVE");
11        $cEvent : GlimpseBaseEventImpl(this.machineID == "hubble.eclipse.ime.usp.br", this
          after $bEvent, this.data == "ALIVE");
12        then
13        $aEvent.setConsumed(true);
14        update( $aEvent );
15        retract( $aEvent );
16        $bEvent.setConsumed(true);
17        update( $bEvent );
18        retract( $bEvent );
19        $cEvent.setConsumed(true);
20        update( $cEvent );
21        retract( $cEvent );
22        ResponseDispatcher.NotifyMeValue(... ...);
23      end
24    </RuleBody>
25  </Insert>
26  </ComplexEventRuleActionList>
```

Listing 3. SLA Violation due to uncorrect service behaviour rule

According to this case study, three rules have been implemented in order to cover the possible behaviors of the services involved. Such implementations correlate the events notified from the BSM related to a violation of an SLA, with the status/overload events coming from Ganglia.

Listing 1 reports a first rule that reveals if any of the machines used in the infrastructure is overloaded. Specifically, in this case the rule matches if two events are triggered to the CEP : the notification of an SLA violation form the BSM about service WF (see at line 9); the notification that the specific machine hosting the service is overloaded (see at line 10). In this case, the body of the rule specifies to consume the event about the SLA notification (see lines 12-14) , and it notifies possibly to an entity (e.g. a Choreography Governing Board) responsible for the correct operativeness of the choreography (see line 15). Similarly, the rule reported at Listing 2, matches if any SLA violation has been notified by the BSM at the service-level, and if one of the machine at the infrastructure level failed to send the "alive-notification" to the CEP. This rule highlights the case that either a machine crash occurred, or anyhow that it is not reachable anymore. Finally, the last rule (see Listing 3) correlates a notification from the BSM that the service WF is violating the SLA (see line 9), with the monitoring of the infrastructure revealing that the machine hosting the service is not overloaded. Specifically, in this case study a machine is not overloaded when the CEP receives at least two "alive" messages after the notification of the SLA violatoin (see lines 10-11). As introduced above, in this case the rule infers that the violation might be due to the incorrect (non-functional) behavior of WF. Note that, in these examples we used a hard-coded hostname here, but more sophisticated means of defining this or querying a remote list of machines might be feasible. For example, within the scope of the CHOReOS project we will rely on the specific API that the CHOReOS IDRE will provide.

6   Related Work

As we are arguing in this work, also [11] discusses how monitoring in SOA cannot separately address layer-specific issues. In fact, problems that from one layer affect the others cannot be captured and understood. Nevertheless, the work in [11] focused on the monitoring and adaptation of service orchestrations (i.e. BPEL processes) that are deployed onto a dynamic infrastructure. Thus, the solution does not directly refer to distributed choreographies where service aggregation is coordinated in a decentralised way. In this sense, our approach cannot rely on any entity that is specifically responsible of enacting the choreography, or of restructuring and adapting any running instance.

Also in [17], a multi-layered service-oriented monitoring framework that focuses on both the platform and the infrastructure layers is presented. The primary goal of that approach is to collect and aggregate monitored information with regard to specific performance constraints. Two are the main differences with our framework. First, our architecture is based on a distributed service bus implementing publish/subscribe communication mechanisms, while the core of the monitoring framework in [17] is implemented as a centralized orchestrator (i.e. a Globus Service) monitoring all the applications on the connected virtual environments. Thus, our architecture appears more scalable, since the publish/-subscribe paradigm natively allows to adapt the number of component instances by replicating them over the bus. Note that also the DSB can be implemented by federating several distributed instances of a bus. As a second difference between the two solutions is that our Multi-source Monitoring framework explicitly supports a correlation technique that makes use of complex event processing, while the approach in [17] mainly focuses in collecting, and storing the monitored indexes in suitable repositories.

In [18] the authors proposed a monitoring approach that enables autonomous service provisioning in federated clouds. Among the others, the framework was mainly conceived to support either the deployment, or the decommission of the requested services as virtual machines on a specific IaaS. Thus the main difference with our approach is that such solution conceives the sources of the monitoring mainly as layers of the same kind. In our approach we combine events that happen onto different abstraction layers.

Another family of works related to this paper concerns those monitoring solutions that are tailored to capture events at a specific abstraction layer (i.e. the infrastructure level). Accordingly, basic monitoring of hardware system resources is an essential component of virtually any production environment.

There are many reasonably similar monitoring systems available today that focus on hardware resources[8].

Furthermore, a lot of sophisticated monitoring systems that deal with large-scale computing environments such as grids also exist [12,19,20,21]. Some of them have been designed with a specific environment in mind [22,23,24] and, therefore, are either tied to characteristics of these environments or serve some specific purpose within them. Most, however, try to be generic. Accordingly, a proposal for the general characteristics expected of a monitoring system has been prepared [25].

7   Conclusions and Future Work

The FI world challenges the SOA by raising scalability, distribution and hetero-geneity issues. In this vision, either the services, or the things are discovered, chosen and bound at run-time. In this context, usually cooperations are regu-lated by means of choreographies, modeling dynamic and flexible composition of services/things. Nevertheless, as choreographies are abstract specifications, they may include interaction schemas that can evolve after the design phase, so that unexpected events or scenarios may actually take place at run-time.

In this work we presented a Multi-source Monitoring Framework, through which the non-functional properties of choreographies can be kept under obser-vation. Specifically, it supports the observation at run-time of anomalies that are due to phenomena originated from sources operating at different abstraction layers.

Both the overall architecture of the framework, and the application case study are developed within the context of the CHOReOS project. So, as future work we will keep working of the refinement of the implementation we already have, and we are planning to extensively validate our framework by applying it on final version of one the use-cases of ultra-large scale service choreographies that will be released by the CHOReOS project.

Acknowledgements. This paper is supported by the EU FP7 Projects: CHOReOS (IP 257178), NESSoS (NoE 256980), and CONNECT (FET IP 231167).

References

1. Barker, A., Walton, C.D., Robertson, D.: Choreographing web services. IEEE T. Services Computing 2(2), 152–166 (2009)
2. Besson, F.M., Leal, P.M., Kon, F., Goldman, A., Milojicic, D.: Towards automated testing of web service choreographies. In: Proc. of AST, pp. 109–110. ACM, Waikiki (2011)

---

[8] Popular examples are Nagios (www.nagios.org), Big Brother and Xymon (www.bb4.org, xymon.sourceforge.net), cacti (www.cacti.net), and zabbix (www.zabbix.com).

3. Bertolino, A., De Angelis, G., Kellomäki, S., Polini, A.: Enhancing service federation trustworthiness through online testing. IEEE Computer 45(1), 66–72 (2012)

4. De Angelis, F., De Angelis, G., Polini, A.: A counter-example testing approach for orchestrated services. In: Proc. of ICST, pp. 373–382. IEEE CS, Paris (2010)

5. Bertolino, A., De Angelis, G., Polini, A.: Validation and verification policies for governance of service choreographies. In: Proc. of WEBIST. SciTePress (April 2012)

6. Bianculli, D., Ghezzi, C.: Monitoring conversational web services. In: Di Nitto, E., et al. (eds.) IW-SOSWE, pp. 15–21. ACM (2007)

7. Campos, J.: Survey paper: Development in the application of ict in condition monitoring and maintenance. Comput. Ind. 60(1) (2009)

8. Hofmann, R., Klar, R., Mohr, B., Quick, A., Siegle, M.: Distributed performance monitoring: Methods, tools, and applications. IEEE Trans. Parallel Distrib. Syst. 5(6), 585–598 (1994)

9. Maia, J.L., Zorzo, S.D.: Socket-Masking and SNMP: A Hybrid Approach for QoS Monitoring in Mobile Computing Environments. In: Proc. of JCC, p. 106. IEEE CS, Washington, DC (2002)

10. Wang, C., Xu, L., Peng, W.: Conceptual design of remote monitoring and fault diagnosis systems. Inf. Syst. 32(7), 996–1004 (2007)

11. Guinea, S., Kecskemeti, G., Marconi, A., Wetzstein, B.: Multi-layered Monitoring and Adaptation. In: Kappel, G., Maamar, Z., Motahari-Nezhad, H.R. (eds.) ICSOC 2011. LNCS, vol. 7084, pp. 359–373. Springer, Heidelberg (2011)

12. Sacerdoti, F.D., Katz, M.J., Massie, M.L., Culler, D.E.: Wide area cluster monitoring with ganglia. In: Proc. of CLUSTER (2003)

13. Bertolino, A., Calabrò, A., Lonetti, F., Di Marco, A., Sabetta, A.: Towards a Model-Driven Infrastructure for Runtime Monitoring. In: Troubitsyna, E.A. (ed.) SERENE 2011. LNCS, vol. 6968, pp. 130–144. Springer, Heidelberg (2011)

14. Lesbegueries, J., Ben Hamida, A., Salatgè, N., Zribi, S., Lorrè, J.: Experience report: Multilevel event-based monitoring framework for the petals enterprise service bus. In: Proc. of DEBS. ACM (to appear, 2012)

15. Bertolino, A., De Angelis, G., Polini, A. (eds.): V&V tools and infrastructure – strategies, architecture and implementation. Number Del. D4.2.1. The CHOReOS Consortium (2012)

16. Chatel, P., Leger, A., Lockerbie, J. (eds.): "Passenger-friendly airport" scenarios specification and requirements analysis. Number Del. D6.1. The CHOReOS Consortium (2011)

17. Katsaros, G., Kousiouris, G., Gogouvitis, S.V., Kyriazis, D., Menychtas, A., Varvarigou, T.: A self-adaptive hierarchical monitoring mechanism for clouds. JSS 85(5), 1029–1041 (2012)

18. Kertész, A., Kecskemeti, G., Marosi, C.A., Oriol, M., Franch, X., Marco, J.: Integrated monitoring approach for seamless service provisioning in federated clouds. In: Stotzka, R., Schiffers, M., Cotronis, Y. (eds.) PDP, pp. 567–574. IEEE (2012)

19. Newman, H.B., Legrand, I.C., Galvez, P., Voicu, R., Cirstoiu, C.: Monalisa: A distributed monitoring service architecture. In: Talk from the Computing in High Energy and Nuclear Physics (2003)

20. Truong, H.-L., Fahringer, T.: SCALEA-G: A Unified Monitoring and Performance Analysis System for the Grid. In: Dikaiakos, M.D. (ed.) AxGrids 2004. LNCS, vol. 3165, pp. 202–211. Springer, Heidelberg (2004)

21. Andreozzi, S., De Bortoli, N., Fantinel, S., Ghiselli, A., Rubini, G.L., Tortone, G., Vistoli, M.C.: GridICE: a monitoring service for grid systems. Future Generation Computer Systems 21(4) (April 2005)

22. Boulon, J., Konwinski, A., Qi, R., Rabkin, A., Yang, E., Yang, M.: Chukwa, a large-scale monitoring system. In: Proc. of CCA (2008)
23. Park, K.S., Pai, V.S.: CoMon: a mostly-scalable monitoring system for PlanetLab. OSR 40(1), 65–74 (2006)
24. Wolski, R., Spring, N.T., Hayes, J.: The network weather service: a distributed resource performance forecasting service for metacomputing. Future Generation Computer Systems 15(5-6) (October 1999)
25. Tierney, B., Aydt, R., Gunter, D., Smith, W., Swany, M., Taylor, V., Wolski, R.: A grid monitoring architecture. Memo GFD-I.7. Global Grid Forum (2002)

Supporting Field Investigators with PVS: A Case Study in the Healthcare Domain

Paolo Masci[1,*], Dominic Furniss[2],
Paul Curzon[1], Michael D. Harrison[1], and Ann Blandford[2]

[1] School of Electronic Engineering and Computer Science
Queen Mary University of London
{paolo.masci,paul.curzon,michael.harrison}@eecs.qmul.ac.uk
[2] UCL Interaction Centre
University College London
{d.furniss,a.blandford}@ucl.ac.uk

Abstract. This paper reports the lessons learnt about the benefits of using a formal verification tool like PVS to support field studies. The presentation is based on a field study in the healthcare domain which was designed to investigate the resilience of human behaviour in an oncology ward of a hospital. The automated reasoning tool PVS was used systematically to compare actual practice observed during the field study with normative behaviour described for example by user manuals for the devices involved. The approach helped (i) identify latent situations that could lead to hazard, and (ii) suggest situations likely to warrant further investigation as part of the field study. The main contribution of this paper is a set of detailed examples that illustrate how we used PVS during the field study, and how the tool led to insights.

Keywords: Experience report, Field study, Socio-technical system, Automated reasoning, PVS.

1   Introduction

One approach to understanding complex socio-technical systems prior to introducing new technology is to undertake field studies. Field studies involve going to the real workplace to investigate how work is actually done, e.g., by observing workers and asking them questions. Little research addresses tool support that would help investigators during these field studies. To date, software tools developed and used by field researchers mainly focus on storing and encoding information — see for instance [14]. This paper explores how an already existing tool typically used to verify hardware and software can be used to reason about the field study data that is collected in a way that is accessible to field researchers. The aim is to automate routine checks, for example how consistent the information is, as well as to identify systematically those situations that are likely to warrant further investigation. The concern is to identify situations

---

* Corresponding author.

P. Avgeriou (Ed.): SERENE 2012, LNCS 7527, pp. 150–164, 2012.
© Springer-Verlag Berlin Heidelberg 2012

where gaps in the way artefacts and information resources support user actions may create sufficient preconditions for unsafe user actions potentially leading to harm. Previous work [2,6,7] has explored the benefits of using verification tools when re-analysing data from already completed field studies. In particular, we were able to gather additional insights about the socio-technical system, and we argued there that such an analysis could help when performed *during* the field study. However we had no direct evidence to support the claim. This paper builds on that research, in the context of a live field investigation. We report on our experience and the lessons learnt.

Contribution. We illustrate in detail how we used the PVS verification system to support investigations as part of a field study. The focus relates to specific situations faced during a field study carried out in the oncology ward of a hospital. Relatively simple use of the PVS verification system (i) helped identify latent situations that could lead to hazard, and (ii) suggested situations that warranted further investigation as part of the field study.

The rest of the paper is structured as follows. Section 2 makes clear how field studies and formal methods complement each other, and the benefits that can be obtained from their combined use. Section 3 describes artefacts and technologies involved in a particular procedures relating to glucose monitoring that were considered during the field study. Section 4 briefly introduces the PVS verification system and describes the modelling approach and the developed PVS models. Section 5 illustrates how a relatively simple use of PVS can provide useful insights for the field study. Specific real situations we faced during the field study in the oncology ward of a hospital will be the focus. They illustrate the obtained results and the lessons learnt. Section 6 contrasts and compares the approach with related work in the area and draws conclusions.

2   Integrating Field Studies and Formal Methods

Formal methods and field studies are traditionally seen as alternative approaches to analysing a system derived from completely different paradigms. On the one hand, formal methods are typically used to verify whether given properties hold for a model of the system under certain assumptions, and they are typically concerned with normative behaviour described in manuals and protocols. On the other hand, field studies focus on empirical approaches and aim to analyse how a system works 'in the wild' when deployed in the real world.

An alternative and more constructive perspective is to see the two approaches as complementary [15], and use them within a cyclical process where they feed each other. This paper illustrates the lessons learnt from a successful story of integration of field studies and formal methods to analyse the resilience of a complex socio-technical system — a hospital ward where a new device has been introduced with the aim of making the overall system more robust and efficient.

The field study proved invaluable in that it enabled: (i) identification of the information resources required by participants in the work; (ii) understanding of the difference between work as intended and documented as procedures, and work as practised; (iii) understanding of the gaps in the way that actions are resourced; (iv) a broad exploration of safety goals that are not achievable because circumstances conspire against them.

The formal reasoning tool has been used at the same time as field study to inform it and be informed by it. It provided essential benefits in: (i) making the categories precise; (ii) analysing the links between information resources and actions systematically; (iii) exploring the consequences of prescribed procedures systematically.

The rest of this paper develops these points and illustrates in detail our pragmatic use of field study data and formal methods.

3   Glucose Monitoring Procedure in the Oncology Ward of a Hospital

This section illustrates some relevant observations made in the field about the actual use of the introduced technology in the oncology ward under investigation. The technology adopted is a handheld wireless device to help clinicians get frequent blood glucose readings from patients. The field study was performed during the first months of introduction of the device.

The ward has 24 beds for accommodating patients that need to stay overnight in the hospital whilst they are treated. Whilst in hospital, patients who are diabetic need their blood glucose levels managed. These levels can be affected by the patient's glucose intake, treatment and condition, so they need to be monitored closely to make sure they are not too high or too low. Either could lead to further health problems. The introduced device is used to monitor these levels. Information recorded on the meter during a reading can be automatically stored in the patient's record.

The main features of the device and the procedure described in the manual to perform the blood glucose test are the focus of attention in what follows. This information is compared with the procedures followed by clinicians observed during the field study. The description we give here is provided at a level of detail that is adequate to illustrate the benefits of using the verification tool during a field study. These descriptions are translated into a PVS model (Section 4) so that PVS can be used to analyse the model (Section 5).

3.1   Blood Glucose Meter and Accessory Box

The blood glucose meter adopted is a palm-sized portable device [9] that allows clinicians to measure blood glucose levels by means of small test strips that are inserted in a slot at the top of the device. The device has a touch screen that can be used by clinicians to view the patient's previous blood glucose test results as well as the patient's record. A reproduction of the device layout is shown in Figure 1. The device also has an integrated barcode scanner located close to the port that receives test strips used for identification purposes. The device supports a number of features, which we summarise.

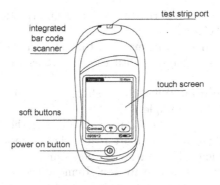

Fig. 1. Reproduction of the blood glucose meter

Clinician and Patient Identification. The device has a built-in barcode scanner that allows a clinician to identify a patient as well as the clinician taking the reading. This feature aims to guarantee that (i) only authorised personnel can use the device, and (ii) blood glucose readings are automatically associated with the right patient.

Wireless Connectivity. The device can be configured to communicate with a central server through a wireless connection. This makes it possible to synchronise in real-time with a central data management system that contains information about patients.

Quality Control. Device functionalities and accuracy must be checked regularly using special liquid compounds ("control and linearity solutions") that make sure that the glucose testing is accurate and reliable.

The glucose meter ensemble includes an accessory box for convenient transportation of meter and consumables. The accessory box contains: two test strip vials to perform the test, single use lancets to puncture the patient's finger, small boxes for disposable white swabs, control and linearity solutions to perform quality control tests. The glucose meter is battery-powered. A base unit is provided to recharge the meter's batteries when docked in the unit. The unit can be hard-wired to a local area network to enable data transfer to and from a central data management system.

3.2   Normative Procedure from the User Manual

The normative procedure described in the device user manual [10] and various training material [13] is given as a sequence of steps. The procedure is the following (we adapted the original text here to match the level of detail needed for our illustrative example).

1. **Identify clinician.** Power on the device and scan the clinician's badge.
2. **Identify patient.** Enter the patient's account number by either scanning the patient's bar coded wristband or manually.

3. **Verify test strip code.** Verify the strip code information by pressing "scan" and scanning the vial barcode.
4. **Insert test strip in the meter.** Insert a test strip with the test strip window facing up. Insert the end with the silver bars. Insert test strip before dosing.
5. **Obtain blood sample.** When the flashing drop icon appears on the meter display, obtain a blood sample
6. **Wait for the results.** An hourglass will appear on the display while waiting for the result. When the results are ready, choose an appropriate comment from a list of pre-loaded comments, as necessary.
7. **Remove test strip from the meter.** Remove the test strip from the meter and discard it according to infection control policy.
8. **Turn off meter and dispose gloves.** Press the power off button to turn the meter off. Remove gloves and dispose of them.
9. **Document test results.** Document the blood glucose result with date, time, and clinician's initials on flow sheet or chart as required.

3.3   Actual Procedure Observed at the Hospital Ward

The field investigator provided the following notes after spending some days on the ward. He observed various clinicians during their visits to patients for the blood glucose test, and talked to them to obtain explanations of what they did. In the following we report some relevant observations (we adapted the original text from the field notes to match the level of detail needed for our illustrative example).

Prepare Trolley. The blood glucose test was performed on a series of patients. Because of this, the clinician prepared a wheeled trolley to carry all the necessary equipment. The wheeled trolley contained two platforms to separate clean apparatus from waste. The top platform was used to hold the accessory box and a box of disposable gloves. The bottom platform had a bin for sharps and special refuse. A cardboard tray was also carried on the trolley for temporary location of used items, e.g., used swabs or used test strips, before they were transferred to the bin for sharps and special refuse.

Annotate Bed Numbers. The numbers of the beds that are to be visited are reported on handover sheets. The clinician scribbled these bed numbers on the cardboard tray so as to create a checklist that was easy to access and update.

Unlock Device. The glucose meter is undocked from the base unit, powered on, and unlocked to initiate a new session. This is done to check whether the device is functioning properly and whether the device requires a quality control test. The badge number of a trained member of staff is needed to unlock the device and initiate the session. Such a number can either be scanned or manually entered.

Visit Patients. The visit starts after checking that the trolley and the accessory box has sufficient consumables for the whole set of patients that must be visited. At each bed, the clinician carried out the following sequence of activities:

- Ask the patient consent to perform the test. Some patients may refuse to do the test, or may be away from their bed for other reasons, e.g. treatment in other areas of the hospital. In these cases, the clinician skips the patient and goes to the next bed in the list.
- Scan the patient barcode. If the device is not able to correctly scan the barcode (e.g., because the wristband is crumpled), the clinician enters the number manually. Sometimes the device does not have information about the patient; in these cases, the device allows the clinician to continue and they proceed.
- Scan the strip container.
- Puncture finger.
- Insert test strip in the device (this activity is sometimes performed before puncturing the finger).
- Put blood on the strip.
- Wait for the test results.
- Record the test results in the glucose chart. The chart includes a number (the current test result), and a graph reporting the history of results (the clinician updates the graph with the current result). If the result is too high or too low, the clinician must report this to the nurse looking after that patient.

Visit End. When all patients have been visited, the device is docked to the base unit and the trolley emptied.

4 PVS Models

In this section, we illustrate the PVS models we developed out of the gathered field study data. The field data were organised according to the DiCoT method [3]. This method encodes relevant categories that are employed by the various users within the system and their means of communication. Inevitably the field data are open to alternative interpretations. The advantage of a less formal approach like DiCoT is that it enables an appropriate representation of a complex and rich system. However in order to assess the adequacy of the resources in supporting the actions needed to achieve goals, the PVS models go a stage further to make precise certain assumptions. These models can be seen as hypotheses about the meaning of the information resources within the activities. As hypotheses they are open to alternative interpretations that may have different more or less consistent implications. A PVS model is therefore not intended to be definitive and a number of alternatives could be developed in order to explore different assumptions about the circumstances.

4.1 Modelling Approach

The modelling approach used has been outlined and illustrated in the context of other field studies including incident analysis in [6,7,5,8]. It involves the following steps: (1) modelling information resources reported in the field study data (e.g., glucose meter displays, information on staff badges, content of the accessory box); (2) modelling how information resources propagate within the system (e.g., how a staff ID is entered into the glucose meter); (3) formulating and verifying conjectures about how resources were used (e.g., were relevant resources available at critical moments to relevant actors) and facts about the prescribed use of information resources (e.g., according to procedures and regulations). The first two steps of the procedure aim to help field investigators externalise facts about what information resources are available to users and how such resources are used. The third step aims to check whether information resources provide constraints that are correct and tight enough to support safe user actions.

4.2   Modelling Language

PVS models are specified in a strongly typed higher-order logic, which allows quantification over propositional functions to be formulated. The language includes the usual base types (e.g., `bool`, `nat`, `integer` and `real`), function type constructors `[A -> B]` (predicates are functions with range type `bool`), and abstract data types. Models are packaged in modular components called *theories*, which can be parametric in types and constants. They can use definitions and theorems of other theories by importing them. A language mechanism used extensively in the models considered here is *predicate subtyping* [12], which makes it possible to express complex consistency constraints. When using expressions with subtypes, PVS automatically generates proof obligations, called type correctness conditions (TCCs), that ensure the valid use of the type. We will rely on this automatic generation of proof obligations to check various consistency constraints for the use of information resources.

4.3   Developed Models

We model artefacts and information resources used by clinicians during the blood glucose monitoring procedure. The models aim to enable a systematic analysis of consistency of collected data and safety checks. The concern is to identify situations where gaps in the way artefacts and information resources support user actions may create sufficient preconditions for unsafe user actions potentially leading to harm, such as wrong patient identification or unsafe disposal of refuse.

In the developed models, each information resource and artefact is specified using a different PVS datatype. The level of detail used in the PVS models was discussed with the investigator in relation to their findings as it must be consistent with the level of detail understood by the investigator. The aim is to create a model that embeds the facts observed by the investigator during the field study in a precise way, but without the need to be too specific when certain information is not available or not deemed relevant by the investigator. In the developed models, the collection of information resources and artefacts represents the state of the system. The use of information resources and artefacts is modelled as transition functions over system states. This will be illustrated by demonstrating some relevant features of the specification of the models. The complete PVS models relative to the field study data described in Sections 3.3 and 3.2 will be made available online [1].

Blood Glucose Meter. The device is modelled with a PVS record type. The record has thirteen fields, and each field specifies either data stored in the device, such as patient account numbers, or device screens, such as "results ready". The selection of the specific type for each field is adapted to the understanding of the field investigator of the system and to the availability of information from the field study data and user manuals. In some cases details are only partial and PVS makes it possible to express partial information. An example of this can be found in the definition of patient account numbers. The observations and the user manuals reveal that they are integers, but additional details about specific constraints on the range of these numbers was not available. As a result of this the modelled patient account numbers are specified as bounded integer numbers where the bound is an uninterpreted constant (`max_patient_ID`) rather than a specific value. For other aspects, we had access to several details, but the investigator deemed it sufficient that an abstract view was given as additional information was not contributing to a better understanding of the situation. An example of this is the screen shown by the device when the clinician needs to unlock it – the specific content of the screen is not relevant to an understanding of the work. This is captured in the specification. The information is abstracted into a Boolean field, `session_unlocked`, that keeps only a high-level view about that particular device screen. Consistency constraints can be embedded as subtypes at this stage, e.g., the device must be powered on before messages are shown on the device display. The utility of embedding these constraints will be discussed further in Section 5. An excerpt from the type definition developed for the blood glucose meter follows — the relation of each field in the record type with the actual device is made clear with a comment in the specification, which is the text following the '`%`' symbol.

```
max_patient_ID: posnat  % uninterpreted constant
patient_ID       : TYPE = below(max_patient_ID)
Blood_glucose_meter: TYPE =
[# powered_on : boolean,                  % ON/OFF Led
   patient_IDs: [patient_ID -> boolean], % patient IDs in the device
   quality_check_passed : boolean,       % periodic quality test screen
   session_unlocked: {b: boolean | powered_on}, % unlock screen
   ready_to_analyse: {b: boolean | powered_on}, % test ready screen
   results_ready   : {b: boolean | powered_on}, % results ready screen
   %... more device screens omitted
   result_memory_full    : boolean       % meter memory (results)
   comment_memory_full   : boolean  #]    % meter memory (comments)
```

Accessory Box. The accessory box is modelled with a PVS record type. The record has six fields. Two fields are bounded natural numbers modelling white swabs and disposable lancets that are available in the box, and the other four fields are data types representing information about the test strip vials and the control solutions in the accessory box. The initial data from the field study did not provide information about the maximum swabs and lancets that can be placed in the box. The level of accuracy with which clinicians checked whether they were sufficient for visiting the beds was also not clear. Therefore we had to make decisions about the level of granularity for the models. A sensible solution was to use two symbolic constants (n_white_swabs and n_lancets), which made it possible to reason about the consequences of any possible situation during the analysis phase. In these specific constants only one constraint about the possible range values is embedded, that they are strictly greater than zero. It was known from the field investigation that the clinician (at least) visually checks whether the accessory box contains swabs and lancets before starting the visit. For the test strip vials, we modelled the following information: the barcode on the vial, specified as a new PVS abstract data type with two constructors, one constructor for readable barcodes, and the another one for unreadable barcodes; the number of strips in the vials, specified as a bounded natural number lower than a symbolic constant n_strips; the strip "lot", an enumerated field that specifies whether information about a set of strips is valid, invalid, expired, unknown, or not available.

```
Accessory_box: TYPE =
  [# white_swabs          : upto(n_white_swabs),
     lancets              : upto(n_lancets),
     test_strip_vial_1    : Test_strip_vial_box,
     test_strip_vial_2    : Test_strip_vial_box,
     high_control_solution: Control_solution,
     low_control_solution : Control_solution #]
```

Trolley. The trolley is modelled as a PVS record type with four fields: cardboard, which describes the content of the cardboard (whether it contains used gloves / swabs / other waste, and whether a checklist of beds has been annotated on the board); glovebox, which abstracts the glovebox as a number representing the gloves left in the box; accessory_box, of type Accessory_box defined above; yellow_bin, which models the content of the special refuse bin as an enumerated field whose possible values are full, not_full, empty, NA. The modelling choice for the bin was driven by the requirement to model information resources observable by the clinician. The bin is opaque, and therefore a simple visual inspection from outside is not sufficient to determine its content.

```
Trolley: TYPE =
  [# cardboard     : Cardboard,
     gloves_box    : Disposable_gloves_box,
     yellow_bin    : Special_refuse_bin,
     accessory_box: Accessory_box #]
```

Clinicians. Observable information resources are carried by clinicians during bed visits: whether they carry handover sheets, modelled as a Boolean field (has_handover_sheets); the actual content of the handover sheets, modelled with a field (handover_sheets) given as a function that maps beds in the ward to patient records; whether they have a pen or a marker for updating sheets and bed checklist, modelled as a Boolean field (has_pen_or_marker); whether their badge makes it possible to unlock the blood glucose meter (has_unlocking_code).

```
Clinician: TYPE =
  [# has_handover_sheets: boolean,
     handover_sheets    : [upto(n_beds) -> Patient_record],
     has_pen_or_marker  : boolean,
     has_unlocking_code : boolean #]
```

Patients. Observable information resources carried by patients while staying in the ward include: the wristband code, modelled as a natural number (wristband_code) — we chose to use a natural number rather than the type patient_ID defined for the blood glucose monitor model because the facts collected by the investigator did not provide any evidence that the wristband codes were generated with a system compliant with such value constraints; whether the wristband can be scanned is modelled with a Boolean field (wristband_can_be_s canned) — sometimes the barcode cannot be scanned because, for instance, the wristband has been accidentally crumpled; the patient name (patient_name), a string storing the patient name — we are not including any assumption about whether the names are unique, as the investigation did not provide such evidence; the bed number (bed_number), a bounded integer number identifying one of the beds in the ward.

```
Patient: TYPE =
  [# wristband_code: nat,
     wristband_can_be_scanned: boolean,
     patient_name : string,
     bed_number   : upto(n_beds) #]
```

Activities. The clinicians are involved in activities that are specified as transition functions over system states defined in terms of the data types described in the previous section. The state of the system collects together, possibly multiple instances, of the system elements: trolley, device, clinician, and patient. Since the aim of modelling activity is to describe precisely the observed use of artefacts and information resources to determine whether there are gaps or mismatches, an activity is defined for each step described in Section 3.3. An illustration of the formalisation of the activity is puncture_finger, which specifies the use of artefacts on the trolley during the first phases of the blood glucose monitoring test. The aim of the illustration is to give the reader a taste of the modelling style and of the decisions that need to be made during the modelling process. The formalisation of the other activities will be made available online [1].

From the field study data, the following facts about the use of artefacts and information resources when puncturing the patient's finger to get a blood sample and start the test can be discerned.

– The clinician uses at least one lancet and one white swab for each test. A precise estimate of the total number of lancets and swabs that will be used in each test cannot be identified in advance, because the test might need to be repeated, e.g., because the alcohol used to cleanse the puncture site may lead to error codes or inaccurate reading, or because the collected blood sample was not sufficient or was excessive. This uncertainty is modelled using two symbolic constants (used_lancets and used_swabs) in the arithmetic expression for updating the number of lancets and white swabs in the accessory box. PVS is able to generate proof obligations using these expressions that enables exploration of what may happen for different ranges of values for the symbolic constants. An illustration is provided in Section 5.

– The clinician may use a cardboard container that is either empty or contains used items, e.g., because the test had to be repeated more than once, or because the clinician is delaying the transfer of used items to the bin. This uncertainty can be expressed using a random Boolean variable[1].

– The clinician needs to use disposable gloves. The number of gloves needed cannot be estimated in advance in a precise way because of the particular work environment. For instance, clinicians may be temporarily interrupted during the blood glucose monitoring test because they need to carry out another task. As for the number of lancets and white swabs, we therefore use an arithmetic expression with a symbolic constant used_gloves.

```
puncture_finger(sys: State): State =
sys WITH [ trolley := trolley(sys)
    WITH [ accessory_box := trolley(sys)'accessory_box
    WITH [ lancets := trolley(sys)'accessory_box'lancets - used_lancets,
           white_swabs := trolley(sys)'accessory_box'white_swabs
                                                   - used_swabs,
           cardboard := trolley(sys)'cardboard
             WITH [ used_gloves := choose(fullset[boolean]),
                    used_swabs  := choose(fullset[boolean]) ],
         gloves_box := trolley(sys)'gloves_box - used_gloves ]]]
```

5   Using PVS to Support the Field Investigation: Analysis and Results

The modelling exercise was itself a first analysis step. The modelling approach proved useful as a means of helping the field investigator organise a substantial number of field notes, which were frequently incomplete and interleaved with other observations of devices. The modelling process achieved clarification and made the subsequent stages of the analysis faster and more effective.

---

[1] In PVS, random values for any datatype can be obtained with the **choose** function, which takes as argument the set from which the random element must be chosen.

5.1 Issues Emerged while Developing the PVS Models

Several questions warranting further investigation as part of the field study were raised while developing the models. Some relevant examples follow.

Quality Control. The aim of the quality control performed when scanning the barcode on the test strip vials is to calibrate the device to a specific set of strips and to check whether the strips are valid and approved. Modelling this information from the user manual stimulated further investigation of subtle inconsistencies in the mental models possessed by clinicians. For instance, some clinicians believed that the test strip scanning was only for checking the validity of the strips. This understanding is correct but partial, and opens the possibility of calibrating the meter for a vial of test strips and, in the case the strip vial is empty, using strips from another uncalibrated set — the accessory box has two strip vials and the container is opaque, therefore clinicians are not able to visually check whether the vial has strips in it when scanning the barcode.

Barcode Scanner. The barcode scanner embedded in the device is used to read clinician's badges and patient's wristbands. Whereas the field investigator had accepted the technology as standard, a systematic analysis of the user manuals made clear that different subtle variants of the same technologies could have been implemented in the device. Each technology could be more or less suited to the context. This also helped to clarify the origin of various minor disturbances observed during the study, e.g., when the device was not scanning correctly the barcode on the wristband.

User Manual. Another advantage of the added analysis included an awareness of what was and was not in the device manual. Data solely from the field can be understated because it is assumed by participants and not particularly salient. However, when contrasted with the official and concrete account in the manual the importance of these differences is emphasised, e.g., the manual says that if there is not enough blood placed on a test strip then this can hinder the reading but staff also said that too much can also hinder the reading.

5.2 Issues Raised by PVS When Checking Model Consistency

Proof obligations automatically generated by PVS stimulated further constructive discussion after the modelling step. In the following, we illustrate some of these situations for the `puncture_finger` activity specified above in Section 4. For that activity, PVS automatically generated various proof obligations that could not be discharged using the facts available from the field study. Two examples illustrate this.

Lancets. An undischargable proof obligation automatically generated by PVS related to the arithmetic expression containing the symbolic constants. PVS requires the expression that updates the number of lancets to result in a value that is non-negative. This translates into a request to the field study to check whether the accessory box is guaranteed to contain enough lancets for the tests:

```
% Subtype TCC generated for
% trolley(sys)'accessory_box'lancets - used_lancets
% expected type upto(n_disposable_lancets)
puncture_finger_TCC1: OBLIGATION
 FORALL (sys: State):
    sys'trolley'accessory_box'lancets - used_lancets >= 0
```

This obligation, although mathematically trivial, drew our attention to the lancets and stimulated further investigation about how they are actually used by clinicians. The investigation started as a clarification of whether they were single use, but then allowed the investigator to get useful insight about the risks of not putting them in the sharps bin straight away and also getting them mixed up with the unused lancets (it is hard to distinguish used lancets from unused ones by visual inspection). Some of these latent situations were actually observed in subsequent visits to the ward, when the trolley was not used because only a few patients needed to be checked.

Battery. A second undischargable proof obligation generated by PVS resulted from the reasonable conjecture that the device is ready for the test. The conjecture claimed that a precondition that the device be unlocked be true. We composed the modelled activities to specify a symbolic execution trace and verify the conjecture. Interestingly, PVS generates a proof obligation because of a consistency constraint imposed in the model: in order to be unlocked, the device must be also powered on:

```
% Subtype TCC generated for
% symbolic execution trace
% expected type {sys: State | device(sys)'powered_on
%                              AND NOT device(sys)'session_locked}
symbolic_execution_trace_TCC2: OBLIGATION
 confirm_strip(enter_patient_ID(...prepare_trolley(initial_state)...)
    'device'powered_on
  AND
 confirm_strip(enter_patient_ID(...prepare_trolley(initial_state)...)
    'device'session_unlocked
```

This detail has drawn attention to the fact that the device is battery powered, and that wear and tear inevitably reduces the autonomy of the device. This can be a source of disturbances during visits to several beds, because the clinician powers on the device at the beginning of the visit and keeps the device powered on until the visit completes. In some cases, the device may therefore run out of power and require replacement with another one. This raises a question about latent situations where the trolley may be left unattended for short periods of time in order to collect another device.

6   Related Work and Conclusions

Little work has been done on approaches that integrate formal methods and empirical studies, and hardly any concrete examples can be found of case studies involving real world systems. This is partially linked to the complexity of using formal methods, which require a steep learning curve, and to additional barriers (some real, some imagined) created by the current generation of user interfaces for automated reasoning tools, which are essentially text-based and practically inaccessible to non-expert users.

Wright, Fields and Merriam [15] investigated the possibility of defining a conceptual framework for integrating formal methods and empirical approaches for studying interactive systems. They argue that extant artefacts and informal understanding of the system can provide insights about usability properties that might be of interest. This informal understanding can then be refined through formal methods by generating design questions and evaluating design alternatives, which can in turn be evaluated empirically, e.g., through prototypes. They demonstrate the approach with an example based on a web browser. Fields [4] applied the same approach to the analysis of a remote control system. Rukšėnas et at [11] combined empirical studies and mathematical models to formalise the relationship between salience and cognitive load revealed by lab experiments. The outcome of the lab experiments was used to refine the salience rules defined in the mathematical model, and the outcome of the model-based analysis was able to generate new experimental hypotheses for researchers in cognitive science. These works share with ours the argument that informal approaches and formal methods have complementary roles in the analysis of the system.

In our previous works, we have shown that the integrated analysis proposed by Wright, Fields and Merriam can be extended to the wider socio-technical system. We demonstrated the utility of the approach when re-analysing field study data from already completed field investigations performed in different contexts and for different aims, including: use of drug infusion pump in a day care unit [2], analysis of an emergency dispatch system [6,7], and analysis of incidents reports [5,8].

In this work, we have explored the possibility of using the PVS verification tool to support an investigator while conducting a field study. For the developed models, PVS is able to generate proof obligations and proof attempts in seconds. We have provided some evidence of the utility of the approach. As gaps and inconsistencies are uncovered within and between the various specifications, new questions are generated, which can be used to refine the field study. Also, the formal specification can be refined as new facts are discovered — the two methods feed each other.

Acknowledgements. CHI+MED: Multidisciplinary Computer-Human Interaction research for the design and safe use of interactive medical devices project, EPSRC Grant Number EP/G059063/1. Extreme Reasoning, Grant Number EP/F02309X/1.

References

1. PVS models of field study at oncology ward (June 2012), PVS models
   `http://tinyurl.com/PVS-bloodglucosestudy`
2. Blandford, A., Cauchi, A., Curzon, P., Eslambolchilar, P., Furniss, D., Gimblett, A., Huang, H., Lee, P., Li, Y., Masci, P., Oladimeji, P., Rajkomar, A., Rukšėnas, R., Thimbleby, H.: Comparing actual practice and user manuals: A case study based on programmable infusion pumps. In: Eics4Med, the 1st Intl. Workshop on Engineering Interactive Computing Systems for Medicine and Health Care, pp. 59–64. ACM Digital Library (2011)
3. Blandford, A., Furniss, D.: DiCoT: A Methodology for Applying Distributed Cognition to the Design of Teamworking Systems. Interactive Systems, 26–38 (2006)
4. Fields, R.: Analysis of Erroneous Actions in the Design of Critical Systems. PhD thesis, University of York (2001)
5. Masci, P., Curzon, P.: Checking User-Centred Design Principles in Distributed Cognition Models: A Case Study in the Healthcare Domain. In: Holzinger, A., Simonic, K.-M. (eds.) USAB 2011. LNCS, vol. 7058, pp. 95–108. Springer, Heidelberg (2011)
6. Masci, P., Curzon, P., Blandford, A., Furniss, D.: Modelling distributed cognition systems in PVS. ECEASST 45 (2011)
7. Masci, P., Curzon, P., Furniss, D., Blandford, A.: Using PVS to support the analysis of distributed cognition systems. Submitted for publication to Innovations in Systems and Software Engineering (2012)
8. Masci, P., Huang, H., Curzon, P., Harrison, M.D.: Using PVS to Investigate Incidents through the Lens of Distributed Cognition. In: Goodloe, A.E., Person, S. (eds.) NFM 2012. LNCS, vol. 7226, pp. 273–278. Springer, Heidelberg (2012)
9. Roche. Accu-Chek Inform II System, Professional glucose testing for the wireless age (August 2010)
10. Roche. Accu-Chek Inform System. Operator's manual (November 2010)
11. Rukšėnas, R., Back, J., Curzon, P., Blandford, A.: Verification-guided modelling of salience and cognitive load. Formal Aspects of Computing 21(6), 541–569 (2009)
12. Shankar, N., Owre, S.: Principles and Pragmatics of Subtyping in PVS. In: Bert, D., Choppy, C., Mosses, P.D. (eds.) WADT 1999. LNCS, vol. 1827, pp. 37–52. Springer, Heidelberg (2000)
13. NHS Trust. Accu-Chek Inform II Blood Glucose Meter Standard Operating Procedure (August 2011)
14. Westbrook, J.I., Ampt, A.: Design, application and testing of the Work Observation Method by Activity Timing (WOMBAT) to measure clinicians' patterns of work and communication. International Journal of Medical Informatics 78 (2009)
15. Wright, P.C., Fields, R., Merriam, N.A.: From formal models to empirical evaluation and back again. In: Formal Methods in Human-Computer Interaction, ch. 13, pp. 283–314. Springer, Berlin (1997)

Model-Based Evaluation
of the Availability of a CBTC System

Alessio Ferrari, Massimiliano L. Itria,
Silvano Chiaradonna, and Giorgio O. Spagnolo

ISTI-CNR, Via G. Moruzzi 1, Pisa, Italy
{Ferrari,Itria,Chiaradonna,Spagnolo}@isti.cnr.it
http://www.isti.cnr.it/

Abstract. A metro control system is a software/hardware platform that provides automated mechanisms to enforce the safety of a metropolitan transportation system. In this field, the current technical trend is the Communications-based Train Control (CBTC) solution. CBTC platforms are characterized by a continuous wireless interaction between trains and ground controls. Several degrees of automation are provided, from basic traffic monitoring to unattended train operation. Besides safety issues, a CBTC system is also required to guarantee a high level of availability. These platforms are normally composed of several subsystems and devices, and estimating the overall availability of the system is not a trivial task. Stochastic Activity Networks (SAN) are a powerful formalism that allows modelling and evaluating complex distributed systems. In this paper, a study is presented that shows how SAN models can be employed to evaluate the availability attributes of a CBTC system. The current results show that the SAN technology and the analysis tool adopted, named Möbius, are mature for a profitable employment in industrial practice.

Introduction

Communications-based Train Control (CBTC) is the last technological frontier for signalling and train control in the metro market [8,4]. CBTC systems offer flexible degrees of automation, from enforcing control over dangerous operations acted by the driver, to the complete replacement of the driver role with an automatic pilot and an automatic on-board monitoring system. CBTC systems are typically employed in traffic intensive environments, with strong timing and service constraints. Therefore, such platforms are required to provide high *availability* [7] to ensure readiness of correct service. Another typical issue of the development of CBTC products concerns the *modularity* of the system. Indeed, when developing a CBTC product, a company has to take into account that every metro installation is different from the other, and the customers might have different requirements for the control system that they wish to purchase. Therefore, companies that develop CBTC products are required to provide different versions or configurations of their CBTC platform.

P. Avgeriou (Ed.): SERENE 2012, LNCS 7527, pp. 165–179, 2012.

Formal methods provide powerful abstraction and analysis tools to evaluate availability attributes on systems with high modularity requirements. In metro and rail transport systems, several formal approaches have been applied to perform availability estimation. Among others, Patra A.P. *et al.* [9] evaluates the availability of a railway infrastructure through a Petri Net model. The estimated availability is then used to compute the capacity of the infrastructure. Zhu *et al.* [12] study the availability issue of WLAN-based train-ground communication schemes in CBTC systems. In this case, the availability is analysed using a Continuous Time Markov Chain (CTMC) model. Xu *et al.* [11] study the CBTC communication system considering multiple redundancy configurations. In this work, availability properties are analyzed using a Stochastic Reward Net (SRN) model.

Within an effort of defining a general approach for obtaining customizable CBTC solutions, we have considered model-based analysis to evaluate the availability attributes of a CBTC product. To this end, we have exploited the Stochastic Activity Networks (SAN) formalism. The system architecture used for the experiments presented in this paper is derived through a product line-based method [3]. The method enforces the reusability of the components and the system modularity typically required by the CBTC market. Given the flexibility of the SAN modelling language, the analysis approach can be applied with limited effort also to different configurations of the system (i.e., different product instances). Furthermore, the availability evaluated can be used to tune the selection of the components for the final version of a product configuration, by taking into accout market requirements and cost-related concerns. The presented work is part of an academic study applied to an industrial system that is currently under development.

The paper is structured as follows. In Sect. 1, a description of the CBTC working principles is presented. In Sect. 2, an overview of the adopted approach is given. Sect. 3 describes the system architecture – both functional and physical – employed in our case study. Sect. 4 focuses on the SAN modelling and analysis, and presents the evaluation of the current results of the CBTC availability. In Sect. 5, conclusions and final remarks are given.

1   Communications-Based Train Control Systems

CBTC systems [8,4] are novel signalling and control platforms tailored for metro. These systems provide a continuous automatic train protection as well as improved performance, system availability and operational flexibility of the train. The conventional signaling/control systems that do not use a CBTC approach are normally called *fixed block* systems. In such platforms the distance between trains is computed based on fixed-length sections. The problem with these systems is the limited amount of trains that can move on a line at the same time.

CBTC overcomes this problem by introducing the *moving block* principle: the minimum distance between successive trains is no longer calculated based on fixed sections, but according to the rear of the preceding train. This distance is called Movement Authority (MA), and is the limit distance that cannot be shortened by a running train. This approach ensures a reduction of the allowed distance between two trains running in the same direction. Hence, a larger number of trains can move on the same line.

From the architectural point of view, CBTC systems are characterized by a division in two parts: *onboard equipment* and *wayside equipment*. The first is installed on the train and the latter is located at a station or along the line. A continuous wayside-to-train and train-to-wayside data communication is provided using radio transmission [6]. The main element of the onboard equipment is the Onboard Automatic Train Protection (ATP) system, and the main element of wayside equipment is the Wayside ATP system. The former computes the train speed and location, and sends this information to the latter. Therefore, the wayside ATP is aware about the exact position and speed of any train along the line. This information is used to compute the MAs that are sent to each train. The Onboard ATP receives the MA and computes a dynamic braking curve to ensure safe separation of trains. Furthermore, this system controls that the speed limit is not exceeded.

CBTC systems also allow automatic train control functions by implementing both the ATO (Automatic Train Operation) and the ATS (Automatic Train Supervision) systems. The ATO enables the absence of the driver on board the train, ensuring the fully automatic management of the train in combination with the ATP. The ATS offers functions related to the supervision and management of the train traffic, such as train routing, adjustment of schedules and determination of speed restrictions within certain areas. A CBTC system might include also an interlocking (referred in the following as IXL). The IXL monitors the status of the objects in the railway yard (e.g., switches, signals' status) and, when routing is required by the ATS, allows or denies the routing of trains in accordance to the railway safety and operational regulations.

2   CBTC Availability Evaluation Method

Fig. 1 depicts the process followed to evaluate availability attributes for a CBTC product by means of SAN modelling and analysis. The approach adopted starts from a representation of the functional architecture of the CBTC product in terms of functionalities (Functional Product Architecture). The Functional Product Architecture is derived from a product line-based process described in our previous work [3]. Such an architecture does not represent the system in terms of the devices, but it comprises the CBTC functionalities that are implemented by devices of the product.

Starting from the Functional Product Architecture we identify the devices or sub-systems that are available for building the product. They can be either platforms internally developed by the company, or Commercial Out of The Shelf (COTS) products.

The first phase of the method, named Product Definition (described in Sect. 3), allows defining a physical architecture in terms of components (Physical Product Architecture). In this phase, the desired functionalities are apportioned to

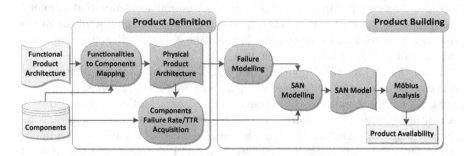

Fig. 1. Overview of the process adopted

a subset of the available components (Functionalities to Components Mapping). Moreover, the failure rates and the time to repair (TTR) of the selected components are also considered (Components Failure Rate/TTR Acquisition).

The second phase of the method, named Product Building (described in Sect. 4), leads to the evaluation of the availability attributes of the product. First, Failure Modelling is performed to model possible failure categories. The scenarios are used to distinguish which failures affect the system availability. After this analysis, a SAN model is built using the previously evaluated failure rate/TTR of the components. The model is finally analysed through the Möbius tool, which produces the Product Availability as output. This information is used to tune the selection of the components for the final product, by taking into accout the required availability of the system, as well as cost-related concerns.

3   CBTC Product Definition

The CBTC product functional architecture is defined in terms of CBTC functionalities. Such an architecture is the output of a process performed according to a product-line based method. The choice of expressing the architecture in terms of functionalities enables major abstraction, and eases compliance with the CBTC standards [4,5]. More details are reported elsewhere [3].

We are here interested to develop a *physical* architecture from this *functional* architecture. The physical architecture is focused on the components that implement the functionalities. The components are selected between the devices and subsystems that are available on the market, or that the company has already produced for previous systems.

3.1   Functional Architecture

A simplified version of the product functional architecture defined for our case study is depicted in Fig. 2. Three main systems are involved: the Wayside ATP, the Onboard ATP, and the ATS[1]. Arrows among functionalities inside a system

---

[1] For the sake of simplicity, the ATO system is not considered in our case study.

are *usage* arrows. If a usage arrow is directed from a functionality to another, this implies that the former uses a service of the latter. Arrows among systems are *message* arrows. If a message arrow is directed from a functionality to another, this implies that the former sends a message – the label of the arrow – to the latter.

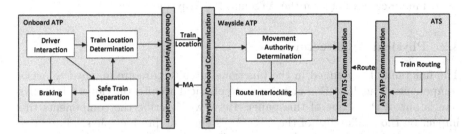

Fig. 2. CBTC functional architecture

The functionalities that the three systems are required to implement are summarized below.

Onboard ATP

- **Driver Interaction.** This functionality manages the interaction with the driver by accessing the information provided by all the other modules;
- **Train Location Determination.** This functionality computes the position of the train;
- **Safe Train Separation.** This functionality uses the location information of the train to compute the braking curve and ensure safe separation of trains;
- **Braking.** This functionality enforces brakes when required by the system (Safe Train Separation) or the operator (Driver Interaction);
- **Onboard/Wayside Communication.** This functionality provides bi-directional communication between the Onboard ATP and the Wayside ATP. It is mainly used to receive the MA, and to send the Train Location information.

Wayside ATP

- **Movement Authority Determination.** This functionality computes the MA message to be sent to the train based on the position of the other trains and on the railway status;
- **Route Interlocking.** This functionality controls points and signals according to the route requested by the ATS (see the Train Routing functionality of the ATS);
- **Wayside/Onboard Communication.** This functionality provides bi-directional communication between the Wayside ATP and the Onboard ATP.
- **ATP/ATS Communication.** This functionality provides bi-directional communication between the Wayside ATP and the ATS. In particular, this functionality allows receiving the route requested by the ATS.

ATS

- **Train Routing.** This functionality allows requiring the route for the train in accordance with the train service data, predefined routing rules and possible restrictions to the movement of the train;
- **ATS/ATP Communication.** This functionality provides bi-directional communication between the ATS and the Wayside ATP.

3.2   Physical Architecture

The functionalities defined in the functional architecture are mapped to actual components. The definition of a complete physical architecture for a CBTC system is out of the scope of this paper. Here, we describe the components that impact on the availability of the CBTC system. The product physical architecture derived for our case study is informally represented in Fig. 3.

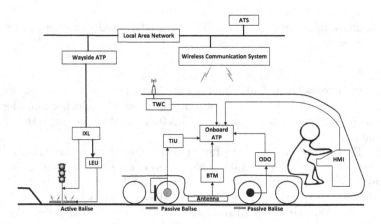

Fig. 3. CBTC physical architecture

Table 1 summarizes the mapping between functionalities and components that have been performed to define the physical architecture. Table 1a collects the functionalities apportioned to the onboard equipment. Table 1b collects the functionalities apportioned to the wayside equipment.

The **Onboard ATP (OATP)** is the core component of the onboard equipment, which was already identified as a subsystem in the functional architecture diagram. This component requires additional devices to properly implement its functionalities:

- **Odometer system (ODO):** the component includes the sensors and the board that are used for the determination of the train speed and location;
- **Train Interface Unit (TIU):** the component has the primary role of controlling the braking and traction system;

Table 1. Mapping between CBTC functionalities and components

(a) Onboard equipment

Functionality	Component						
	OATP	ODO	BTM	PB	TIU	TWC	HMI
Train Location Determination	X	X	X	X			
Braking	X				X		
Safe Train Separation	X						
Onboard/Wayside Communication	X					X	
Driver Interaction	X						X

(b) Wayside equipment

Functionality	Component						
	LAN	WCS	WATP	IXL	LEU	AB	ATS
Wayside/Onboard Communication	X	X	X				
Movement Authority Determination			X				
Route Interlocking			X	X	X	X	
ATP/ATS Communication	X		X				
ATS/ATP Communication	X						X
Train Routing							X

- **Human Machine Interface (HMI):** this is the control panel that allows interaction with the driver;
- **Balise Trasmission Module (BTM):** the component processes the information coming from an Antenna that reads the messages received from the Active Balises (AB) and Passive Balises (PB) (see below for details);
- **Train Wayside Communication (TWC):** the component allows bi-directional communication with the wireless wayside devices.

The OATP processes the information coming from all these devices and controls their behaviour.

The **Wayside ATP** is the core component of the wayside equipment. As the Onboard ATP, this component requires additional components to implement its functionalities:

- **Wireless Communication System (WCS):** provides bi-directional wireless communication with the OATP;
- **Interlocking System (IXL):** provides route interlocking functionalities. When the ATS requires a route, the route is forwarded by the Wayside ATP to the IXL. The IXL verifies that the route is free of other trains and is not conflicting with other routes. In such a case, the IXL locks and sets the sitches belonging to the route, and properly sets the wayside signals.
- **Active Balise (AB):** the component that embeds the aspect of a signal. When the train passes, the Antenna placed below the train can read the information concerning the signal aspect from the AB.

- **Lineside Electronic Unit (LEU):** controls the Active Balises (AB) to embed the aspect of the signal (e.g., red, green, yellow). Information on the signal aspect are received from the IXL.
- **Passive Balise (PB):** the component that embeds absolute position information w.r.t. the beginning of the line. When the train passes, the Antenna placed below the train can read the information concerning its current location from the PB. Therefore, the position computed onboard through the ODO can be adjusted according to the information received.

In our simplified architecture, the **ATS** system requires solely the **Local Area Network (LAN)** component, to communicate with the WATP. Failures occurring in any of the described devices may affect the system availability. Failures occurring in any of the described devices may affect the system availability. For example, if the TIU component fails, the system will brake automatically. Afterwards, the train will not be able to provide service, since the traction system is impaired.

3.3 Components Parameters

The parameters considered for the evaluations are the failure rate of the devices and the time to repair or substitute the failed device (TTR).

Table 2. Parameters values

Device	Onboard				Wayside				
	BTM	OATP	TWC	TIU	IXL	LAN	WCS	LEU	WATP
Failure Rate	10^{-5}	10^{-6}	10^{-5}	10^{-5}	10^{-6}	10^{-5}	10^{-5}	10^{-6}	10^{-6}
TTR	0.5				1				

The failure rate is the frequency with which a component fails (expressed in failures per hour). The TTR represents the time to repair or the time to substitute the failed device (expressed in hours). We assume that the TTR includes also the time due to the detection of the damage, and the time required to the maintenance personnel to travel to the site of the failure.

The values of these parameters are normally available to the system architect. Indeed, they are either evaluated by the company – if the components are internally developed – or provided with the COTS devices – in case commercial components are employed.

In our analysis, we use the default values reported in Table 2. They are hypothetical, but realistic ones, and are used just for showing the potentials of our analysis method. However, to take into consideration to some extent variations of the assumed settings, we performed a sensitivity analysis on the failure rates and TTRs of the devices.

4 CBTC Product Building

The physical architecture described is considered to define a failure model for the CBTC system. Then, a SAN model is defined, and analysis is performed through the Möbius tool to evaluate the availability of the system.

4.1 Measure of Interest

The Availability measure for railway systems is defined in [1] as follows:

$$A = \frac{MTBF}{MTBF + MDT}.$$

MTBF (Mean Time Between Failure) is the mean time between failures of the system. MDT (Mean Down Time) is the average time that the system is non-operational. MDT includes all downtime associated with repair, corrective and preventive maintenance, self imposed downtime, and any logistics or administrative delays. In our analysis A represents the steady-state probability that the system works properly.

4.2 Failure Model

The failure model defines the types of system failures, the types of device failures and the relationships among devices failures and system failures.

The considered system failure categories are the ones described in the EN 50126 standard [1], concerning the Reliability Availability Maintainability and Safety (RAMS) characteristics of railway systems. Such categories are as follows.

A **Significant Failure** is one that fulfills the following description: a failure that prevents train movement or causes a delay to service greater than a specified time and/or generates a cost greather than a specified level.

A **Major Failure** is a failure that is not Significant, but fulfills any of the following descriptions: (1) a failure that must be rectified for the system to achieve its specified performance; (2) a failure that does not cause a delay or cost greater than the minimum threshold specified for a significant failure.

A **Minor Failure** is failure that: (1) does not prevent a system achieving its specified performance; (2) does not meet criteria for significant or major failures. Minor failures do not affect the system availability.

In [1] only *permanent* failures are considered, since transient failures do not affect RAMS attributes.

Table 3 classifies the CBTC system failures according to the failure categories above. Only failures belonging to the major or significant failure category affect the availability of the CBTC system. Hence minor failures are not considered.

Each failure is considered to occur in a set of hardware devices (or in one device only). When one of these combinations happens (i.e., devices fail at the same time) a major or significant failure is generated in the system.

Table 3. Classification of failures

Devices Combination (*: and, +:or)	Failure	
	Major	Significant
(TWC*LEU)+(TWC*BTM)+ (LAN*WCS*LEU)+(LAN*WCS*BTM)	X	
(OATP+IXL)*((LAN*WCS)+TWC)		X
IXL		X
TIU	X	
OATP	X	
WATP		X

4.3 SAN Modelling

In order to evaluate the availability measure A, the CBTC system has been modelled through the SAN formalism [10] and the Möbius tool.

The SAN formalism is a stochastic extension of Petri nets based on four primitives: *places, activities, input gates* and *output gates*. Places and activities represent the state and the actions of the modelled system, respectively. Input gates control the enabling of activities and define the marking changes that will occur when an activity completes. Output gates define the marking changes when an activity completes. Cases (small circles on activities) are used to represent uncertainty upon completion of an activity. The attributes of the SAN primitives are defined by using sequences of C++ statements.

Möbius is a powerful multi-formalism/multi-solution tool, that supports the hierarchical composition of different submodels [2] thanks to the *Join* and *Rep* state-sharing compositional operators. Join is used to compose two or more sub-models. Rep is used to construct a model consisting of a number of replicas of a submodel.

Fig. 4 shows the composed model representing the CBTC system. Each node represents either an atomic SAN model (Submodel), or a model obtained by composing SAN models by means of the Join or Rep operators.

The Join *OnBoard* combines the atomic SAN models of the devices OATP, TIU, ODO, BTM and TWC. It represents the onboard control system. The Rep *Trains* models the presence of multiple trains along the line, through the replication of the *OnBoard* model. The Join TrackSide combines the atomic SAN models of the devices IXL, WCS, LAN, WATP and LEU. It represents the wayside control system. The Join CBTC_zone composes all the onboard systems models with the wayside system model. It represents the overall CBTC system model. The *SystemStatus* model is used to evaluate measures related the CBTC system model. This approach allows performing analyses on different configurations of CBTC systems in order to evaluate how changes in the system can affect the measures of interest.

All devices in the CBTC system are modelled using an atomic model. Each device fails independently from each other. The time to the failure of each device

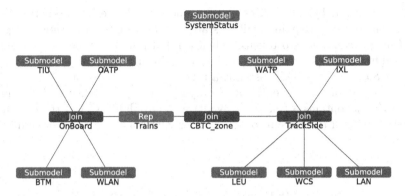

Fig. 4. Composed System

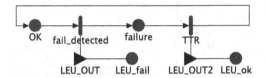

Fig. 5. Lineside Electronic Unit (LEU) SAN

is modelled by a exponentially distributed timed activity. Fig. 5 shows a SAN model representing a LEU device. One token in the place labeled *OK* represents the proper working status of the device. The time to its failure is modelled by the timed activity labeled *fail_detected*. When the *fail_detected* activity completes, the SAN goes in failure status, moving the token from the place *OK* to the place *failure*. At this point, the token remains in the *failure* place until the device is repaired (i.e., until the *TTR* timed activity completes). The *TTR* activity represents the time to repair or substitute the failed device. When the activity *fail_detected* completes, a token is moved in the shared place *LEU_fail*. The place *LEU_fail* is shared with the SAN *SystemStatus*, shown in Fig. 6. This model represents the whole failure status of the CBTC system.

The SAN *SystemStatus* receives a token from the SAN *LEU* through the *LEU_fail* shared place. So the immediate activity *f6* in Fig. 6 is enabled when the shared place *LEU_fail* contains a token. When *f6* completes, a token is added to the place *LEU_failure* of the SAN *SystemStatus*. When the LEU device is repaired, a token is put in the shared place *LEU_OK* of the *SystemStatus* model by the LEU model, so the immediate activity *r6* completes, and a token is moved out from the place *LEU_failure* of the *SystemStatus* SAN. All the other hardware devices involved in the CBTC system, both onboard and wayside, are modelled in a similar way, considering different failure rates and different TTR.

In general, every time a device fails in the system, a token is put in one of failure places of the *SystemStatus* SAN, generally called *DEVICE_NAME_failure*. Each of these places contains a number of tokens equal to the number of the failures produced by the devices of the same type. For example, if two BTM devices fail and they remain in failure state in a shared interval of time, the place *BTM_failure* contains two tokens. When a BTM device is repaired, a token is removed from that place. When a major or significant failure happens, the input gates of *SystemStatus* SAN also put a token in the shared place *fail_in* and so a token is put in the place *failure*. Computing the probability that the place *OK* in Fig. 6 contains a token, we evaluate the availability *A* of the system as the probability of the system to work properly without any major or significant failure.

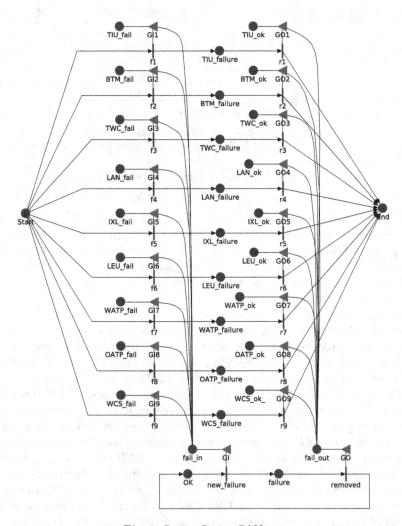

Fig. 6. SystemStatus SAN

4.4   Numerical Evaluation

For the scope of this paper, we evaluated the unavailability U of the system defined as: $U = 1 - A$. For railway systems, unavailability must be at most $2 \cdot 10^{-4}$. A steady state analysis has been performed using the simulator provided by the Möbius tool. Each numerical result is obtained with a confidence interval of 1% and a confidence level set to 0.95.

Fig. 7 and Fig. 8 show the impact on U of the failure rates of different devices, and of different times TTR to repair a device. The straight line $\leq 2 \cdot 10^{-4}$ represents the threshold of maximum unavailability allowed.

Fig. 7a plots the values of the unavailability U, as a function of the failure rate of a single device, for different devices OATP, TIU, IXL and WATP. It is interesting to note that, among the devices considered in the analysis, TIU is the most critical device. In fact, the failure rate of TIU affects more than the others the availability of the system.

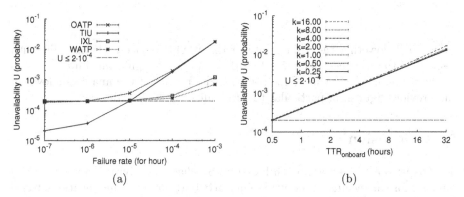

Fig. 7. Expected unavailability U of the CBTS system as a function of the failure rate of a single device, for different devices OATP, TIU, IXL and WATP (a), and as a funtion of $TTR_{onboard}$, for different values of $k = 0.25, \ldots, 16$ (b)

Fig. 7b plots the values of the unavailability U as a function of the repair time $TTR_{onboard}$ of the devices on board of the train. Different values of the repair time $TTR_{wayside}$ of the wayside devices are considered, where $TTR_{wayside} = k \cdot TTR_{onboard}$. This figure shows that, for values of $k \leq 32$, the impact of k on the unavailability U is not significant, and for values of $TTR_{onboard} \geq 0.5$ hours, the unavailability requirement, $U \leq 2 \cdot 10^{-4}$, is not satisfied.

Fig. 8a and Fig. 8b plot the values of the unavailability U, as a function of the failure rate of the single device TIU and WATP, respectively, for different values of $TTR_{onboard} = 0.5, 1, \ldots, 32$. Fig. 8a highlights that, also for values of $TTR_{onboard}$ greater than 0.5 hours (and $TTR_{wayside} > 1$ hour) and only for low values of failure rate of the device TIU, U is under the allowed threshold and satifies the requirement $U \leq 2 \cdot 10^{-4}$. On the contrary, Fig. 8b shows that, when the failure rate of the TIU component is fixed to the default considered

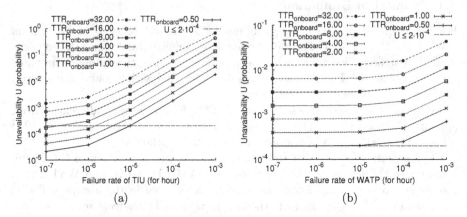

Fig. 8. Expected unavailability U of the CBTS system as a function of the failure rate of the single device TIU (a) and WATP (b) for different values of $TTR_{onboard} = 0.5, 1, \ldots, 32$

value 10^{-5}, lowering the failure rate of the WATP device and the TTR with respect to the assumed default values does not bring significant improvements to the availability measure. This confirms the results of the analyses shown in the previous figures, in particular the criticality of the TIU device.

5   Conclusion

This paper outlines an approach based on Stochastic Activity Networks (SAN) analysis for the evaluation of availability attributes of a Communications-based Train Control (CBTC) system. The approach is applied on a reduced version of a CBTC physical architecture, which is derived through a product-line based approach. Furthermore, we have shown how different failure rates of different components and different times to repair affect the availability measure.

Current results show that the SAN modelling formalism is a proper tool to model failure modes of a system that satisfy the CBTC functional requirements. Furthermore, availability attributes for the system can be computed in a matter of minutes by means of the Möbius tool. Different configurations of the physical architecture can be evaluated and compared with minimal re-factoring effort at the model level.

Future works concern the implementation of the approach on different configurations of a real system, with precise failure rates and well defined components provided by our industrial partners. Integration of the approach with a safety analysis strategy to identify safety-related properties of the system is also foreseen.

References

1. CENELEC. EN50126 Railway Applications - The Specification and Demonstration of Reliability, Availability, Maintainability and Safety (RAMS) (1997)
2. Courtney, T., Gaonkar, S., Keefe, K., Rozier, E.W.D., Sanders, W.H.: Möbius 2.3: An extensible tool for dependability, security, and performance evaluation of large and complex system models. In: 39th Annual IEEE/IFIP Int. Conf. on Dependable Systems and Networks (DSN 2009), pp. 353–358 (2009)
3. Ferrari, A., Spagnolo, G.O., Martelli, G., Menabeni, S.: Product Line Engineering Applied to CBTC Systems Development. In: 5th International Symposium On Leveraging Applications of Formal Methods, Verification and Validation, ISOLA 2012 (to appear, 2012)
4. Institute of Electrical and Electronics Engineers. IEEE Standard for Communications Based Train Control (CBTC) Performance and Functional Requirements. IEEE Std 1474.1-2004 (Revision of IEEE Std 1474.1-1999) (2004)
5. International Electrotechnical Commission. IEC 62290-1: Railway applications: Urban guided transport management and command/control systems. Part 1: System principles and fundamental concepts (2007)
6. Kuun, E.: Open Standards for CBTC and CBTC Radio Based Communications. In: APTA Rail Rail Transit Conference Proceedings (2004)
7. Nyström, B.: The use of availability concepts in the railway system. International Journal of Performability Engineering, 103–118 (2009)
8. Pascoe, R.D., Eichorn, T.N.: What is Communication-Based Train Control? IEEE Vehicular Technology Magazine (2009)
9. Patra, A., Kumar, U., Kraik, P.: Availability target of the railway infrastructure: an analysis. In: 2010 Proceedings - Annual Reliability and Maintainability Symposium (RAMS), pp. 1–6 (2010)
10. Sanders, W.H., Meyer, J.F.: Stochastic Activity Networks: Formal Definitions and Concepts. In: European Educational Forum: School on Formal Methods and Performance Analysis, pp. 315–343 (2000)
11. Xu, T., Tang, T., Gao, C., Cai, B.: Dependability analysis of the data communication system in train control system. Science in China Series E: Technological Sciences 52, 2605–2618 (2009)
12. Zhu, L., Yu, F., Ning, B.: Availability Improvement for WLAN-Based Train-Ground Communication Systems in Communication-Based Train Control (CBTC). In: 2010 IEEE 72nd Vehicular Technology Conference Fall (VTC 2010-Fall), pp. 1–5 (2010)

Author Index